P9-AAY-700

PATH

TO

PERMANENT PEACE

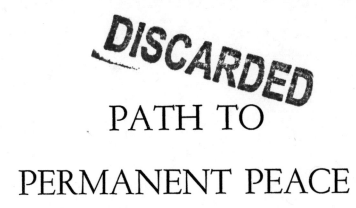

PATH TO

PERMANENT PEACE

Volume I

E. J. PAWLOWSKI, M.D.

VANTAGE PRESS

NEW YORK   WASHINGTON   HOLLYWOOD

PREFACE

These are times of the decline of morality and the increase in school drop-outs, juvenile delinquency, crimes of all sorts, mental and emotional illnesses, divorces, illegitimate children and pathological cultural trends. These are times when the suicidal rate of psychiatrists proves to be the greatest of all medical specialties. These are times when our young people seem to be without purpose and direction in life, imbibing psychic stimulants and other drugs, revolting on college campuses, being involved in protest marches and burning draft cards. These are times of rebellion of youth. We see the Hippies and the psychedelic drugs, long hair and beards, "folk-rock" protest songs and mini-skirts.

These are anxious times in which the free world is becoming smaller, and its leaders are deadlocked as to whether to continue bombing North Viet Nam, whether to escalate or de-escalate the war. There is some talk of "peace at any price." We are now engaged totally in the Viet Nam War, and on the brink of World War III and the annihilation of all mankind.

To have a common-sense philosophy of behavior that the countries of the world, and especially each individual, can live by, is a godsend. The Mature Person-to-Person Philosophy described in this book is the answer to the world's problems. It does not rely on other individuals or leaders to resolve the problems. It is a practical philosophy. It alleviates frustrations, and each single individual can do something about world problems; he can work by himself. Adults and children both can do something about the maturation of the world and not leave things to the leaders. No matter how lowly a position a person holds, he can help correct the ills of the *people* of the world. Hopelessness and frustrations occur because a person cannot do anything about a problem and has to depend upon someone else. This Philosophy gives hope.

Margaret M. Fleming Pawlowski, M.D.

INTRODUCTION

This book is written primarily to be used as a formal course in Peace for the high school student. Ideally, it should be studied by the ninth-grader, age 14 or 15, before he or she reaches the legal age of being able to quit school. Also, adults should read this book and make a total effort toward becoming more emotionally mature.

After taking this course, the prospective drop-out in high school will be better prepared to face life, and, hopefully, he may decide to continue with his education. Also, the incidence of so-called juvenile delinquency and crimes of all types will be decreased, not only in the present for those studying this book, but more important, in the next and future generations as the students become parents, and raise more emotionally-mature children. There will be the prevention of mental illness in one's family. Following in order, there should be a gradual elimination of mental and emotionally-related illnesses with their associated job and social failures, and a decline in divorces and the raising of immature and unstable offspring. The children will grow to be stronger, more morally responsible, self-disciplined, and independent. The undesirable traits of our society and culture will be modified and corrected. Decreasing our numbers of immature people will prevent war.

It may already be too late to avert a world war at this time. There may be too many differences of opinion, and there may be too many people who are set in their ways with ingrained, rigid personalities. There may be too many cultural and nationalistic tendencies that are at opposite ends, and which may not be understood and tolerated by each other. It may already be too late because of the large number of countries with internal unrest, with widespread poverty, illiteracy, and sickness. Their peoples are greatly lacking in the development of their innate capacities. It may be too late because in this country and in other free countries there are racial problems, a general moral decline, and an increase in break-ups of the family unit.

Nevertheless, we must concentrate all our energies now before there is a total world catastrophe, and aim to the future for peace. We must do this for the sake of ourselves and for the future of mankind. Even if we should find ourselves in the midst of a war, we should continue to prepare during the war to avoid more wars in the future. We have to realize the urgency of the world situation and do something about it right now. We have to initiate a chain reaction of thought and action to make ourselves more mature.

Throughout history wars have been fought "to end all wars," to prevent death and slavery, to ensure peace to children and future generations. We would like to hand down to our children and the next generations a movement toward man's emotional maturity and permanent peace. Most of the hard work will have to be done during the present generation, for seemingly-impossible changes will have to be made. In the next and succeeding generations the task should grow progressively easier, as there will be fewer emotionally-immature people, although new problems will arise and will have to be resolved. The movement toward maturity and peace should be forever improved upon and solidified, and totally incorporated into our way of life. As each year passes by, we will have that much more insurance of achieving peace in our own minds, peace in the family, peace in the community, and peace between the nations of the world.

The title of this book, *Path to Permanent Peace,* is meant to be descriptive. It means that you as an individual should make a path during your lifetime through your dealings with people toward a permanent peace. Each of you will have to travel the road to a lasting peace alone, but all of you will arrive at the same ultimate goal. Attaining the peace will be each person's responsibility. The methods used will be similar for everyone. How this is to be accomplished will be explained in detail in this book. For those who may have particular emotional problems, for example, excessive passivity, or extreme rigidity and defensiveness, extra help in the form of psychotherapy may be necessary in the quest for peace. Also, cultural trends may need to be modified, and more individual freedom might have to be provided before a person may be able to fully plan and work for permanent peace. Some people, as those under autocratic rule, may have to bide their time and await "outside" help before they completely realize their goal. However, each person, no matter what the circumstances, should continue to strive to pursue his path toward peace with all the means at his disposal.

We want this book to serve as the beginning of a common-sense plan for permanent peace. Through the use of this book, and especially beginning in adolescence, we would want to interrupt the vicious cycle of immature people raising immature people, which ultimately leads to war. The high school student will be helped immeasurably with his goals and career, and his choice of mate and marriage. He will attain success and security on his own merit, reaching his ultimate potential, and not find a need to get ahead by aggression and taking advantage of others. He will make a study of the meaning of life and his growth toward emotional maturity. He will learn how to raise mature, not pathologically aggressive, individuals, from whose ranks mature leaders will emerge. The Mature Person-to-Person Philosophy will be exercised to the limit by everyone, and all of the time. Problems and aggression of all types will be handled appropriately by mature people, and war will be averted.

* * * *

We should be searching always for the truth. Any suggestions or criticisms would be welcomed by the author. Please address correspondence to:

EMIL JOHN PAWLOWSKI, M.D.
c/o Publisher

CONTENTS

PART I

PLAN FOR A PERMANENT PEACE

PART II

WORKING FOR A PERMANENT PEACE

ILLUSTRATIONS

PART I
Plan For A Permanent Peace

CHAPTER I

AN IMMATURE PEOPLE WITH IMMATURE LEADERS

We are now living in the most dangerous period of history ever. We are all aware of the real possibility of a world holocaust from atomic bombs. We should stop and give serious thought to the fact that there are now devices in the hands of certain people that are capable of annihilating the entire human race. Realizing this, most assuredly we should want those certain people in control of the continued existence of mankind to be of the greatest emotional maturity and wisdom. If they are not, then we and our children have good reason to be living in constant fear of the future.

Some may say that they have resigned themselves to dying today or tomorrow because one has to die sometime. Such a person implies that it is acceptable to him that other individuals may end his life whenever they wish. We must conclude that this person has not made a satisfactory adjustment to living, and more important, he has little or no conception of his place in the universe. If a person is emotionally stable and of average intelligence, he will definitely be concerned with the prospects of war and what can be done about preventing it.

Marked advances have been made in the physical sciences. Man today is healthier and lives longer than ever before. He eats better, dresses more attractively and warmly, and is sheltered more comfortably. He has more conveniences to ease his work and more time for his pleasure. Unfortunately, however, innovations have progressed to the point where a single push of a button can control the lives of millions of people. Although man has made tremendous scientific achievements, he has not progressed sufficiently so that he has learned how to live peacefully with himself and his fellow man. Whereas he has developed intellectually by leaps and bounds, there has been no commensurate emotional growth. This is not to say that the human being of today is not more mature than his counterpart of years ago, but the evidence remains that he is not mature enough to avoid war.

The basic instincts of man seem not to have changed appreciably over the years. The man who shot the crossbow is basically the same man who is now in a position to press the button of an atomic device. The leader who gave the order for the man to use the crossbow is basically no different from the leader of today. Man's basic drives and needs, his desires and objectives, his problems in reference to himself and others, have not changed to any great extent. The fact that today man is thrown into more contact with people should not necessarily make life more complicated for him. It is a rationalization when people state that the hectic life of modern civilization is responsible for the increase in mental and emotional problems. With more people and more avenues of opportunity open to an individual, he should be able to divert his frustrations more easily and direct his energies toward more satisfying relationships and objectives.

In the following chapters we will see that immature people are responsible for wars, and immature people are involved with Communism. Also, there are immature people in the free countries, in France, in Italy, and in the United States, and in every other country in the world. The title of this chapter refers to the fact that all the people in this world, including leaders, are in some areas, to some extent, emotionally immature. This is to say that there is not a single person in the world who is a completely emotionally-mature individual.

By emotional immaturity we speak of the person whose emotional capacity as a human being has not been fulfilled. This lack in emotional development is chiefly due, first, to the nationalistic and cultural deficiencies which have preceded the person, and which have influenced his family and him; and, second, to the immediate family environment in which the person is raised. A deficiency in a person's emotional make-up may impede his physical, intellectual, and social pursuits; he is curtailed in the realization of his potential. He is irresponsible and lacks self-discipline. He is "spoiled" in the sense that he thinks of his own comfort first, and he wants everything his

18

way. He wants "to take" but not "give", and if he does give a little he expects something in return. A mutually-beneficial relationship with another person cannot be maintained. He is excessively dependent upon others, seeking sympathy and acceptance from them, and he lacks confidence in himself. He is indecisive, afraid to act on something, and unable to achieve success through the utilization of his own merits. Being inflexible, he has difficulty in adapting to new situations. There is present emotional instability and unpredictability of behavior, with the possibility of the development of hostile feelings, thoughts, and expressions.

A state of immaturity will weaken a person's ability in having an "open mind" so that he will be ruled by feelings of jealousy and resentment. He will be incapable of studying and evaluating two or more sides of an issue and of reaching a just compromise. This includes the critical examination of knowledge from the past as well as the present, so that prejudices and bigotry may be eliminated in arriving at sound judgments. Also, it means the inability for objective introspection, and not having love, understanding, and empathy for other people. All of this means, among other things, the immature voter, for personal gain, supporting immature leaders. It also means the immature leaders, for their own personal gain, allowing themselves to be influenced by outside sources, and supporting issues which are not for the common good.

The immature person is insecure, and in his search for security he will be taken advantage of or will take advantage of others in word and deed. The people in those countries are individually and collectively immature where they have been living under a form of government which is not for the common good—where man is being exploited, yet they are unable to do anything about it. Individually, the people have not attained emotional maturity because of the lack of freedom, denying them the fulfillment of their potentials, and because of deficiencies in their cultural and family environments. As a group, they are immature in not having been able to change their way of life, which is an insult to the dignity of man. Even more immature are the people of the rest of the world who are in a position to more readily do something about it, but who permit such mass-exploitation. Without saying, immature are they who comprise the aggressive government and subjugate the people.

Some people are, over-all, more mature than other people. One person may show more signs of maturity than another in a certain area—for example, in his behavior at work; but he may appear less mature in his social relationships. However, in most instances we might expect to see a person who is considered to be mature to exhibit maturity in most areas. To have the entire population of the world attain maximum maturity, each person will have to reach an ultimate in maturity within himself. In order that this may be achieved, man must be free, cultural changes will have to be made, and families will have to learn how to raise mature children. Also, each person will have to work, utilizing his potential to the fullest, in the direction of becoming more mature and of helping mature others— the method for this to be discussed in the chapters which will follow.

We will be extremely severe in our appraisal of Communism. Also, we should bear in mind that if we were not contending with Communism, it could be Fascism, or any other type of government where there is a banding together of people who are influenced by cultural trends and the need to take advantage of others. In his search for gratification and personal security, any immature leader will exploit others; and invariably the poor people will suffer the most. In this chapter we are going to be equally critical of the freer peoples of the world, like those of the United States, and the democratic way of government. An equal amount of criticism could be directed at the German or Swedish or other cultural trends which have contributed to the immaturity of its people. A bad cultural trend lends to the immaturity of an individual and opposes his being able to utilize his potential to the fullest, to succeed and find security for himself. Pathological cultural trends are a real threat to world peace. Because all the people in one area or country may have similar traits, these may be accepted as being normal and mature. Distorted ideas and values might be handed down to the people of succeeding generations who will incorporate them in their own personality patterns. These people so influenced will strongly feel that only their ideas and way of life are right, and that other nations with their ideas are wrong.

Even though most of this discussion is going to pertain to the United States, similar situations are everywhere, and each person in every country should make a similar analysis of its own people and leaders. The United States has much to be desired; however, it is the foremost country in the world today where an individual can unfold himself as a human being. There is no other nation where its entire population has such unlimited opportunity. There is no other country where man can exercise his potential to such a degree as in the United States.

Many people in this country tend to look condescendingly at the people of other countries. Perhaps because of this country's achievements, the better living conditions and material possessions, these people may feel superior to foreigners. They do not realize that it is our land of opportunity which is superior, and not the basic individuals themselves. Unfortunately, many of these immature, obnoxious Americans, not true representatives of the American people, are the center of attraction, appearing in the movies and newspapers, and they are in a position to tour foreign countries. They provoke anger and resentment toward the United States. The foreigners see them as pompous, ignorant, narrow-minded weaklings, who seem to have more money than they know how to handle, while others in the world are living in poverty. Their weakness invites attack. These immature Americans seem to not remember that their ancestors came from those same foreign countries, and that it was through their efforts that this country is what it is today. The characteristics of the ancestors, combined with the product of their intermixing with each other, have produced what we see in the present-day people of United States. From the time that our country was first founded there have been rapid developments in science, economics, travel, and the means of communication. There have been wars and other events involving this country and the rest of the world which influenced the growth of this country. Our country has been spared devastation, and we have capitalized economically both in war and peace in producing goods for ourselves and other countries.

Based on a search for freedom, individual initiative, and the opportunity to exercise one's potential in a free-enterprise system in a conducive culture and climate, the pioneers came to this country; and this country made progress as the world had never seen before.

Today, we find that the people in the United States, as in the rest of the world, are immature and insecure. Because of a basic insecurity, the people are bringing upon themselves stronger governmental controls. The United States is becoming more and more a Welfare State, and it is heading in the direction of Socialism, and inviting Communism. The people falsely believe that they will gain security from a government which cares for them and gives them immediate gratification in the form of hand-outs. These are the same immature people asking for favors from their politician friends—the veterans wanting unjustifiable increases in pension benefits, and the workers through their unions placing excessive demands on management. They are seeking something for nothing, or more for the same amount or even less effort.

The more hand-outs that are given to people, the more they want, and the more they expect. Their appetites become insatiable. They feel that the government owes them a living. They actually are ungrateful for what is given to them. Only those who put forth time and effort for something fully appreciate its worth. These passive people, and the remainder of the population, are being engulfed and overprotected by the government because of their desire for dependency and security. In the process they are losing their freedom without realizing it. By becoming dependent upon the State, they have no choice but to take what the State offers them. They will ultimately lose whatever initiative, incentive, and talent for success they may have had when functioning independently.

Dependency for anyone is not good, for it carries with it hostility and rebellion toward the one on whom one is dependent. The dependent person may experience enjoyment from the feeling of being cared for, but he will be made to feel subordinate and more inadequate, having to depend upon someone else. He will be resentful and afraid that the relationship might end, and he will ultimately be more insecure than in the first place. Therefore, charity, lend-lease, or aid of any type given indiscriminately fosters dependency and resentment, and invariably proves to be more harmful than helpful in the long run.

Of most importance is that the government is usurping the people's opportunity for the attainment of real security. This security could be obtained by the people exercising their potential, and gaining success and self-worth in the free-enterprise system. All freedom of the people could be lost eventually, not due to an outside aggressor, or to subversive action within the country, but due to the basic insecurity of the people themselves, coming under the domination of the government.

The number of government employees is steadily increasing far in excess of the total population increase. Statistics reveal that now one out of every five workers is employed by the government. There is tremendous government waste because of the many inefficiently-run bureaus and the innumerable needless jobs created by politicians for their constituents. Governmental agencies do not in reality ask for appropriations based on what work has to be performed. They ask for and receive budgetary allowances in excess of that of the previous year, and then proceed to distribute the money to those gaining the newly-provided positions.

As the government grows more powerful, with more members, and the people in private business who pay the bulk of the taxes become fewer in number, we could reach an intolerable situation. We wonder who in the end will support the governing body. This is realistic; because all of us know, or should know, that the efficiency of the average governmental agency is much less compared to that of private industry. With some exceptions, governments—federal, state, and local, including all their branches—draw to them a certain type of individual who does not function at the same peak of efficiency as his counterpart in private enterprise. Lack of initiative, incapability, insecurity in a person and his search for security, might be some reasons for this. Too often one sees government workers expending more time and energy figuring how to get out of work than it would actually take in doing the work. Yet frequently they are resentful of those in private industry for the profits that are gained. It would be interesting to conduct a survey and compare the over-all work performance—that is, the competence of the workers themselves, the attendance records, and the amount and calibre of the work accomplished—of the employees of a private concern and a typical city government. From observations, one could speculate that if the personnel from almost any private business were to replace similar personnel of almost any government agency doing similar work, and given a few weeks' indoctrination period, they would perform their new duties in one-quarter of the time now utilized.

It was mentioned how the people, due to their immaturity and insecurity, are turning toward what they think is security offered by a strong Welfare State. Now, it should be explained that the politicians, the leaders themselves, are immature and insecure if they offer government hand-outs to the common person. Such leaders are really exploiting the common people. They are playing on the immaturity and ignorance of these people, most of them with a small amount of education and in the lower income brackets. These are the people who will be most apt to reach for government aid. The leaders, in the process of gathering votes, make promises and give the people federal aid and other forms of immediate gratification. The promises are not unlike those given by the Communists to their deprived peoples. Under the guise of working chiefly for the welfare of their fellow man, the Communist leaders promote their own interests. Many of our leaders may not realize that they are seeking personal gain and security for themselves in making the promises, and many more will not know that the people, too, are searching for a basic security in accepting their promises, thereby voting for them. However, some of the leaders do realize that they can derive more personal gain by "feeding security" to the common person, and they have even crossed party lines to accomplish this end. True, some leaders have good intentions in wanting to really help the people, thereby offering them the hand-outs. But these leaders are acting in ignorance, and therefore they should not have been chosen to lead in the first place. They, the leaders, will gain personal satisfaction and self-value in believing that they are necessary for the people, which feeling will be reinforced the more dependent upon them the people become. Again it should be stressed

24

that they are fostering a dependency which is to the ultimate detriment of the people and the country. Dependency, weakness, and lack of initiative is what we accentuate in people if we subject them to a Welfare State or Socialism. In the old days it was subjugation by rule; now it is subjugation of people by making them dependent. The people and the country would be stronger, more secure, more mature, and freer if the people were pressured to work for their gains and to achieve on their own merit. The only form of government aid which should be condoned is that given to deserving, destitute people based upon individual need.

It is interesting how the politicians offer to provide services to people, such as medical care to the aged, and others, beyond what anybody really needs—just so they can gain personal favor in the way of votes. The politicians, mostly lawyers, are not proposing government-sponsored free legal clinics, for apparent reasons. Perhaps the health fields have been exploited because of their essential nature; more probably, however, because of the altruistic and passive nature of the physicians. Physicians for the most part are preoccupied with intellectual pursuits and the welfare of their fellow men, and they are not interested, nor do they have the time, to concern themselves with other matters. They are prone to exploitation. The politicians are promising and giving away the people's money chiefly for their own gain.

A strong government means that there is a majority of strong, mature people in the country from whose ranks strong, mature leaders are elected. A strong government is an ideal government. A weak government is the result of immature, weak people and their chosen leaders. Measured in terms of the people it represents, an excessively strong or large government means that the majority of its people and leaders are immature and weak. It means that the majority of the people, due to insecurity-feelings, are seeking security in the form of paternalism— that is, hand-out legislation; and because of it, they are making the leaders and government in support of the hand-outs excessively strong and large. It means that the leaders, due to their own insecurity-feelings and in search for personal gain and security, are catering to the people's weakness, offering them the dependency and security which they seek, though it will ultimately prove to be a false security. It also means that the leaders are overcompensating for their basic insecurity in having been chosen to leadership positions. A dependent, insecure people are a weak people; and weak people provoke the Communists and others, who are immature and aggressive, to dominate them.

If there is but one relatively-mature person who is intimidated by the government, or who even stands in awe of a government official, then the government is too powerful. To that person the government is no longer serving him and his community for a mutually-better existence. To that person the government official is not a true representative for him and his community.

With all of the people being insecure and yearning for security, the masses believing that they can obtain it through welfare aid, government jobs, and similar means, the government leaders seeking it through providing it to the masses, we are heading toward a stronger Welfare State, Socialism, and beyond. The movement has begun; and theoretically, if the Communists could remain patient—which they cannot because of their immaturity—without too much effort they would rule the world within the next few generations. But who can really be blamed for not recognizing this movement or trend when we find that American psychiatry, with its analysis and objectivity, is heading in the same direction? Actually, the psychiatrists are advocates, most of them unknowingly, of socialized medicine. The costly state mental hospitals, community mental health centers, and court and school, state-operated mental clinics are the forerunners of socialized medicine in the United States today. Under the guise of only helping the mentally-incapacitated people, the federal and state legislators, community leaders, psychiatrists, and others who support these programs, are unconsciously or consciously seeking self-gain at the expense of the people themselves. The ultimate goal of treating the mentally-ill person should be to make him more independent, mature, and secure, so that he can realize his optimal potential. The proponents of these mental health programs, including the actual practice of psychotherapy, purport in word to aim at helping the patient

26

attain this ultimate goal. However, in their actions, by enticing the patient and the patient's family to reach out and cling to them, they are fostering dependency, and are actually counteracting what they are telling the people.

The policy of the state-controlled clinics is to have the patients pay what they can afford; but invariably the charges are less than what would be paid to a private practitioner, and the people naturally reach out for the clinics. The nominal fee paid by the patients is low enough that they will feel they are getting something for nothing. A person generally values a thing more if he expends work, time, and money for it, and he usually gets out of something that which he puts into it. For the clinics to raise their fees is not the answer, because the patients readily recognize that the structure of the state-run agencies is not unlike that of the other government-controlled projects which are being operated at about twenty-five per cent efficiency. Just knowing that something is being operated by the government denotes to the public that products and services are at "rock-bottom" prices, and that they would not be cheated. The average person seems not to be aware that, due to governmental inefficiency, he is not getting the most from his tax dollar. It is true that the individual in need is paying slightly less for a service, which more than likely will be inferior; however, over-all taxes involving everybody will be increased. The total population is paying fourfold for the service which could be performed by the private practitioner. The fact that the one person reaps the maximum benefit while all the people pay for it in itself should not be frowned upon. The issue here is that the person would be ultimately benefitted more if he were not offered a crutch so readily, if he and his family were pressured to unite and "stand on their own two feet".

The politicians, hearing about the need for mental-illness preventive measures, and just as they are being able to offer to the people other "give-away" legislation in order to gain votes, leap at the opportunity to promote the mental health centers. The psychiatrists, most of whom are dedicated to the helping of their fellow man, mindful of the enormous and seemingly unconquerable task before them in the form of unanswered mental problems and the vast numbers of people involved, lend support to these programs. They readily admit to the tremendous need for psychiatric assistance, but they are not necessarily admitting that the government-operated facilities are the answer. Because the psychiatrists are already harassed with their own practices, or involved in teaching or research, or attached to state institutions, or in government positions which are foreign to them, and in awe of the politicians, or for any other number of reasons, they have allowed these programs to become established and have fallen in line with them. The people of the ancillary services, such as the psychologists, social workers, and others, already struggling for recognition in the mental health field, quickly have filled the gap provided by the lack of psychiatrists. The community leaders, in some cases seeing the need for psychiatric help, in the other cases going along with other communities "to keep up with the Joneses", and in still other cases seeking personal gain in the form of recognition, have supported and even initiated the establishment of these government-controlled centers. Once a government agency is established there seems to be a need for it, as there are usually long waiting lists of people awaiting their turn for treatment. However, the long waiting lists prove to be the result of inefficient administration.

To summarize, the need for preventive mental health has been recognized, and something is being done about it in the way of establishing federal and local government-controlled community mental health centers. Unfortunately, what is being done is basically not what the people need or should want. The proponents are telling the people one thing, that is, for them to "stand on their own two feet"; but by their actions in setting up the centers and condoning dependency, they are encouraging them to be the opposite. The people are readily relinquishing their independence and individual responsibility because of their passivity and basic insecurity. Because of their own immaturity and insecurity the proponents are taking this course, fostering the people's dependence upon them. Because the public schools and the government are taking over the special education and treatment of children with behavior, speech, reading, and similar emotionally-related problems, the parents are being deprived of a basic responsibility for the proper raising and training of their own children. Of course, immature parents welcome this. This applies also to the newly-initiated Head Start programs in which government-sponsored pre-school training, medical examinations, and even breakfast and lunch, are offered to the children of so-called deprived families. If this trend continues we can speculate that eventually our pre-school children will receive guidance in government-controlled nurseries, similar to what is seen under Communism. The parents will lose control of their families, and there will be less emotional fulfillment for both parents and children. More and more emotionally-immature children will be raised.

The answer to this particular problem rests with psychiatry itself. The psychiatrists should "shift for themselves" in the attainment of their goals as psychiatrists, without government aid. They, because they are supposedly more mature, more independent, and more secure, should practice more what they preach, and set an example for their patients and for all people. They should become more involved in private enterprise and strive for individualism, and not seek salaried positions, as is the growing trend.

In the case of severe hardship and deserving people who need help—for example, destitute people and abandoned children—the federal and local governments, or, better still, a charitable organization supervising the patient, should compensate the psychiatrist and those providing ancillary services. The courts, schools, and other institutions in need of consultative services should do the same. There would be a saving of money in the long run, and this practice would promote independence, not only for the patient but for the psychiatrist and others as well. The government or the charity would have more control over the finances set aside for the psychiatric services. They could be more selective as to the need for treatment and of the professional people who would provide the services. It would be a simple matter not to refer patients to anyone who was not performing adequate and honest services. Now, it is virtually impossible to fire a government employee. Upon the patient or his guardian would fall the burden of his proving his need and inability to pay for the assistance, personally seeking a therapist, and convincing the therapist and agency sponsoring him that he continues to be in need of help. He would have the opportunity of free choice of therapist. All involved—the agency, the therapist, and the patient—would serve to keep each other in check, pressuring the other toward maturity, independence, and doing good work. For the patient with little or no motivation for treatment, external pressure, as from a court or school, would have to be applied for him to gain the help that he requires. In this respect there would be no difference from what is seen in today's clinic-type of practice. Ultimately, as people mature more, face their responsibilities, and prepare more adequately for themselves and their families in times of disaster and old age, there should be less and less need and demand for governmental help. Medicare and Medicaid are not good because they provide health services to all people based on age and low income, and not on individual need.

Just as community mental health should be subsidized—that is, financial aid for patients based on individual need given directly by the governments to the private practitioners—so should the government agencies on all levels strive to operate in a similar manner. As many functions of the government as possible should be placed in the hands of private enterprise. Even the postal service and the public utilities could be managed by individual concerns. By the setting of rigid specifications, and through the use of competitive bidding, coordination of agencies, rotation of companies, and overlapping of services, these organizations could be run with the same continuity and with more efficiency. The government should keep only the minimum amount of work for itself and serve the people primarily in a supervisory capacity to see to it that the jobs are carried out effectively. The present government-operated welfare agencies, and others, are extremely lax. Their liberal practices condone and encourage laziness. The federal aid for medical care and housing for the aged, the many other similar government programs, and even social security, tend to negate the fact that man is born an individual with the basic ability, responsibility, and initiative to care and plan for himself and his family.

It seems that the basic essentials which have made our country great are now ceasing to exist. With more government workers, more government controls, and more dependence upon the government and its agencies, the people are becoming more dependent, weaker, lazier, and insecure. With our affluent society has come an excessively-large government and a weak new generation. If our country should not continue on to greatness, and there should be a tendency to decline, there might also be an unconscious tendency to engage in war to strengthen the economy. This would prove to be a false economic prosperity.

Today, fewer and fewer people know how to save and to arrange for their own future. With jobs with sick leaves, holidays and vacations with pay, insurances, retirement plans, and other fringe benefits, much of the planning is taken out of the individual's hands. This is not unlike the parent-like programs of the government which foster a weakness in its people. It encourages laziness and removes man's incentive to work every day at the peak of his efficiency. He is not utilizing his capacity to the fullest. In old age he finds himself dependent upon others. His children have been raised as selfish, irresponsible, inadequate people who shift the care of their elderly parents to the government. With their grandparents in nursing homes, the grandchildren are deprived of the three-generation unity which offers maturity and security, and a better appreciation of their life in time and space. In the end the people would become more independent and the country would grow stronger if they were pressured into assuming more individual responsibility at a young age, so that they could care for themselves in their old age. If the people were offered higher wages for the amount and calibre of work performed, but with an elimination of the fringe benefits, they would be forced into "standing on their own two feet." Of course, with the widespread use of fringe benefits, having been given in the first place to appeal to man's basic insecurity, the people would now only very reluctantly relinquish them. They not only would want a continuation of the benefits, but an increase in hourly wage or salary as well. The situation is something similar to the offered redeemable trading stamps in a grocery store where the people would want the stamps in addition to lower prices. If fringe benefits were eliminated, people would more accurately know how much

31

they were being compensated for their work, without being offered guarantees which they might never receive. Of most importance would be the development of individual responsibility mentioned earlier.

We have discussed how the people of the United States, due to immaturity and insecurity, are heading in the direction of a strong Welfare State and Socialism. In turn, the excessively-large government is making the people more dependent, weaker, and insecure. The alarming thing is that, without our realizing it, our country is being transformed into one whose people are going to be even more immature and insecure. A cultural trend is taking place in which immature, insecure parents are raising more immature, insecure children. This trend is gaining momentum and it could reach a point where it would be impossible to change it. Of importance is that the increase in numbers of immature people may not be as apparent as it would be if there were merely an increase in the incidence of, for example, the psychoneuroses and psychoses—in which, incidentally, there is underlying immaturity. Not being apparent makes it doubly dangerous, because there will be a change for the worse without anyone realizing it. The people will have adopted pathological cultural and character traits unknown to anyone, including themselves. In the strong position as supposedly successful parents with wealth, education, and high status in the community, these immature people will influence their own and other people's children. It is unfortunate that many of these people, due to a good memory, family affiliations, favoritism, neurotic motivation, but lacking in emotional maturity, attain high positions and have an influence on society and culture, national and world policies.

Immature, insecure parents cannot relate to each other in a balanced "give-and-take" relationship, that is, satisfy each other's needs in a mature way. They cannot "give," only "take." The husband and wife tend to belittle, dominate, or, by some other means, take advantage of each other to build themselves up and feel secure. Something has been lacking in their past lives in the form of recognition, acceptance, understanding, discipline, love, security, and other factors, which now makes them immature and insecure adults. They may have retained pathological attachments and resentments with the members of their own immediate families which will interfere with a balanced husband-wife-children relationship. They, as marriage partners, are still searching for what they have missed in infancy and childhood from their own parents as a result of immature relationships, and they are trying to find it in the relationships with each other, with their children, and from outside sources.

Immature and insecure, preoccupied with their own feelings of inferiority and inadequacy, with their own problems, lacking in emotional warmth, and striving for gratification and security, the parents cannot give to their children the concern, the warmth and security for which the children are searching. The parents feel they cannot give up what little they have. The children feel rejected. The more children there are, the more pressures on the parents, and on the children themselves from vying with each other—and even with one of the parents—in attempting to gain attention and approval from the parents. This promotes teasing, envy, jealousy, resentment, greed, hatred, and hostility in the children. Not finding the security in the parents frightens the children, making them pressure the parents for it all the more. This sets up vicious circles of anxiety involving both the parents and the children. The family situation becomes worse, and the children grow even more insecure. These children who feel that something is lacking—things which in reality are recognition, acceptance, understanding, discipline, love, security, and an over-all mature relationship, but of which they are unaware—will continue to strive for that something of which they were deprived as they grow older, feeling that they do not have enough of everything. They become extremely possessive of people and property. Their demands may grow to be insatiable, and this becomes a source of aggression and of wanting to take advantage of others in their drive for self-satisfaction and security. Also, this type of person will readily reach for government hand-outs.

Today, we find the people of the United States enjoying a higher standard of living, and with more leisure time, than any other people in the known history of the world. With the coming of such affluence we have seen a change in the family in which the mother's role is not merely one of subservience and of doing

33

housework. With automatic dishwashers and other labor-saving devices, she has more free time. She is better educated and more involved in the community and other affairs outside of the home. One unfortunate aspect of this is that the modern-day mother, because she frequently has had advanced training in some specific field, and because she feels she has to lend support to her husband's income, may engage herself in full-time work and leave her children in the care of a nursery. She may feel inadequate in dealing with her children and may want to get away from them, but basically the reason for her behavior is due to immaturity and her search for personal security. The more well-to-do might have their children enrolled in private schools during the winter and camps during the summer, both being away from home. The father generally has work and social commitments away from his house. If he is a part of big business, he may have to travel a great deal, and both he and his wife may have to entertain business associates. Both the mother and father, despite the amount of leisure time, are spending more and more time away from their home, each other, and their children. Due to this, and feeling guilty for it—plus a number of other reasons, such as having had deprived backgrounds themselves, wanting to be liked by their children, showing that they have been financially successful, ignorance, lacking in "warmth" and unable "to give of themselves"—but basically due to immaturity and insecurity, the parents saturate their children with material objects. Lax credit systems and installment plan buying have encouraged this irresponsible practice. The immature people frequently over-extend themselves financially in order to satisfy their own and their children's demands for immediate gratification. The further-incurred debts give more reason to the wife that she has to work in order to supplement the family income. The end result is a family trend toward materialism, and less time spent as a family unit.

In addition to the materialism to which today's children are being introduced by their parents, lack of discipline, with consequent disrespect for and rebellion against the parents and all authority, is being implanted in our culture. This is as a result of inadequate controls over children; again, due to immature, insecure parents. The immature parents are afraid that they will not be liked by their children if they impose the restrictions. An immature parent, not finding the security for which he or she is looking in the relationship with the spouse, may be more apt to seek it in the relationship with the children, and not set limits. Very frequently the mother doesn't live up to her end of the bargain in disciplining the children, and the father is looked upon as an ogre by the children when he comes to the mother's rescue. The mother may even prevent the father from punishing the children. In many instances, both parents are equally ineffective in setting limits, or the father may even be worse than the mother.

Because they have not had a mature parental relationship and have not been limited in their behavior, the children do only what they want to do—that which comes easily and which gives immediate pleasure. They are impatient and cannot wait for anything; therefore, they cannot set goals and work for the future. They want everything that everyone else has. The more that something is out of their reach, the more they will want it. To ward off temptation is very difficult for them. At age sixteen they want an automobile; they cannot wait until marriage before they indulge in sexual relations. Immediate gratification is foremost in their mind, and they may even lie and steal to obtain it. Pain and discomfort, hard work, disappointment, failure, unhappiness, or stresses of any kind are not well-tolerated. Because they feel inadequate they find it difficult to accept sickness and weakness of any kind, such as dependence and indecisiveness, in themselves and in others. They don't know the meaning of the word "sacrifice." They become self-centered and selfish, having no real interest in others. They have not learned "to share, to give and take," only "to take." They have not learned to work for things and to complete a job without supervision. They cannot accept responsibility. They will not keep their promises. They will become defiant, domineering, and even aggressive, taking advantage of others, including their parents, in order to get their own way. Because they have been given things without exerting any effort, they hold little appreciation or value for them. In fact, for the above-mentioned reasons, and perhaps others, their entire value-system, their goals, and even their purpose for living, are distorted. From their immature parents, who all too frequently are directing their energies in "keeping up with the Joneses," they have gained the impression that money and material possessions, such as expensive homes, cars, and boats, are of most importance. They become envious of those who possess these items, and later in life they will be jealous of fellow employees and others, even if the others have achieved success via their own merit. Laziness is a key word here. Initiative is lacking, and there is little or no motivation for trying to get ahead on one's own merit. These children do not really know what is expected of them, yet they feel as though they are indispensable. They complain that there is "nothing to do," and they engage in bizarre activities "just for kicks"— that is, for the thrill involved. They adopt a "how much can you get away with?" philosophy. They do only what they want to do and are pressured to do. They feel that parents and teachers are taking advantage of them when they are asked to do something. These are the children who give attention only to the subjects in school which are easy and might interest them, or they might refuse to study altogether. In later life they will not want to pay their bills or meet their other obligations. They will blame others for their failures. They will tend to take advantage of their job situation and their superiors, and do only a minimal amount of work. Because they are crippled in the use of their own potential, they may be driven by neurotic motivation in striving for success by the exploitation of others. Virtues and strength of character will be lacking.

In addition to the lack of limits and controls to which the children are subjected by their immature parents, there is frequently present an over-protective or over-controlled environment. The parents, due to their own inadequacy-feelings, and not believing that their children are capable, tend to do too much for the children; and the children grow up feeling that the world owes them a living. The parents, frequently perfectionistic, feel that they can do things better than the children, which, of course, they should be able to do. Also, they cannot wait for the children to do things themselves. Actually, the parents unknowingly are dominating and taking advantage of their children in doing this, imposing their will upon them; for they are not letting them grow gradually into independent and responsible adults. The parents are deriving pleasure, a feeling of adequacy, and a sense of security unconsciously in doing for their children, and feeling themselves to be valuable and necessary. By over-protecting the children and making them dependent upon them, really exploiting them, the parents are breeding anger, resentment, hostility, and aggression in the children which will be directed at them. The children rebel from being subjected to the inadequate controls and demands of the parents, whom they feel are weak and ignorant. In the extreme they become non-conformists, trying to be individualistic and different from others, especially their parents, yet being very dependent and basically insecure. They shun football and other organized sports which require strict discipline and teamwork. A power-struggle is set up between parents and their children, which serves in later life as a pattern for pressures and conflicts between all people. The children are raised as passive, dependent, insecure, immature people, with no self-reliance. Even upon graduation from college they will experience fears of getting married, going to work, or joining the military service. Due to basic insecurity, they will date anyone in order to feel popular and accepted. The women may rush into a marriage for fear of being left an old maid. Some are afraid to leave the secure school environment, where they can gain prestige for their knowledge, and they continue to work for advanced training and degrees. They grow up incapable of functioning on a mature competitive level, and are unprepared to attain goals by the use of their own potential. Because of their immaturity and weakness they invite exploitation; and when they come into contact with someone weaker than they, they will become the exploiters.

Some of these situations and symptoms mentioned are not necessarily related as cause and effect, and there may be an overlapping of other factors contributing to the behavior which is seen. Also, the difficulties pointed out may not all be present in one individual, or in the same degree in every individual. What is important is that this pathological personality and behavioral trend is in evidence in our society today.

Without realizing it, we are witnessing the evolvement of this culture in the United States, influencing the rest of the world, in which materialistic-oriented, pleasure-seeking, undisciplined, dependent children are being raised into immature, insecure adults. The situation will worsen as these adults raise their own children. With the extension of immaturity, the problem of exploiting and being exploited will grow. The children have been exposed to material possessions and easy living by their parents, and they believe that they are deserving of material things, success, and security. However, they find themselves to be inept in gaining all of this by themselves. Due to their insecurity and immaturity, they are confronted with not being able to function up to par—not being able to utilize their potential to the fullest in order to achieve these things. Because of the fear of failure, since failure would accentuate their feelings of inadequacy and insecurity, they frequently do not try to succeed. They find it difficult to trust anyone and always feel cheated. They are over-demanding, and attempt to get more than the other person. This is the type of person who might resort to cheating and stealing, and who will readily accept hand-outs, and will reach for what he believes to be security through a Welfare State and Socialism. This cultural trend of raising immature people in the United States and the rest of the world has to be interrupted if man is to live under freedom. Insecure, dependent people lack the confidence to make decisions and to act on ideas, which is essential for one to succeed in a free-enterprise system. More important, this cultural trend has to be interrupted if we are ever to have permanent world peace, for it is incompatible for an immature people to live in peace for any length of time.

There are countless everyday examples of immaturity and insecurity involving people of all age levels and in all walks of life. It would be impossible and impractical to attempt to cover all of them. However, enough should be said to convince even the skeptics that we are in fact an immature people, and that the future of mankind rests with our doing something about becoming more mature. These examples are not given with any malicious or hostile intent, and they should be accepted in the spirit of promoting understanding and brotherhood in the world.

We see today that there are more and more children who play in pairs and not in groups. Whether this is due to the

38

children not wanting the rivalry of a third or more persons, or not having to deal in the "give-and-take" relationship of a group —it being easier to take a dominant or subordinate role in a twosome, or for other reasons—it suggests a basic insecurity in our younger people. There are the many behavior and learning difficulties that are present in our population of the so-called normal children, not to mention that there are also a large number of those who are severely emotionally-disturbed. We are all familiar with the general unrest of the adolescents, the "rumbles" and demonstrations, the defiance of authority, the unwillingness to respect adults and conform to an orderly way of life. Many of them do not seem to realize that to be individualistic is everyone's right, so long as it does not impinge upon the rights of others. They balk at being drafted into the military service, but this is understandable if we recall that their parents raised them as not being able to accept discipline, and having too much in the way of material things and luxury. They expect that someone else will serve and care for them. The teenagers of today may have advantages in education, travel, and material possessions, but, like their parents, they are lacking in emotional maturity. It was mentioned that they are frequently criticized for being impatient, for not respecting their elders, and for not following their directions. In many instances, however, the parents do not merit respect and do not set a good example for their children to follow. Some parents are preoccupied with their own adjustment to a fast-changing world, and they do not really know how, or are too immature and insecure, to deal effectively with their children. They may rationalize letting their children dictate to them as an indication of the children's growing mature and independent. There is little wonder that so many of our children are turning toward "the easy way" and dishonesty when their parents lead lives of connivance, unfaithfulness, and general dishonesty. It is alarming that the parents rationalize their own misbehavior and accept it as a way of life, being self-righteous and even religious in public, not aware enough of their actions that they feel a need to change their ways.

We have seen that many indecisive parents will accept their neighbor's line of reasoning and will permit early dating for their own children. Due to their own insecurity the parents will encourage their children to "go steady"—that is, be accepted and be popular. They frequently condone, even initiate, the organization of "canteens" and other activities where the children will be introduced to dancing and socializing with the opposite sex at a very young age. These are the same insecure parents who either "push" their children to start school at an early age, or keep them home an extra year so that they will have "the edge" over their peers. We have only to see the numbers of immature mothers who cannot refuse their children all kinds of sweets which produce tooth decay, who do not enforce brushing after meals, and who cannot get their children to the dentist for proper care and instruction. Actually, dental caries should be called the "Immature-Mother Syndrome."

How many teenagers do we see dressing in the same manner and joining groups and cliques in order to feel accepted, "to belong," to prove their self-worth, and to feel secure? How many school drop-outs and juvenile delinquents are there? Statistics reveal that those who have personality problems and mental disorders of all types are on the increase. Increasing is the incidence of divorces and family break-ups, crimes of all sorts, the so-called psychosomatic illnesses, drug and alcohol addiction, smoking, obesity, immorality, infidelity, and illegitimacy, to list a few—all related to immaturity. These exist in people in all walks of life, including our leaders.

The immature parents of today in this country are raising children who lack self-discipline. But of at least equal importance, although it may not be realized, is that the schools, the courts, the government, and others in positions of authority, are setting a bad example and reinforcing the children's patterns of misbehavior. The people in authority, most of them parents themselves, are erring, not only in the handling of their own children, but also, in the handling of other people's children. They do not enforce decisive and immediate restriction and punishment, due to ignorance and immaturity. The people in authority—that is, ultimately, the government—err in overprotecting the children and making them more dependent by giving them hand-outs. The people in authority, the government, use the same bad method of permissiveness in dealing with the older children and adults as was used by the parents when they were raising the children. This gives confirmation to the parents that they must have used the right methods with their children, and it encourages new parents to proceed in the same bad manner.

Apropos of this, there are too many lawyers who, under the guise of offering fair treatment and justice to their clients—but in reality seeking personal gain, such as exorbitant fees—detain and deter the carrying out of justice, "stretching the law to the limit." Only the rich can afford this "justice" in serious crimes. They, the lawyers, give false reassurance to their clients that they have been wronged. They minimize criminal acts and magnify accident cases for greater compensation and payments. The lawyers, through their actions, condone and encourage the patterns of misbehavior which were formulated in childhood. More important, they are giving license to other unstable people, especially children, to misbehave. Also pertinent in this discussion is the large number of people who give the "I don't want to get involved" excuse. These people have been witness to some type of wrongdoing, but they will fail to help a person in distress, and fail to assist in the prosecution of the defendant. They are insecure, and feel that they will make their positions even more insecure in that the wrongdoer and his attorney might retaliate against them. They fear being sued for libel or slander, or even being physically harmed. In the same vein but on a larger scale are the private citizens and leaders of our country, supposedly mature individuals, who "turn their backs" on the widespread existence of pornography, gambling, political corruption and graft, public Communist demonstrations, and other provocative activities, not being able to adequately curtail them. The offenders are behaving immaturely in impinging upon the rights of weak people in seeking personal gain and gratification. The participants in such activities are also immature and vulnerable in their search for self-gain and gratification. Of most importance is the presence of immaturity in the judges of the courts of law, the civil and church leaders, the politicians, and the masses of people tolerating the exploitation and not doing anything about it. They are giving tacit consent that the offenders continue their practices. All of this is taking

41

place because of weak laws, weak law-makers, and weak law-enforcers. Hypocrites and immature are those using double standards, "bending" the law to suit their own purposes, and not desiring equal justice to all.

We have all been guilty of it ourselves, or have seen people who have gained pleasure from others' misfortunes. This is, in reality, evidence of immaturity in which our positions are seemingly strengthened and we feel more adequate in comparison to the unfortunate person. We have seen people measure a person by his possessions and station in life, and not by his potential and the methods he used in the attainment of his personal achievements. These are the people who are brand-name conscious, the "social climbers" and status-seekers, who want only to mingle with the intellectuals, the famous, the wealthy, and who ignore others felt to be beneath their level.

We have all been witness to those who tell half-truths and who distort facts in order to make themselves "look good." In all walks of life there are people with inadequacy-feelings who "look down" at other people, and who, through disparaging remarks and actions made to their faces or behind their backs, try to "hold down" the other people—thus, in comparison, building up themselves. They might be critical of a person's work, manner of dress, his house, or his friends. There are those who would discredit and blackball someone from being generally accepted. In degrading someone they feel that their own status will be elevated in the eyes of the others. This type of person comes first, and he disregards other people's property, time, and feelings, especially if the other people do not object too much. Of danger to the average individual is the immature, insecure person in a position of responsibility, such as a doctor, social worker, clergyman, or teacher, who cannot admit to himself that he does not know the answer; and who gives false reassurance that a condition is not serious, thereby detaining the person from obtaining the proper help that he needs. There are a great many people in all walks of life who give ill advice, not maliciously, fostering dependency in the listener because they want to feel adequate and thereby gain security.

Immature people discourage and even obstruct others from doing things because, as the others progress, they feel even more

42

inadequate that they are being bypassed and left behind. Intent upon belittling somebody, they will not accept anything that the other person says or does as being right. We have seen those who have the least knowledge being the first to criticize and berate anyone who might make an error, or who seems to be inferior to them. These people will make an issue of the error and "rub it in." If his worker has a good idea, an immature boss might claim the idea to be his own and accept the praise and reward for it. However, if the idea is a bad one, he will be sure to let it be known by everyone. Many blame others for their own mistakes and failures. There are those who are constantly "leaning" on others, depending upon them for food, money, companionship, or for other things, and those who take advantage of friendships. How many people try to impose their will upon others, and how many have been "talked into" or "high-pressured" into doing something that they did not really want to do? Many people will not ask questions or make statements for fear of being ridiculed for not knowing anything. Many will not "let go" of their emotions for fear that someone will take advantage of them and hurt their feelings.

More subtle is the leech who "picks others' brains" for information, and who uses the ideas in his way of life as though they were originally his own—even belittling those from whom he stole the information. This might be a person who literally steals a business idea from another, and along with the idea he receives enough assurance and enthusiasm to beat the originator in making a venture using the idea. He may have even been inferior intellectually and emotionally, but he was able to make a decision based on the originator's confidence in the idea. Under the guise of being shrewd businessmen, there are some who take advantage of other businesses and their products, hoping to elevate their own positions and security by defamation. Some resort to misleading advertising and outright lying about their services and products. Due to neurotic motivation, many people become successful in the sense that they achieve a great amount of education, money, power, or fame. They even contribute to the progress of civilization in their sporadic endeavors, although it is the more mature people who account for the gradual and stable advancement of all. Invariably, those with neurotic motivation succeed at the expense of others. They are never truly happy and satisfied; because of their immaturity they never feel that their goals are fulfilled, and they never really feel secure. As evidence of man's growing immaturity and insecurity, we see men who are fearful and lacking in confidence to start their own businesses. They frequently seek group practices, salaried positions, partnerships, and associations in business ventures, and desire conferences so that they can share other people's views. These insecure and dependent people lean to joining others so that they might gain support, protection, and security for themselves.

We all are familiar with the conceited person, and the one who overcompensates to be charming. Also, we have met the "dogooders," who openly support all charities, racial integration, and the like, to gain praise and security, but who personally contribute nothing, and who would be intolerant if a person of a different race were to move next door to them. A person who states that he has little trust or faith in doctors, for example, or in religion, or in anyone, for that matter, is one who feels inadequate and has little faith and confidence in himself. There are those people who, in order to feel important and valuable but because they feel basically insecure, engross themselves in their work, not even taking time out for vacations. We all have had experiences with waitresses, store clerks, gas station attendants, and others, who have had no pride in doing a good job, but who have wanted to be compensated well for slipshod and even unnecessary services. How many of us have accepted this without demanding better work of them, even tipping them? Anyone in business is aware of the "deadbeat" and problems relative to collecting money. Just as immature is the person who is easy prey to the "deadbeat," not insisting that he make his payments. How many people do we see today who are unhappy and dissatisfied with their positions in life? An example of an insecure person is one who goes to extremes in helping others in order to feel worthwhile. Also insecure is the person at the other end of the scale who is observed as not wanting to help anyone, the selfish person who holds on to the little that he feels he possesses—the inadequate amount of money, ability, and energy—so that he won't be depleted and others won't go ahead of him. There are those who are too withdrawn, and those who are too much "on the go," always having to be with people, and not able to tolerate being alone.

Some people accumulate great wealth because of other people's immaturity and insecurity. The entire insurance business is prospering due to the ever-increasing insecurity of people. Alcoholic beverages, smoking, gambling, and prostitution are big businesses in which the operators are catering to the needs of, and taking advantage of, immature and weak people. Television is another business which for the most part caters to weak-willed people. It fosters laziness and decay of the body and mind in those who already do not want to expend much energy. In many instances it presents sex and violence to the young people as being fashionable and modern. Too often it glamorizes and romanticizes war. It abounds with "give-away" programs, fostering a "get rich for little or no effort" theme. Liberal credit systems also cater to immature people who cannot forestall immediate gratification. The immature people cannot save money and are enticed into over-extending themselves financially with installment-plan buying. Living on a budget, they might claim that they can pay a certain amount per month, not caring too much for how long a period of time they will have to pay. They make commitments not on what they can realistically afford, but on what they can afford to pay today. They may take out one large loan to pay off their many smaller loans.

Observed is the practice for doctors and hospitals, sign painters, plumbers, garage mechanics, and others to charge a set fee for a service, but to increase it for "someone who can pay," or if the client is covered by insurance. The irony of this practice is that a person will complain if he has to pay more for something, yet he, himself, will overcharge someone else in the same manner. Some of these people rationalize their actions by saying that their overcharge fee is the usual one, and that they are lowering the price for most of the people who cannot pay more. In overcharging, the person is acting like an immature child in trying to get as much as he can get. When he receives his exorbitant price, due to the demand exceeding the supply, he now believes he is worth it, and he has a false value

45

of his own worth. A mature person, a conscientious person, will perform a service to the best of his ability all of the time. His service to a rich man should not be worth more because the rich man has the money to pay more. A rich man should not have to pay double the price of a loaf of bread that a poorer man would have to pay. Actually, these people are immature, and they are exploiting others with this practice. The people who are exploited are immature, also, in allowing themselves to be exploited.

Nowadays, with larger schools and classrooms, and greater numbers of people working for the same concerns, with people being given numbers for social security, credit cards, etc., and there being more and more depersonalization, there is good reason why people who feel insecure might feel even more insecure. Being "just a number" in an expanding, complex society, without favoritism, places pressure upon a person to produce, to exercise his own potential in proving himself worthy and secure. The pressure can become intolerable to the immature person who is not independent and self-reliant.

Indicative of man's insecurity is the trend of more young people studying sociology and becoming social workers and psychologists because they "like people and want to help people." On a deeper level, they want to be with people and see what they are like; they want to learn from them, be like them, and be accepted by them. Too many psychiatrists, social workers, guidance counselors, ministers, and the like are in their type of work because they are looking for answers to their own emotional problems. Many of them vie with each other in trying to help others, being primarily concerned with building up their own feelings of adequacy and security.

We are all familiar, or should be familiar, with biased news reports. Unfortunately, the greatest majority of people do not and cannot "read between the lines" in order to formulate their own objective versions of an issue. A story may have been written, for example, praising a leader for the manner in which he tactfully handled a controversy, yet it is not realized that he may have blundered and was responsible for the controversy in the first place. In the same vein, prejudiced news reporters speak of the "Chinese hordes", the "treacherous North Viet Namese", and the "Arab terrorists". This gives readers the distorted view that all the people of those nationalities are Communist sympathizers, and that they all are our enemies. It paints the picture that we, including our leaders, are free from fault. The newspaper coverage, especially in small towns, is quite poor. Certain episodes of vital concern involving town, and even higher, governments are invariably kept from the public. Events involving the wealthy with influence are, for the most part, squelched. Even news of national and world significance is censored "in order not to alarm the masses".

An immature person's dealings with another person are all consciously or unconsciously measured in terms of what benefit the relationship will be to him. He offers favors in return for favors. We all know of people who show favoritism, in schools, in business, in the armed forces, and in all other walks of life. Many people go to extremes in favoring those of the same organization, religion, or nationality, and of being intolerant of all others. They are not being objective, not rewarding someone for a job well done; but they are giving reward to an undeserving favorite, to one who is not best qualified, and this is immature behavior. This discourages another person from wanting to utilize his potential to the limit in seeking merit, and it denies him opportunity, satisfaction, success, and security. Furthermore, in accepting a favor one becomes indebted to the giver; and when another situation arises between them, a mature, objective evaluation regarding the situation cannot be made. This is extremely important in politics, where favoritism is an accepted practice in all levels of government, from the federal to the smallest municipality. A certain leader might offer patronage to legislators so that they will vote for his bill or offer a job to a favorite constituent. The leader in making political appointments is furthering his personal gain, and the taxpayers are being exploited in paying the salaries of those who are not the best qualified to represent and to work for them. This applies to the practice of "balancing a ticket" by nominating a person of a certain race, nationality, religion, or geographical area, for public appeal and voting power, not for

47

his qualifications and potential service to all. These practices are an insult to mature people; and, in fact, if people were truly mature, the practices would not exist.

The practice of patronage is a forerunner to secret deals, and to corrupt ways, and to a weakening of the government and the governed. The politicians are seeking personal gain. The recipients of the patronage are growing more dependent, losing their freedom of thought and action, by becoming indebted to their leaders. The public is not getting the best representation. Too frequently, powerful factions "behind the scenes" who supported the leaders in becoming elected are influencing the leaders in important decisions involving the country and the world.

Decisions influenced by favors are not arrived at in a mature way. They are not made with the thought in mind of what is best for the people, but with the thought in mind of what is best for the politician himself. He, the politician, is seeking personal gain and security. There are countless instances of the flagrant abuse of political power. Legislatures voting themselves pay raises, unjustly taking land by eminent domain, and awarding constituents contracts at exorbitant prices are just a few minor examples. Such behavior is an insult to the taxpayer. Favoritism and patronage are not far removed from discrimination, prejudice, and bigotry. Some people are favored, while others are opposed and not given equal consideration. Immature are the politicians, "small-town" and "big-time" politicians alike, who, under the guise of helping people and working for the common good, use political influence and legal maneuvering to benefit themselves. Also immature are those in subordinate positions who accept this exploitation. Too many of our present-day leaders attain their positions because of neurotic motivation and aggressiveness. And too many voters go along with the crowd in electing these men, and others who are dishonest and who have even served jail sentences.

Man has always exploited fellow man, from making him a slave to even enjoying seeing him tormented. Men of learning have knowingly duped large masses of ignorant people into accepting the idea of reincarnation. While the select live in comfort, the masses are expected to accept poverty with the belief

48

they will return to this life as better people and deserving of more—the implication being that they are now bad people and do not deserve anything better. In Communist China, for their own gain the leaders "brainwash" the children to step on the United States flag every day and shoot a picture of Uncle Sam. There is little wonder that dissension exists between countries when we see people in the same country resentful of their own kind. Everywhere there are examples of this—for instance, the caste system, racial discrimination, class distinction, etc.

Today, as in the past, some men grow extremely powerful and fabulously wealthy at the expense of others. For their own personal gain, some leaders make commitments which prove to be detrimental to large numbers of people. Where objective studies were made that for the common good of the country it would be best to eliminate certain out-moded, inefficient and costly government installations, local politicians supported and even led people to oppose such action. Monopolies have been in existence, safeguarded by the government from competition, benefiting mostly a comparatively small number of early investors. For their own gain, in order to make money, greedy, immature businessmen have sold and continue to sell food and material to hostile nations. And for their own gain, in order to obtain votes, greedy, immature leaders have supported and continue to support these sales. In the past, and still in the present, selfish capitalists have taken advantage of the so-called lower classes of people. So long as they are well-off financially, served by the less fortunate, they show little concern that the less fortunate might improve their position in life. They feel more secure to have the masses of people remain in poverty and ignorance. Because of this type of immature behavior and the exploitation of the masses of people by the wealthy, and in the hope that these laboring masses could elevate their position in life, Communism was originated. However, as will be pointed out, the Communist leaders, being immature themselves, but under the guise of wanting to help the impoverished, continue the same pattern of exploitation, even to a worse degree.

There are those who are called philanthropists—not all—who accumulated a large amount of wealth by the exploitation of others. For a number of reasons, such as the desire of feeling

49

secure, guilt feelings, gaining satisfaction and fame, feeling superior to the recipients, leaving a monument to themselves, they begin to give away some of their money. In like manner, there are some leaders who turn to benevolence after having ruthlessly reached the top. The only time, it seems, that man can offer help to his fellow man, with the exception of his being influenced by neurotic motivations, is when he himself is sufficiently mature and secure, and he does not feel threatened that the other person will surpass and be superior to him.

The immature, insecure people in the upper income brackets —management in big business, due to their greediness and the desire for more profits for themselves—take advantage of the working people by offering them substandard wages and working conditions. Without their realizing it, their actions pressure the working people to seek more protection and hand-outs from the government and labor unions. On the other side of the coin, those in the lower income brackets, the workers, also due to immaturity, take advantage of the capitalists by not working up to capacity. They do not appreciate what is offered to them in the way of opportunity to advance themselves, but are interested only in immediate pleasure and comfort for the least amount of effort. They provoke and pressure the immature rich to even more exploitation. Something else which may not be realized is that the leaders of the labor unions, even though they are representing the workers, are too frequently more concerned with their personal gain than the plight of the workers. Their personal interest is not unlike that which exists in most other leaders of all types throughout the world. This pressure between the working classes and the well-to-do has always existed and still exists. Not until all the people mature, the rich and poor alike, and stop taking advantage of each other, but instead seek to primarily advance their own potential to the limit, will there be a more stable, mutually-beneficial existence for all, and a veering-off from our present-day Socialistic and Communistic trend. Not until all the people mature, and act more for the common good of the country and the world than for themselves, will there be a more stable economy with less chance for depression or inflation, and peace for all.

A problem encountered, more so in the past, is one of immature nationalism, where people are led to believe that their country and its leaders can do no wrong. They feel that even to the death and at the expense of other nations and people, they must defend their country, right or wrong. On the other side of the coin, more prominent today than in the past, there are those who are quick to overlook their responsibility and allegiance to their country. These people are insecure and selfish, thinking of themselves and their own safety first. They do not consider what will be best for their country and their children in the future.

We have all read how, during disasters, such as wars, hurricanes, and floods, certain people have not only not helped others, but have resorted to looting and even killing in order to help themselves. Many of us may have been witness to the so-called stable person's experiencing a state of panic with only a minimal amount of stress, let alone when he is confronted with an emergency situation. All of these people are basically immature, their actions being motivated by selfishness, and they have little or no inclination to help anyone else.

One who might dispute the present-day immaturity of man need only be reminded of the annihilation of over five million Jews by a civilized mankind during World War II. If someone might argue that only a relatively small number of people were involved in that massacre, he must still admit that there were not enough mature individuals in the world so that the extermination of the Jews, and even World War II itself, might have been prevented. It is an insult to the decent people of the world that the guilty few even dared to carry out such a crime against humanity. It is an insult to the decent people of the world that any type of exploitation exists. When the time comes that more people have grown to be mature, they will not have to tolerate any form of injustice.

The constant struggles which exist between countries, between the different factions within a country, between the governments and the governed, between management and labor, and between any people who have entered into a contractual arrangement, are a reflection of the immaturity which exists in people. It is not surprising that so much discord exists between relative strangers when people within immediate families find

51

it difficult to get along with each other. People are unable "to give" as mature people in a reciprocal exchange. The need "to take" is overwhelming, and creates conflict.

Mentioned before was that a dependent people are a weak people, and weak people provoke the Communists and others, who are immature and aggressive, to dominate them. Lack of self-discipline and immorality are aspects of immaturity, just as is dependency upon others. A decadent society is an immature and a weak society, and it invites domination from aggressors. It should be stressed that in the United States we are seeing more people employed by the government and the development of an excessively-large government, which means a weakening of the people and a deterioration of the true function of a democratic government.

We see daily evidence of the softening and weakening of the people in this country and throughout the world. We see more and more people, particularly the young people—which is all the more depressing and serious—who want reward with little or no effort. They tend more to choose the "easy way" with cheating, lying, and stealing. We see the same thing with the adults in the business world with their double standards, taking advantage of people by performing unnecessary services to obtain more money, overcharging, and doing inferior work and the least amount of work possible—but expecting others not to do it to them. We see the movement of the masses toward shunning work, wasting time and materials, and believing that they deserve more pleasure and leisure time. Advertizers capitalize on selling the idea to these people that they deserve special things, such as a certain brand of whiskey, or a winter vacation in Florida.

There are those who cannot give up the immediate pleasure of smoking, although it might prove injurious to their health. There seems to be a confusion in identification in our children, with the boys dressing more effeminately, and the girls dressing and behaving more like boys. There are now more observers of sports than participants, as compared to years ago. In football there are more fair catches and field-goal attempts being made. Statistics reveal that over fifty percent of the youth in this country are rejected by the draft for military service because of emotional, intellectual, and physical disabilities. What is more distressing is that many of the parents of these young people are actually pleased that their children will not have to leave them, apparently not being fully concerned or aware that they have raised inadequate, dependent, and immature children. Being selfish and undisciplined, many of today's children have little desire to embark upon careers such as medicine, nursing, teaching, or the clergy, where they might devote their lives to helping others. These jobs require unselfishness and self-discipline, and the feeling of wanting "to give" more than wanting "to take." Too many of those who do enter these professions are emotionally-immature and neurotically-motivated.

A common complaint is that the present-day specialist physician is "cold" and does not extend sympathy and reassurance, as did the old-time family doctor. Actually, it is the immature people who missed something in their family relationships in their childhood who are seeking this. Also, the specialists themselves may be immature, and it is true that they cannot "give" to their patients.

Weakness is seen in the laxity of discipline in the family, and the increase of immorality in social spheres. Parents are using their influence in getting their inept, ambitionless children into college. Educators are more and more "spoon-feeding" the students, making them more dependent, and allowing for misconduct in the classrooms and on campuses. Even the courts and religious bodies, due to unsureness of their positions, are yielding to the so-called changes of the modern world—actually, the pressures of immature people.

In this country there has been a recent surge for even more freedom. This may seem amusing to those of other countries who have always been oppressed. It is ironic that some of the so-called intellectuals complain about the lack of freedom of self-expression. Under a democratic government, they want the freedom to be able to eulogize Communism and express themselves, yet they certainly would have to keep their thoughts to themselves if they were living under the Communistic system.

There have been public demonstrations, dissension and protestation, mostly by students, opposing adult power, racial discrimination, and government foreign policy regarding wars.

There have been pleas for more sexual freedom, less censorship of obscene literature, and more freedom of speech and press, among other things. It is immature people, seeking personal gain in the forms of vicarious pleasure, monetary rewards, and the like, who take advantage of other immature and weak people when they offer them smut. They are inciting those with little emotional control to sexual misbehavior, and are promoting the degeneracy of the family unit. Unfortunately, many adults in positions of high authority have supported these young people —saying that they, the students, are capable of arriving at the right decisions themselves. It seems that these adults are resorting to wishful thinking in expecting the students to make correct judgments when they, themselves, have not had the wisdom to produce adequate guideposts for them. Those who are fighting for more freedom in these cases are invariably the ones who are most immature, lacking in self-discipline and in need of more rigid controls. History reveals in most instances that these people as children were rebellious with their parents and all authority in general. They are fighting for more freedom and independence, wanting more of everything, even though invariably they have not taken advantage of the freedom that they already possess. Frequently, they attempt to live in an apartment, even in another city, away from their home and family, "to prove" to their parents and themselves that they are mature and independent. They indulge in drinking alcoholic beverages, sexual relations, and the taking of drugs for immediate gratification, to escape their responsibilities and for other reasons; but principally because they associate these habits with adulthood, more privileges, and more freedom. Mistakenly, adulthood is equated to emotional maturity. It should be recognized that some people never attain a maturity commensurate with their chronological age. The young people are seeking this maturity, acceptance by each other, and security. They are acting like adults, but not like mature adults. They mistakenly believe that rebellion and non-conformity mean they are thinking for themselves and are independent. They are basically dependent and insecure, and they are not mature enough to be able to take advantage of any additional freedom and independence in a mature way.

Many more examples of immaturity could have been given, but suffice it to say that we, the people of the United States, are an immature people. The same can be said of the people of all the other countries of the world.

* * * *

To summarize, we have to draw the conclusion that all the people of the world, including the leaders, are immature. Man is not advancing in the emotional area as rapidly as in his various other areas of growth. Emotional immaturity has been defined. Democratic government and its cultural trends have been severely criticized.

The United States is heading in the direction of becoming a total Welfare State. Not only are the people who accept governmental controls immature, but also immature are the leaders who are proponents of the hand-out legislation. Our entire way of life, from the immature parents' attitudes in the raising of children, to the immature parental attitudes of big business, the government, and American psychiatry, is geared in the direction of over-protecting and over-controlling immature, insecure, dependent people and making them even more dependent. Not only are the people being over-protected and over-controlled on the one hand, but also we see on the other hand that they are not adequately limited, controlled, and disciplined. The parents, the government, the law-enforcing agencies, the schools, and others in authority, are all not setting right and decisive restrictions, due to their own immaturity. More and more immature, insecure people are being raised.

Many examples of immaturity in all walks of life have been given. It was stressed that dependence and lack of discipline in a people amount to weakness, and a weak people provoke aggressors to attack them. It is an insult to the decent people of the world that exploitation of people exists, and it is immature of the people that the exploitation has not been curtailed.

CHAPTER II

WHY DO WE HAVE WARS?

Instead of asking, "Why do we have wars?", it might be more appropriate to ask, "Why do PEOPLE have wars?" Wars do not just happen. It is PEOPLE who are involved in their inception and who fight in them. Disputes involving property rights and other factors, some real, some rationalized, have been given as the causes of wars; but it is fundamentally because a peaceful resolution is not reached by PEOPLE with opposing opinions that wars begin.

War is basically senseless and unnecessary. It is true that people's fighting in some wars has prevented their becoming slaves of the aggressors. Yet enslavement could have been prevented, and war could have been averted, had enough people been strong enough emotionally, intellectually, and physically to have thwarted the aggressors in the first place. Almost always it is the innocent and uninvolved people who suffer the worst agony in a war, and it is the strongest and healthiest who are killed and incapacitated. The leaders responsible for the war usually get along best, with their access to food and shelter, and even escape.

War is not natural and inevitable. It might be said by some that wars are necessary periodically in order to limit the population of the world. It is true that many people are killed during a war, but it is also true that there are more marriages and babies born immediately following a war. If there is a shortage of food and land area, and overpopulation is considered to be a real threat to the survival of mankind, then the problem of overpopulation should be approached primarily and directly. It should be decided to evaluate if other forms of food can be developed, if new places to live might be discovered, and if the population growth can be controlled. If it should be decided to curtail the population growth by the extermination of people through wars, then it should be realized by us that this is what we desire, and this is the reason that we are engaged in a war. We would understand that war is a necessary means to handling the population growth. We would not accept the control of the population as being a secondary consequence of war. We might even plan and start a war in order to reduce the number of people, although this would be inconceivable of people who have become aware of their rationalizations.

Other reasons can be given why wars might seem to be necessary. One of these is for the maintenance of a national and world economy. Because of the enormous production of expendable arms and equipment, the vast destruction of property, and the lag in creation of civilian consumer goods during a war, one can readily see why there might be a spurt in the economy. This may be true in a sense, and one is fortunate if he survives a war to be able to capitalize from it. However, any spurt in the economy is actually a spurt that has come about under false circumstances. A country's economy may not have been functioning on sound principles; and even if they are sound, the presence of an unpredictable catastrophe has made it possible for the economy to prosper. It is true that some wars may be termed as having been predictable, but those wars were instigated by an immature and unpredictable people. The apparent prosperity from war is a false prosperity. Any progress that may have been made because of a war is progress made during unstable and abnormal times.

One might speculate that perhaps the only time we will ever have a permanent peace on this earth is when all the peoples are intermixed and there is a complete unity, with the possibility of just one country. This could come about gradually through intermarriages, an international law, and the sharing of educational facilities and other resources. There could even be an acceptance of one main existing religion, or the formation of a universal religion. All of this could be attained more rapidly if, for example, we were attacked by another planet and the earth peoples united in a common effort for survival. Although such an eventual union is conceivable, the prospects of a durable peace would not be good if people remained as they are now. We need only be reminded of the existence of civil wars.

Basically, all the people in this world are the same. No one nationality or color of people is essentially superior to another. This means, for example, that intrinsically the Americans are no better than the French, and the Germans are no better than the Chinese. It is true that the people of a particular nation, in comparison to those of other nations, may possess more physical and mental endowment. Certain peoples may be able to tolerate the hot climates better, jump higher and run faster, advance scientifically and industrially more, and persevere in the exploitation from others to a greater degree. However, given improved conditions for a few generations so that they could have opportunities to exercise their potentials, one would suspect that the backward peoples would be elevated in their areas of deficiency. The reasons that they have been unable to provide themselves with improved conditions, and that they have not advanced so rapidly, may have been beyond their immediate control—such as unsuitable climate, epidemics, superstitions, pathological cultural trends, and, especially, very immature and greedy rulers. Due to possessing admirable traits—for example, steadfastness, loyalty, and dedication to family, friends, and country—they probably did not move from their original environment.

Every person develops an individual sense of values and attitudes as time goes on. He becomes influenced in his thoughts, feelings, and actions, and in how he will react to people and situations throughout his life. Of most importance in determining these traits in an individual are, first, hereditary factors; second, his nationalistic and cultural heritage, including his racial characteristics and religious beliefs; and third, his immediate environment. The latter refers to a person's parents, family, and close acquaintances—that is, his over-all upbringing—which principally account for his individual personality patterns. The three combined—the hereditary predisposition, the cultural traits, and the immediate family influence—make up a person's total personality. Concerning the nationalistic and cultural aspects, some groups of people in general are very emotionally-demonstrative. One nationality, more so than others, might tend to be more impulsive and emotionally-explosive. Another, with its paternalistic, authoritative orientation, may have more tendency to superiority feelings and have more inclination to engage in war. These cultural factors are extremely dangerous because the people, especially the children of a particular nation, might believe, since all other people immediately surrounding them have the same traits, that these are normal and acceptable. However, an entire culture and an entire nation can be wrong. In addition to their individual personality-problems, these certain people must cope with the broader abnormal cultural characteristics which have been passed down to them. We can see that peoples brought up in radically-different cultures might find it difficult to agree on the definition of terms in attempting to settle a dispute. They may claim to have no recognition of the dignity and rights of man, and they may not abide by any set rules of morality.

All human beings have similar drives and needs, and are faced with similar frustrations. How they will go about dealing with these needs and frustrations will vary according to their personality make-up. There may be emotional conflicts present blocking a person from attaining his fullest potential, and his direction in life may become neurotically-motivated.

Also important in how a person will think and act are the form of government under which he is living—that is, the amount of freedom and opportunity he has to exercise his potential; and the sum total of his position and possessions. How successful and secure a person may be will influence how he will feel toward others, and if he will offer the others help. It is much easier for someone with a full stomach and not wanting for anything to be understanding and compassionate for others. By the same token, if a person is struggling for existence due to poverty and oppression, most probably he is going to be lacking in feeling for his fellow man, and it will be more difficult for him to take into consideration the problems of others.

Throughout the world in every country, in the United States and in Russia, there are immature people and immature leaders. These immature people, because they feel insecure and frightened, believe that other people—especially strong, secure people—in word and deed are taking advantage of them. Of course, that mature, secure people would take advantage of them is not true. However, immature people are taking advantage of them. In their attempt to attain success and security, consciously or unconsciously these immature, insecure people themselves tend to take advantage of and dominate still other people—especially weak, insecure people. In fact, these still other weak people, and all weak people, because they are meek and an easy target, will provoke or entice other immature people to try to impose their will upon them.

An insecure person is not certain of his standing, and he compares himself with others to see how he measures up to them. In order for him to think of himself as being worth something and to feel secure, in order for him to elevate himself and to believe that he is at least up to par with the others, he may try to "step on" the other people. In other words, such a person boosts his ego, "builds himself up", or feels secure by "knocking others down." Of course, the "build-up" is a false one, for he himself has not improved; only in comparison to the "knocked-down" person does he feel on the same level or superior. Nevertheless, in his search for security his behavior in one form or another has taken aggressive trends.

Now, the insecure people and leaders of a certain country, especially if the other country's leaders are secure and strong, will feel that any controversy between the two nations is a threat to their own security. They, because of their basic feelings of inadequacy and of not measuring up to par, will react in a negativistic, retaliatory way in search for security. Of course, because of the opposition's strength, direct action may not be taken; nevertheless, a smouldering hostility remains. Also important is that the insecure people and leaders of a nation, consciously or unconsciously, by the nature of their immaturity and insecurity, may take initial aggressive steps against another country in order to gain security, especially if the other country is weak and invites an attack. The leaders of a country, in wanting to feel superior and secure, may instigate a war with another country and then give the excuse that they are only protecting their own rights. Again, it should be stressed that this might take place on a strictly unconscious level. No matter which way you look at it, problems are created by immature people; and, because immature people do not examine problems objectively, eliminating their personal feelings, the problems do lead to aggressive actions, fighting, and war.

All people are seeking self-preservation and personal security. They usually find them in infancy from their relationship with their mature parents, and in later life from successes through the realization of their potential. If they have not gained security, due to their having been raised by immature parents to be immature, dependent, and inadequate people, they will look for it from the exploitation of others. Their demands are insatiable, and they strive to have more than other people, even if they have to resort to aggressive and violent behavior to obtain it.

So long as there are two people in the world, if they are immature, there will be jealousy and resentment between them. One will want more than the other, will want to be the dominant one, and will want to be thought of as the more valuable one in his own eyes and in the eyes of the other. One will attempt to take advantage of the other. A mature person or nation cannot exist peacefully, advancing its own position, not impinging upon anyone's rights, in the presence of an immature person or nation. The immature person or nation will attempt to gain for itself what the mature person or nation possesses, not by exercising its own potential, but through the means of exploitation.

The fundamental factor, then, that causes war is immature people. We should call this the Immature People Concept of the Origin of War. There are not enough mature people in the right places in different countries throughout the world. There are not enough people who will stop others from taking advantage of them, and who have no desire to take advantage of others. There are not enough people with the emotional maturity, wisdom, and physical support to recognize and limit an aggressive nation and prevent war.

Some of the immature, insecure people actually overcompensate in the area of subjecting others to their will, and through their taking advantage of others they find themselves in positions of leadership. This is not to say that all leaders necessarily have to be immature, and that immature leaders are found only in an aggressive nation; for they are present in every country. That is, the leaders of opposing countries involved in a dispute, whether they be Communists, Fascists, or Capitalists, may have similar personality patterns. With a situation such as this, one can see the difficulties that two countries might encounter in trying to reach a compromise. If no compromise is reached, the result might be a war, with the possibility of millions of people fighting, suffering, and dying. It is regrettable, because the people are really fighting for their emotionally-sick leaders who are trying to fulfill their pathological needs.

Now, in addition to the top leaders, there are people occupying subordinate positions of leadership. These people will have personality patterns similar to those of the leaders, and for want of identifying with them, or for other reasons, they will have close association with them. The followers will be varied, and there may be many different motivating factors behind their giving support to a particular leader. Some followers may have failed to make a satisfactory adjustment to living—that is, the social misfits, who are still searching for contentment and a secure place for themselves. They will readily attach themselves to something new and promising, even if it means the exploitation of others. Some may look upon going to war as "a way out," a means of interrupting their life of strife. Any gains that they may acquire through war might surpass any of their peacetime achievements based on their own merits.

Other followers of leaders who are heading in the direction of war might be the students of a country, those who are still unstable and unsettled. Because of their restlessness and malleability they are prime targets for the rabble-rousers and the revolt-minded leaders. People who are poverty-stricken, lacking in education, and passive in personality will be more readily tempted to follow leaders with glowing promises of prosperity and security.

A constant struggle exists between immature people where they are continually pressuring each other to get the better of each other. Many of these immature people cannot satisfactorily cope with others, and they cannot succeed by themselves. It is these people, driven by the search for personal security, who will group together to take advantage of others.

There is a certain amount of romance, glamor, and glory associated with war—for some people, bordering on hysteria. It is seen in young people who have had no actual experience with war. The young males perhaps feel they will attain manhood and prove themselves adequate. It is even seen in the so-called normal individual, the housewife and the working man, especially if the person may feel bored and restless and dissatisfied with life. To some, war will serve as an excuse for a release of their hostile drives. If the cause of going to war appears to be worthwhile, such as fighting for liberty, this adds to the excitement of wanting to participate. Those who may look upon war with disfavor might be apt to keep their thoughts to themselves because of the general enthusiasm to the contrary. One can understand why wars seem to occur in cycles, as it takes a new generation of people to be emotionally prepared to accept and involve itself in a war. Once a war begins, through fear and the desire to survive, the people must fight or be conquered. For a period of time after a war the people, realizing the futility of the war and being exhausted physically, mentally, and emotionally, might be prone to succumb to yet another aggressive power.

*　*　*　*

In summary, we have seen that wars are caused by immature people. Factors such as cultural trends are part of one's personality, and they enter into how a person will feel about another person. There may be many apparent reasons given as to the cause of a war, but these really amount to immature people creating a threat to the security of other immature people and their country. Not enough people now exist who have the relative emotional maturity, wisdom, and strength to prevent immature, aggressive leaders from starting a war.

CHAPTER III

WHY DO PEOPLE BECOME COMMUNISTS?

Communism is the greatest threat to world peace today. Almost one-third of the world's population, about one billion people, is now under Communist domination. We must concentrate in coping with it because we are faced with an immediate danger. More important, however, which most people may not realize, is that Communism will pose even a greater threat in the future. The reason is that the future generations living under Communism will be "brainwashed" in regard to Communism, and it will be the only form of life which they will know. Of extreme importance, and this cannot be overemphasized, is that the new generations will be comprised of so-called human beings lacking in full emotional development. The children, being raised in nurseries without parental influence, which is the practice under Communism, will be stunted in their capacity for feeling. The people will grow to be more and more emotionally-immature, unable to reach fulfillment of their emotional potential, and they will function as an army of automatons.

In addition to the problems of immaturity which the people of a free country with limitless opportunity suffer, Communist-controlled people are faced with the deep-seated and ingrained problems of immaturity associated with a distorted culture. Without fulfillment of his emotional needs, a child may tend to overcompensate in other areas. He may exploit people all the more in his search for more of everything, something which he feels he lacks—in reality, the mature parental relationship which he missed in his developmental years. He may or may not be deficient in his intellectual functions; in fact, he could be superior, secondary to the emotional deprivation and neurotic motivation. The significance of this is that the Communists of the future will not possess the empathy and understanding to

64

deal with a problem on the same level as other people. As time goes on, the gap between the personalities of the people of the free world and the personalities of the Communists will widen. We could reach a point when it would be impossible for people living under democracy and Communism to co-exist even for a short period of time.

Too many people think too lightly about the Communist menace. There are many well-meaning, influential people in this country today who, due to either ignorance, wishful thinking, or other reasons, are stating that Communism now is not such a bad system of government. Many Americans do not appreciate that the Communists are really at war with everyone who is not a Communist. They do not realize that the Communists have as a purpose to dominate the entire world. More important is that most people not living under Communism do not fully understand that, if you were living under Communism, you would be existing as a slave. Communism exploits a person's right to be free. It does not allow an individual to evolve according to his potential, but rather, it permits one person, in the name of the State, to impinge upon the rights of another person. To read about the enslaved peoples behind the Iron Curtain is just so many words to most free people, and they do not grasp the significance of the word "slave." Most free people, because they are preoccupied with their own problems, or for other reasons, do not want to think about the threat from Communism. If each free person were to live under Communist rule for one week as a native and not as a tourist, and were told that he would have to continue living under Communism for the rest of his life, he would enlist in an all-out effort, even go to war, to preserve his freedom. For a free person to accept Communism would suggest that the person has an emotional or a mental problem, that he is immature and dependent, that he has not developed emotionally and intellectually.

We should acquaint ourselves with the fact that a very small percentage, under ten per cent, of the people in a Communist country are active Communists. This means that the countries behind the Iron Curtain, including Russia and China, are really Communist-dominated. Over ninety per cent of the general population in those countries are dominated by the members of the Communist Party. A very small number of immature people control the lives of millions of people. It is a shame that millions of innocent people are slaves of a few, and that the entire population of the world hinges upon the whim of those few who might embark everyone upon a war.

The Communists are using a new method of world domination which is foreign to most people, and this might be the reason for the complacency seen throughout all nations. Before, one country, such as Italy, France, or Germany, tried to conquer the rest of the world. Now, the immature leaders of many different countries are in alliance as Communists, ruling and exploiting their own people, and aiming at ruling and exploiting all the people of the world. They promote subversion and civil strife, revolt and war, within their own country and in other countries in order to gain control.

The questions are sometimes asked: "Why do people under a Communist regime tolerate it?" "Why do they not revolt?" When Communists come to power in a given area, they eliminate the old leaders and replace them with their own. All the key positions are taken over by the Communists—that is, the officials in all levels of government, the police, water, transportation, and other departments, are Communists or Communist sympathizers. The common person, the worker, cannot rebel, or else he will be fired from his job, or even deported and killed. If he should escape punishment, a member of his family might be sent to a concentration camp. The people, and even the Communists themselves, live in constant fear that an informer might claim that they are unfaithful to the cause of Communism. Some of them join the Communist Party out of frustration, not seeing any help forthcoming from the free world, so they may be able to get ahead and live better.

People under Communist domination experience feelings of depression and hopelessness. Even though they may be seen in large numbers on the sidewalks or in overcrowded buses, a marked silence prevails. Many people have two jobs in order to exist, and there is an air of seriousness and industriousness as they hurry from one job to another. A laborer may average two dollars and fifty cents ($2.50) a week (in United States currency). He would have to work several months for a suit of clothes which, because of other expenses, he could not afford to purchase. Individual property-ownership is impossible in most instances, and all property will be ultimately controlled by the State. The living quarters are such that the State allots a certain number of square feet per person. The apartments are crowded, frequently with strangers sharing the kitchen and toilet facilities. There is no refrigeration, so that food cannot be stored. The food is rationed, and it is necessary frequently to wait in long lines at stores in order to buy one day's supply. Travel is restricted, and one cannot move from place to place without State authorization. All religious belief is discouraged: people have been fired from their jobs because their children have attended church services. There is strict censorship of radio, newspapers, and magazines. The people hear and read only what the Communist leaders want them to know. They do not know what is really happening outside of the Iron Curtain. They are unaware of what their leaders are thinking and doing, and they have no actual choice of leadership. They might be forced into fighting a war with no true knowledge of the surrounding circumstances. People under Communism may not be shackled by ball and chain, but they are restricted in their activities, and through propaganda they are restricted in thought. Because of the distrust that prevails, the Communists themselves are virtually slaves of each other. It is as though they were caught in a spider's web with almost no chance of disentanglement and escape. The irony of the Communist system is that it was conceived to free the laborer from working under slave-labor conditions, but it has become distorted so that today it has made slaves of the laboring class—in fact, of everybody.

Already mentioned in what we might call a Communist cultural trend is that children born under the Communist system will be deficient in emotional development and one-sided in their views about their system and the free world. The children of the future will have been taught that Communism is the best form of government, not having been exposed to any knowledge to the contrary. Even if, at a later age, they were exposed to democracy, the odds are that they would disbelieve and reject it. People living in an environment of bitterness, distrust, and fear become hardened, and they are preoccupied with the serious, desperate business of survival. They are living in a state of insecurity, from the lowliest peasant to the topmost ruler. They may resort to ruthless tactics to maintain their uncertain stations in life.

In Russia, the people might have good reason to believe that the Communist system is a very effective one. Nearly one-half of all the farm produce of the Communist-dominated satellite countries is shipped to Russia. Also, the United States, Canada, and other countries have shipped large quantities of wheat to Russia, which the peasants assume was raised in their own country. Therefore, the Russian people's standard of living has been elevated. The majority of the people probably do not realize why they have such prosperity, and the peasants, understandably, may not care to know, since they have "never had it so good". The factors mentioned comprise a cultural trend in Russia which will grow more dangerous in future generations. It means that people living under Communism will accept it as time goes on, and that they will be more apt to fight in the defense of it.

Immature people become Communists. In fact, Communism is a system that draws to it immature, maladjusted people. They find the opportunity, and are actually encouraged through Communist doctrine, to dominate people. The people that the Communists attempt to control are usually in a weakened condition physically, intellectually, and emotionally, as in the underdeveloped nations, so that unknowingly they provoke and entice the Communists to dominate them. Under Communism, the Communist leaders will find a "happy hunting ground" in their being able to take advantage of others. Under the guise of working for a classless society which would provide the best possible life to the common man, the Communists find an outlet for their immature personalities, and advance themselves at the expense of others.

The same motivating factors are present in those who become Communists as in those who might become involved in a war. Immature people, with deficient personalities and inadequacy feelings, will react in such a way to seek security through Communism. Some security will be achieved through the feeling of belonging, and of being a member of a group or organization with a common purpose. More security will be hopefully attained from the promises that the State will take good care of everyone. In the search for their basic security—that is, self-worth and personal gain—the people who are leaning toward Communism are actually acting like any other people, as in a democracy, for example. They are striving for security through a realization of their own potential. They seek self-gain in one form or another through their actions. They are striving for individuality, and their primary concern is their own security, and not the State itself. They will most likely deny this, for they may be unaware of it themselves. Nevertheless, the people who are becoming Communists have the same needs that are present in all other people. The main difference with them is that they may lack the opportunity, or lack the ability to recognize and capitalize on an opportunity, and therefore be unable to achieve the security which they desire. As a result, due to frustration, these people would become more prone to exploit others, and one can see that they might readily accept the Communist system. Of course, the degree to which they exploit, where human life itself has little meaning, is much different from the behavior of most of the other people of the world.

The Communists express that the State, and not the individual, comes first. However, they really believe, even though they may deny it—and this is proved by their actions—that the individual is supreme. Because of their exploitation of people, one might not suspect that they recognize the supremacy of the individual. However, they exploit others in order to further themselves, to feel more personally secure; and they themselves are individuals. They, as individuals, act so as to come first, to be supreme, to be ahead of everybody else, including the State. In his dealings with others a Communist shows no recognition of the dignity of man, that is, of his fellow man. Yet, through his actions, through showing a primary concern for his own life, he really does recognize the dignity of man, when the man is himself. Communists may say they sacrifice people for the good of the State, or for others, and not for themselves; but how many of them would be willing to sacrifice themselves for the good of the State or for someone else? It is true that there are some people who do not seem to respect the dignity and rights of man. They, through cultural trends and religious beliefs, have been raised to believe that a leader or doctrine is supreme, and that their lives are secondary. But, these peoples' views would undoubtedly change in time if they were given that benefit of a broader education. The Communists of the present do not fall into this category because they value their own lives more than the State. However, their "brainwashed" children, and the Communists of future generations, will believe the State is supreme and that man has no dignity or rights. The individual really is supreme, and all civilized people not mentally, emotionally, religiously, or culturally perverted, accept this. The State should be comprised of individuals, the individuals working together as a representative body with a purpose to serve individuals, including themselves.

If the State did come first, the individual would be curtailed in his being able to exercise his individuality to the fullest. Adults coming under the domination of Communism would lose their individuality. To the child born in the Communist system, never really having experienced individuality—that is, the development of himself as a person to the fullest degree—the concept of individuality would be foreign to him. It is for the remaining people of the world to maintain a "life-line" to these people so they may have glimpses of what others are like. If we fail, and Communism should encompass the entire world, the human species would become different from what it is today. People would become mechanical in their actions. They would lose their capacity for emotional response.

The Communists say that their system would be of most benefit to all of mankind. Yet they persecute and purge people by the thousands in order to gain control, so how much actual desire can they have to help mankind? They say that in order to achieve total world Communism it is sometimes necessary to exploit people, but later all the people will derive the most out of it. Why is it necessary to have worldwide Communism before all under Communism could benefit? If that type of government is best, why is it necessary to impose it upon people? If it were truly the best form of government for the people, in time this would be recognized and all countries would want it for themselves. They say that if the world became totally Communistic there would be a completely classless society, and all would be content. However, there would still have to be leaders and policy-enforcement, and not an equality, without problems, among all people. If each individual were not permitted to determine the extent of his own potential and ability to work, then leaders would be necessary to determine this for him. Likewise, the leaders would have to decide the needs of an individual, which would prove to be an impossible task, especially when dealing with the insatiable needs of all immature people. The Communist leaders now have a much higher standard of living than the standard of the people they control, so is it likely that they would give up this balance? It would take a lot of ruling to try to make the people buried under Communist domination happy. It would take generations before the people would be completely stifled as far as their intellects and emotions are concerned, so that they would more or less accept slavery as a way of life. Even ultimately, a system of Communism could not endure because the people would remain immature, and it is opposed to the nature of man that he not grow and mature. If Communism ever took over the entire world, the progress of civilization would be set back over a thousand years. There could be no peace with it.

It was stated in the previous chapter that unstable students and social misfits might be susceptible to ideas leading to war. These disgruntled intellectuals, too, might be prime candidates for the Communist Party; but, as mentioned, the largest numbers of people who find themselves subjected to the subversion and force of the Communists are the people living in poverty and lacking in maturity and education in the underdeveloped countries. In the emerging nations there is disorganization, instability, and weakness, which appeals to the Communist philosophy of easy exploitation.

In the more advanced, free countries, people have the opportunities to sublimate their aggressive drives to socially-acceptable and personally-profitable ends. As it is, in the free countries there is more living comfort and basic security, and man need not be too anxious and aggressive in his striving for personal security. There is no problem of self-preservation. With the

71

many opportunities provided for through philanthropies, investments, business, the professions, and other media, the already-wealthy can achieve more self-worth and security. The middle class and the working class of people, with the use of initiative and intelligence, can gain security through the professions, business, and other ventures. The working class has labor unions through which a worker can express his grievances and make meaningful gains for improved working conditions, a better home, and relaxation. With adequate food, shelter, and clothing, and the prospect of being able to work for the comforts of living, a person achieves satisfaction, self-assurance, and independence. Living in a state of freedom, where an individual can gain successes and prove himself valuable through the utilization of his potential, so that he and his family can advance and earn a better life, the individual is using his aggressive drive in gaining personal security. In a democracy where there is more freedom, it is true there is more opportunity for a person to seek self-gain and security in the way of honest endeavors. However, unfortunately, there is also more opportunity to look for self-gain and security in the way of dishonesty and corruption.

Under Communism and other similar forms of government, the people do not have the opportunity for intellectual and emotional fulfillment, self-expression, and realization of their potentials. This is a threat to peace because it lends itself to unrest, dissatisfaction, and frustration. One human being is limiting and enslaving another human being, and the result is resentment. It has been argued that the peoples of the underdeveloped countries are "not ready" for independence, that they are incapable of ruling themselves, and they need outside help. It is true that they may need help, but they do not need and should not want to be exploited. By being helped to help themselves, those peoples will, in due time, become independent, be best able to govern themselves; and they will have a fuller appreciation of freedom and its rewards when they achieve it. In the beginning, because of their heritage and environment, they may have no inclination to want to exert themselves and to work for something better in life. It may seem that they want to be subjugated, and that they do not desire the right for freedom and fulfillment of their potentials. They may settle for small favors offered them by the Communists, anything being better than what they have had in the past. In fact, due to their poverty, lack of education, and emotional immaturity with inadequacy feelings, the people will actually reach out for immediate gratification and dependence offered by the Communists; not considering that freedom, even though it might be farther away, would hold immeasurably more promise for them. It could take another generation, with family and cultural changes, before the people of such an underdeveloped country would desire self-fulfillment as individuals.

Just being given food for the day has been enough motivation for soldiers to want to join a Communist-dominated army. This, coupled with their frustration at being stifled and resentment of others with plenty, gives purpose to soldiers to want to fight for Communism. It should be stressed that the backward peoples are not basically inferior to those people of more advanced nations. The backward peoples, the Communist-dominated peoples, and even the Communist leaders themselves would, in the last analysis, prefer freedom and the opportunity for a realization of their potentials.

* * * *

In this chapter we have examined Communism as a growing threat to peace. As each day passes, it becomes more of a threat, and we come closer to the brink of total war. We have seen how people live under Communist domination, and how the same psychodynamics prevail in the Communists as in people who have a tendency toward war. Also, we have seen that there are similar motivating factors in all people, whether they are living in the United States or in Russia or in China. Some of the ideas of Communism have been refuted. We can understand why certain people, especially those of underdeveloped countries, would more readily be susceptible to Communism.

Chapter IV

THE MATURE PERSON-TO-PERSON PHILOSOPHY

We frequently hear people exclaim that "The world is in one big mess", or "It is a rotten world". Actually, it is not the world itself which is in a turmoil but, rather, the people in it. The world itself is beautiful, with its blue sky, stars, and planets, its green mountains and blue waters, its flowers and animals, and even its towns and cities. Of course, there are storms and droughts and poverty and sickness, but all of these serve as fuel for man's ingenuity in making the world even a better place in which to live. Basically, it is the people in the world who are responsible for causing most of the troubles for themselves and others. They have to live together, yet they make it miserable for each other. If one thinks about it, one has to admit that the greatest single problem in the world today is the inability for man to get along with his fellow man. Obviously, with the ever-increasing population, people have to develop a better way of getting along with each other. It is true that, as man gains more insight into the behavior of himself and of others, and how people interact, he will be able to deal with everyone more effectively. However, more and speedier action will have to be taken if the people of the world want a more satisfying existence, and if, in fact, they hope to survive at all.

An immature person cannot check or control his behavior adequately. In his constant search for pleasure and personal security, he tends to spread out and impinge upon the rights of others. Also, he has difficulty in containing the behavior of other immature people who encroach upon him. To merely ask for forgiveness of our trespasses and forgive our trespassers is not the solution in helping people to mature. The people have to learn how to control their own and other people's behavior if they expect to be able to get along with each other.

In order to survive, man must learn to live with his fellow man. He must adapt to a philosophy of life which will enhance both his and everybody else's life. People differ so much as to their beliefs that it seems quite certain no one premise will be accepted by all the people in the world in the near future. For example, to expect that all people would live in harmony under one type of government, or that all people would accept one religion, would be hoping for too much. That a common ground acceptable to all will ever be found in any religion, or in any type of political or cultural ideology, is possible, but not in the foreseeable future. It could be found now, however, in a very personal type of philosophy, one involving an individual's behavior in relation to the behavior of other individuals. Such a philosophy would be meaningful to each and every person in the world. Because of its intimate and beneficial nature, all people would ultimately accept it. It would become a way of life for everyone, helping the person practicing it, and also all those who come in contact with him. Such a philosophy could become a reality. It is one in which a particular individual wants to behave decently, and wishes that others will behave in the same way. He has no inclination, no need or desire, to trespass, nor does he want anyone to trespass against him. He will not take advantage of anyone, nor will he allow anyone to take advantage of him. It does not matter that another person may claim not to recognize the dignity of the human being, or the equality of men. It does not matter that another person denies it is the nature of man to mature and fulfill himself as an individual. In fact, it does not really matter if the other person does not accept such a philosophy, or that he not agree about anything at all. This particular individual wants to emerge as a more mature person. He will use his energies, really aggressive energies, in bettering himself as a person, and seeking self-worth and security—actually striving for self-preservation. The energies will be used also in his forcing others to deal with him maturely, the success of this again making him feel more secure—and again in keeping with his drive for self-preservation. In the last analysis, the others will benefit from their relationships with him. They will have their aggressive energies curbed until they can control them themselves, and the energies will be directed in their seeking security and preservation for themselves. When they learn from experience and habit, and when they fulfill their own potentials, they will also use their energies in forcing still others to mature behavior, thus gaining more in the way of security and self-preservation. This particular individual is a relatively emotionally-mature person who knows how to get along with people. He is doing something about teaching people how to get along with each other.

A philosophy which involves the behavior of one man in relation to another is particularly necessary for Communists, certain scientists, and others who do not believe in God. For them—the atheists, agnostics, and other non-believers—a philosophy dealing with man, a being which they admit exists here and now, and is of the highest order in the universe, should be accepted. Generally speaking, those people who do not have a great amount of self-confidence and personal security will not have a great amount of confidence, trust, and faith in others—and, especially, in a super-being. They are immature and insecure; they are indecisive and prone to waver as to their beliefs. However, according to their upbringing and religious background, and in times of strife, they may tend without much success to seek comfort and security from becoming involved in religion. At the other extreme are people who are strong-willed and opinionated, and who appear to be self-confident and very secure. Due to their cultural, familial, and educational backgrounds, they have adopted rigid psychological defenses and have overcompensated for their basic feeling of insecurity. They are dogmatic and bigoted, or agnostic and atheistic. Actually, they are more immature and insecure than the people at the other end of the scale who are indecisive and lacking in confidence. These over-confident people lack sensitivity, understanding, and true feeling for others, and they are farther removed from the attainment of emotional development and fulfillment as a human being. The most mature people have firm convictions and beliefs, yet they are open-minded, and are subject to amending their ideas. They are critical of concepts, and flexible enough to accept some, reject others, and to think of new ones. Those who believe are more moral and virtuous, and they will be more accepting of a philosophy regarding the decent behavior of men, although they will be the least in need of it. The more truly self-confident, secure, and mature a person, the more apt is he to have faith in others, and in God, and the more able will he be to exercise such a philosophy. Those who disbelieve will least accept any such philosophy, but they are the ones who really need it the most. They need a guide which will govern their own actions and the actions of others. Until they, or their descendants, mature, it is left to the relatively mature people of the world to keep them in check.

A mature person is one of any age who can effectively deal with any other person of an approximate age or younger. After one reaches the age of so-called manhood or womanhood, about age twenty-one, however, one should be fairly close to being able to deal effectively with anyone of any age. The mature person should have attained the fulfillment of his potential which would be average for his chronological age-level. A mature person will not have any need or desire to exploit anyone, nor will he allow anyone to exploit him. A mature man will not try to take advantage of women, children, the elderly, or immature and weaker males. In like manner, a mature woman or child will not try to take advantage of any weaker person. A mature person will be in opposition to any immature person, group, organization, or government if he or anyone else is being exploited by them. He must have the emotional maturity, wisdom, and physical strength or support to be able to successfully cope with an aggressor.

Emotional maturity is commensurate with a person's chronological age. There is an average amount of maturity for boys and girls at each age level. If a person has not achieved his full potential for any particular age of his life, he is not to be considered as being mature for that particular age. A person is not to be considered mature based on the fact that he reached adulthood or old age. This means that achieving maturity is progressive and dynamic, beginning in infancy and continuing until one dies. Every day of one's entire life, in every relationship, one should work at becoming more mature. In continuing this way, a person should be more mature and wiser at age seventy, barring senility, than at age thirty or fifty. One never attains complete or perfect maturity, but one becomes relatively more mature. With more freedom, the removal of bad cultural trends, and more relatively-mature parents raising children who are capable of achieving their potentials, there will be more mature individuals and mature populations in future generations.

This concept of maturity differs from the old static and complacent idea in which a person was said to be emotionally mature if he, for example, reached a supposed age of reason, were able to make good judgments, were not impulsive, and learned to "give and take". All of these features are traits of an emotionally-mature person, but they are not an end-point in themselves, because they can be improved upon as a person gets older and more intelligent. As a person grows older he can become more reasonable, make better judgments, become less impulsive, and become better at "giving and taking".

Some people slow down in the attainment of maturity as they get older. They may be fifty years of age, yet are functioning at an emotional level which is average for twelve-year-olds. Relatively speaking, an eight-year-old can be more emotionally-mature than a fifty-year-old. If the eight-year-old is functioning closer to the average for his chronological age level than the fifty-year-old is functioning to the average for his own age level, then the eight-year-old is relatively more emotionally mature. Of course, the fifty-year-old is in all likelihood absolutely more mature than the eight-year-old.

Generally speaking, if a child is being raised by mature parents to be a mature individual, unless there is any interruption in this relationship, he will continue to grow more emotionally-mature year by year, commensurate with his chronological age. If he is mature up to par at age five and six, for example, and if the environment does not change drastically, he should continue to grow more mature as he becomes age nine and ten. It is conceivable that a person may fall behind in maturity for some reason, and then catch up at a later date.

If a person is mature, he should and will deal in a mature manner with any other person, regardless of age. An immature fifty-year-old man operating at a twelve-year-old age level of maturity can, and probably will, if the occasion arises, take advantage of a mature eight-year-old boy. The man will exploit

78

the boy even though he, the man, is absolutely more mature, though not relatively more mature; because immature people of any age tend to exploit other people. It should be remembered that the child is relatively more mature because he is functioning closer to the average of maturity seen in boys of his chronological age. The man is absolutely more mature, however, though not relatively, than the eight-year-old boy since he, the man, is functioning as a twelve-year-old. The fifty-year-old may be immature only in certain areas, although, generally, one who is immature in one or two areas is found to be immature throughout, but varying in degree. In the case of the eight-year-old being exploited, mature people should come to his aid. The same boy at the age of twelve may be close to being capable of dealing with the fifty-year-old on an emotional level. Of course, the man's age, strength, size, appearance. facial and vocal expressions, status in life, experience, and intellect will serve to intimidate in his exploitation of the boy. When the same boy reaches the age of fifteen or sixteen, if his emotional maturity still coincides with his chronological age, he should much more readily be able to cope with the man. Over the age of twenty, he would not allow the man to take advantage of him. Being mature, this boy at any age will have no desire to take advantage of the fifty-year-old, or of anyone else, even though the opportunity may present itself. He will behave in a humble manner, learning from the comparative wealth of information and experience of all adults.

There are many means by which people can exploit or take advantage of other people. These may be conscious, in which a person may act with awareness and deliberateness, or unconscious, when he acts without full realization. The act may be physical, or by the spoken or written word. Also, it may be performed actively or passively. For example, a person can actively and deliberately scandalize and belittle another person because he is jealous of him, and he wants to build himself up in comparison to him. One can passively sulk, or refuse to speak and withhold information in order that a person may experience some grief, or shirk one's work because one is resentful of his boss. A businessman may not be fully aware of his exploitation of a competitor, rationalizing his actions as being a part of everyday business practices. Some Communists may likewise be unknowingly and actively exploiting their subjects by believing what they are doing is for the subjects' own good. Passively and unconsciously, some people may be exploiting the people under Communist domination by giving tacit consent to the Communist exploitation in not recognizing it as such. Countless more examples of people taking advantage of people could be given, all the way from the bully at the schoolyard to the dictatorial leader of a nation. It is necessary for everyone to recognize the various means of exploitation, the ways that demanding people overstep their bounds, so that they can maturely deal with them.

The Mature Person-to-Person Philosophy is an extension of what we shall call Pressure Psychotherapy. Pressure Psychotherapy involves the relationship of a patient with a psychiatrist who knows how and is able to practice this type of psychotherapy, really the ultimate of all psychotherapies. The patient is pressured or forced to deal in a mature manner with the psychiatrist. The psychiatrist does not impose his will upon the patient in any other way than to pressure him to act maturely with him, and with every one of his other relationships. The well-being of the patient is foremost in the psychiatrist's mind. The psychiatrist has an expectation for the patient to behave in a mature way. He does not really care too much, only insofar as how it influences the patient's actions, how the patient thinks or feels; but he does insist that the patient act, including what he says or writes, in a mature manner. In the process, however, the patient is pressured to organize his thoughts and gain an understanding of his feelings. The content of what the patient analyzes, and even how he feels about it, are not so important; but the fact that he did the analysis, that he thought, felt, talked, and acted, that he did his part in figuring out and solving a problem, and that he is gaining independence, are important. He is growing less dependent and more independent, more mature and secure, due to reacting to the Pressure Psychotherapist. The most important factor necessary for the successful use of Pressure Psychotherapy is that the psychiatrist be a mature person, so that he can give the patient a mature relationship.

To the psychiatrist practicing Pressure Psychotherapy, the unconscious is of secondary importance. In Chapter X we will concentrate on a person's unconscious motivations—the importance of the fact that he be raised as a person who is decent and of good intent, empathic and understanding, a person who is not malicious and evil. He will be raised to be not neurotically-competitive and exploitative, but to be motivated to desire the fulfillment of his potential, based on his own merit and hard work. There the value of the unconscious will be given more significance, since a more emotionally-mature and healthier personality is more amenable to the utilization and response of the Mature Person-to-Person Philosophy.

The psychiatrist, in using Pressure Psychotherapy, says the least amount necessary to the patient, depending upon the patient's intelligence and perceptiveness. Through having confidence in himself and in his patient, knowing the patient's capability and potential, the psychiatrist is able to convey to the patient a similar confidence which will make the patient want to try to succeed. The patient will recognize that the psychiatrist has good will and good intent toward him, and understands his problem. He will accept that the psychiatrist is on his side, and he will gain the desire to work together with him in achieving success. The patient will anticipate that the psychiatrist wants and expects him to change from being a passive person to one who takes the initiative, and who initiates thought, feeling, talk, and action. This will take place, first, in respect to the psychiatrist, then with all others. Through various techniques, such as making the patient keep his appointments and pay his bills, periods of silence, facial expressions of expectation, and, especially, learning and using different means peculiar to an individual which will make him express himself and act, the psychiatrist will have gotten the patient to comprehend his, the psychiatrist's, expectation of him. The patient will then be pressured through similar techniques to act upon what he feels the psychiatrist wants him to do—to set mature goals, to follow through, and to succeed. Eventually, the person will initiate talk and decisive, mature action completely on his own. He might resist by doing nothing, which could cause irritation and anxiety to a relatively immature therapist. A fine balance has to be maintained between the patient and the psychiatrist, the weight of pressure tipping the scales in the direction of the patient. Too much pressure may cause the patient to become too anxious and defensive, irritable, angry, and negativistic, which will worsen the problem, or the patient may refuse the treatment altogether. The psychiatrist from experience learns to exert the right amount of pressure so that the patient will unfold his potential in the most efficient manner possible. He knows when not to pressure the patient at all, and when to pressure him so that he will perform with maximum efficiency. An immature, greedy, unknowledgeable, and inexperienced therapist might err in procrastinating the application of pressure, prolonging the treatment, thus causing undue anxiety in the patient and fostering his dependency.

By being a relatively-mature person himself, the psychiatrist has been able to get his patient to act, and to act maturely. In the process the person has most probably experienced feelings of embarrassment, uneasiness, irritation, dissatisfaction, anxiety, guilt, insecurity, and anger at the psychiatrist, others, and himself for his own inaction, or his past and present ineffective action, or the fact that he is not improving rapidly enough. The psychiatrist has not ridiculed, belittled, or made him feel more inadequate. To the contrary, he has been responsible for the patient's achieving self-confidence and security from having gained self-understanding and success in the world. He has diverted the patient's hostility and aggressive energies from being directed at him, others, or the patient himself, which could cause depression and a worsening of the problem, and turns them to the patient's trying to accomplish things, succeeding, and gaining security, happiness, and peace of mind. He has helped the patient to seek the different avenues open to him, and he has motivated him to attempt to further himself through the realization of his potential.

When the patient behaved, or tried to behave, immaturely with the psychiatrist, or others, the incidents were discussed objectively, with the least amount of interference from the doctor; and the patient came to the realization that what he had said or done was immature. The doctor did not permit the patient to take advantage of him, or others; nor in any way did he take advantage of the patient. The patient, through his relationship with the therapist, has been pressured to "stand on his own two feet", to think, to feel, to socialize, to work, to act, to advance himself, to succeed, and to feel secure, all in a relatively-mature manner. He has been made to become an independent and responsible person, and to assume his obligations, including the obligations for the care of his family. Because of the success, security, and happiness which he has derived from the realization of his potential, he has no need or desire to seek these things through the exploitation of others.

Pressure Psychotherapy is applicable and successfully used in the treatment of all emotionally-related mental illness, which includes the personality disorders, psychoneuroses, psychoses, and psychophysiological disorders. Failures are seen only when the patient is able to get away from the influence of the Pressure Psychotherapist. This is seen in adults quitting treatment—sometimes condoned, and even encouraged, by their well-meaning, but ignorant, family doctor or clergyman. It is seen in children being withdrawn from further treatment by their parents for many reasons, such as the parents not wanting to be shown that someone else can help their child, and that they are responsible for the child's problems.

It is only through the thorough education of all concerned that Pressure Psychotherapy can be truly effective to the patient. Even then, there are circumstances beyond one's control in which the patient can escape the pressure of the therapist. Of course, the greatest burden for success depends upon the therapist's exerting the right amount of pressure, and enlightening those closest to the patient as to what he is trying to accomplish. Those in association with the patient will in turn pressure him to return to the psychiatrist if he makes attempts to escape his influence. The more widespread the Pressure Psychotherapy concept, the more effective it will prove to be.

In the Mature Person-to-Person Philosophy, this Pressure Psychotherapy is carried over to all people, the relatively-mature people acting as the psychiatrists, pressuring the immature people in relationships with them to behave in a mature manner. The relatively-mature people will not impose their wills upon the immature people, only insofar as forcing them "to do unto others as they would want others to do unto them". The mature people will not take advantage of any people in any way, and they will pressure everyone to behave in a mature manner, not letting anyone take advantage of them or anyone else.

The Mature Person-to-Person Philosophy means literally what it says. It is a mature person dealing maturely with another person, mature or immature. The mature person will not take advantage of the other person, and he will not allow the other person to take advantage of him. He will not have the desire or need to exploit anyone, because he has lived as a virtuous person, one who has realized the fulfillment of his potential, and attained success, self-satisfaction, maturity, and personal security appropriate to his age level. He will stop anyone trying to exploit him or anyone else, because a normal person does not want to be exploited, and he will have the emotional, intellectual, and physical strength or support to carry out his wish. By his acting in a mature way, he will force all people coming in contact with him to react to him according to the same mature methods. The people's newly-learned mature behavior in relation to the mature person will then carry over in some degree to their other relationships. They will be more amenable to the mature methods of the next mature person they meet. From their contact with the mature person, the people will not only learn how to behave maturely from his actual curtailment of their immature behavior, but also from experiencing and observing his manner of behavior. He did not allow them to exploit him, and he did not try to take advantage of them. The mature person will have curtailed the people's immature behavior so that their aggressive energies become directed at fulfilling their potentials through legitimate, not exploitative, channels. When the immature people have gained success and personal security through the fulfillment of their potentials from socially acceptable channels, they will then be ready to more fully accept and practice the Mature Person-to-Person Philosophy themselves. The immature people themselves, now actually relatively-mature, will expend more of their aggressive energies in their use of the Mature Person-to-Person Philosophy. In other words, an immature person's aggressive energies are turned away from exploiting another person to realizing his

84

own true potential, and then to curbing still another immature person's aggressive, exploiting-type of behavior, forcing him to behave maturely. From hurting people, he has turned to truly helping himself, and still other people.

The more emotionally-mature the other person, the more amenable he will be to the Mature Person-to-Person Philosophy, and the easier it will be for the mature person to exercise it. The mature person himself will want to be amenable to any other person practicing the Mature Person-to-Person Philosophy. He will raise mature children who possess love and understanding, with the desire to help their fellow man. There will be an improvement of the culture for future generations. The people of the future will be progressively more emotionally-mature. They will utilize the Mature Person-to-Person Philosophy as a way of life. The mature person-to-person relationship will be extended to mature group-to-group, and mature country-to-country, philosophies. Mature people will unite with one another to practice the Mature Person-to-Person Philosophy with individuals, groups, and countries.

In pressuring a person to a mature type of behavior, it makes little difference how his personality has been influenced by hereditary, constitutional, cultural, or family backgrounds. Of course, he will be more amenable to the use of the Mature Person-to-Person Philosophy if he has been raised in a more mature environment. Whatever the person's character, psychological defenses, patterns of behavior, education, and experiences, he will be forced to reciprocate with the same type of mature behavior exercised by the relatively-mature person. The person can think and feel as he wishes, but he should not be allowed by the relatively-mature person to take advantage of him, or anyone else.

The Mature Person-to-Person Philosophy can and should be exercised by all the people, of all ages, of the world. It should be kept constantly in mind by everyone so that, in each person, a mature pattern of behavior will be created. The mature person using it is really only relatively mature, there not being any entirely mature people in the world. In the beginning a relatively-mature person may, on the one hand, be guarding himself from being exploited by another person; yet on the other hand he may be exploiting the same other person concerning the same or a different matter. Also, the relatively-mature person may find himself being exploited by certain people, and he in turn is exploiting still other people. It should be remembered that it is a natural reaction for immature, insecure people to take advantage of others in their search for security. They gain a false sense of security from feeling themselves superior to the person they have dominated.

Most immature people appear very dependent, passive, inadequate, and insecure, and they invite most of the exploitation. Immature people tread upon other immature people who appear to be weak, and who seem not like the type to object. They exploit them because they think they can get away with it. At the other end of the scale, there are the people who are even more immature, but they may appear to be full of self-confidence and towers of strength. Actually, the latter group is neurotically overcompensating for its insecurity, and upon close examination one sees opinionated, hostile people with rigid defenses. These people have little or no insight as to their basic insecurity, and they will revolt at the idea that they are immature, and that there is any need for a Mature Person-to-Person Philosophy. These people who will protest the most are the people who need it the most. They, with their seemingly-firm convictions and overwhelming personalities, readily convince the immature masses that they are mature, and they frequently get themselves elected to leadership positions. The people of this latter group invariably succeed in not permitting themselves to be exploited, and they also succeed in the exploitation of others. They do not spend much time in trying to exploit people like themselves, however, as they usually do not succeed and end up in a fight. Interestingly, the first group of insecure, dependent, inadequate-appearing people, although being exploited most of the time, will exploit others more insecure and weaker than they when given the opportunity. In fact, most of the immature people of whom other immature people take advantage are the ones who would most readily take advantage of the same or of other immature people. All of the people of the world, of all ages and in all walks of life, belong in these three categories, or variations of them. (*See Illustration 1.*)

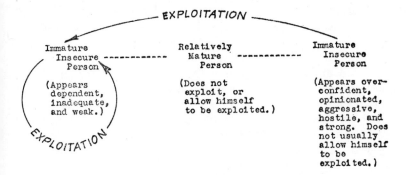

Illustration 1: Exploitation

If a person is exploited, he should handle the problem by himself whenever possible, depending upon the seriousness of the situation. He should respond immediately with appropriate personal action according to the circumstances, or seek the help of an effective higher authority, such as that of a parent, policeman, or the court. This does not mean that he should take the law in his own hands if he can handle the problem, or if it is one of minor consequence. It means that every person should learn to cope with his own problems, and direct the action leading to the resolution of the problems, whenever possible. Each person should try, and should be pressured, to be as independent as possible. Still, even if help is not requested, due to any number of reasons, including the assailed party's believing he is not in need of help, all mature people should become involved and provide the exploited one with assistance when it is needed. Serious attacks—for example, false statements made to injure the reputation of another, stealing one's property, or physically hurting another—should be directed to a mature higher authority. Only in self-defense, and for the defense of those for whom he is responsible, when one is physically at-

87

tacked and no mature higher authority is immediately available, should one resort to physical violence. Still, one is obligated to avoid an all-out fight if aid is forthcoming and one can stall for time fighting defensively. If there is no possibility of help arriving before one would be physically hurt and possibly killed, then the attacked should strike back immediately and with all his power. As soon as a mature higher authority becomes available, the attacked should stop any self-defensive measures, and allow the authority to assume the responsibility for providing order and peace.

Immediate and firm reaction to an aggressor is necessary, or he will gain confidence from his success and exploit faster and all the more. One should not "turn the other cheek". So long as a person is strong enough intellectually, emotionally, and physically, or there is available a higher authority with these essentials, there should be no problem in containing an aggressor. If a person and his supporters are weak, there being no effective authority available, their only recourse is to stall for time, realizing their retreat is feeding the aggressor's appetite, and they should muster all their resources to defend themselves. Even if an aggressive person feels he is of about equal strength as another, being immature, and comparing himself and competing with the other, he will make an attempt to dominate him. A person has to be much stronger than the aggressor, and has to show him that he actually is much stronger, before he can expect the aggressor to leave him alone. He not only must be stronger, but he must let the aggressor know that he is not afraid to engage in an all-out fight in self-defense if he is physically attacked.

For protection of one's reputation or property, there is no urgency for immediate action, and one is not justified in resorting to physical violence, even if an effective higher authority is not immediately available to intervene. It should not be that the attacked, just as the attacker, should take the matter in his own hands, beyond voicing a protest. If he did, he would be acting as immaturely as the aggressor. In our present civilized society, a mature higher authority is almost always available to come to the aid of individuals.

If an immature person attempts to exploit someone and he is

thwarted, he will invariably find another, weaker person to exploit. In fact, he will probably test every one of his relationships, and in some manner exploit the people who will permit it. Of course, the means and the degree of exploitation will vary from person to person. In exercising the Mature Person-to-Person Philosophy with such a person, you would find that in not being allowed to take advantage of you, he would in fact stop trying, and seek out someone else to exploit. He would not necessarily terminate his friendship with you, but he would behave maturely in your presence. If your relationship with such a person begins on this level, he usually learns his limitations quickly, and there is no problem. However, if from the beginning, the person is permitted to overstep his boundaries with you, and later an attempt is made to restrict him, there will be much more difficulty in getting him to accept the limits. He will be confused as to your behavior, and irritated with you. He will keep on trying to take advantage of you as he once had done, and if he becomes frustrated, he may terminate the friendship with you. If you had not been dealing maturely with him from the very beginning, it will be difficult for you to change to a consistently-mature type of behavior with him. He will have gained a sense of self-confidence and personal security from his early successes in exploiting you, and he will want to continue his domination over you.

For the Mature Person-to-Person Philosophy to be truly effective, it is necessary for everyone to practice it. There are now too many people who are unable to thwart others taking advantage of them, so they turn to taking advantage of still others. These people should be pressured to try harder in thwarting their aggressors; for, in succeeding, they, along with the aggressors, will have less inclination to exploit. An immature person should not be allowed to seek out and take advantage of another person if he is thwarted by a mature person. The mature person should aid those people for whom he is responsible, and others who need help, in repelling the immature person's attempts to exploit them. All other people should try to behave maturely and repulse the immature person's attempts at exploiting them. Of course, the immature person will not be trying to exploit everyone, as it will be obvious to him from the start that it would be a waste of time to even try with certain people.

The immature person has to try to exercise the Mature Person-to-Person Philosophy himself, as he will be relatively more mature than others he meets, and the others will be making attempts to take advantage of him. He will have to be alert in his every relationship. He will have to be on guard in not taking advantage of others, and in not allowing others to take advantage of him. The more relatively-mature people will be exercising the Mature Person-to-Person Philosophy with the relatively-mature people. This will not be as necessary and as difficult to do as with the more immature people, but it will serve the two-fold useful purpose of practice for the more relatively-mature, and reinforcement of what constitutes mature behavior for the relatively-mature.

Everyone will have to concentrate upon pressuring everyone else to behave maturely. This includes every person, that is, man, woman, and child. It includes people in the roles of parents, teachers, doctors, clergymen, policemen, judges, legislators, employers, and all other authority figures. It also includes husbands and wives, workers, and students. No one should be excluded. Everyone should act as a Pressure Psychotherapist, forcing others to mature behavior. They should pressure people to seek and follow through with any help that they may require in order to mature, and to follow through with all of their goals. As stated, all relatively-mature people should not allow relatively-immature people, if thwarted by another mature person, to now seek them out for exploitation. They should not permit immature people to now take advantage of them, after escaping from the person who thwarted them, and now seeking another victim. The immature people should be forced by everyone with whom they come in contact to behave maturely, to accept their responsibilities, and not to find an easy way to gain a sense of personal security such as that derived from the domination of others. Mentioned before was that the feeling of security gained from the domination of others is a false security.

We are aiming for the production of the mature man. It should be everyone's goal to strive for more emotional maturity, to concentrate in his everyday relationships with all people to deal with them in a mature way. They will be working to become more mature beings by cultivating their potential, practicing for perfection in the emotional area. Since people do behave more immaturely at certain times, they will now focus upon better behavior all of the time. Each person will be trying to behave more maturely himself, and through the use of the Mature Person-to-Person Philosophy he will aid the immature people to become more mature, whether they are seeking maturity or not, whether they like it or not. Ultimately, they will all benefit from it. Merely a person-to-person type of philosophy would not be sufficient for the advancement of man's emotional development. Immature people deal with other immature people, with the foremost thought in mind of achieving personal gain. It is necessary for a person, even an immature person, to desire to be a relatively-mature person, (Illustration I, Page 87), and to seek not only personal gain but mutual gain. He should want fair and just treatment for the other person as well as for himself. It requires the Mature Person-to-Person Philosophy for our civilization to advance in the emotional area.

Not only will people grow more mature, but the numbers of more mature people will increase also. Being raised by mature parents will make the children more prone to accept the Mature Person-to-Person Philosophy; in fact, being raised as virtuous people, with a fulfillment of their emotional needs, they will be more amenable to both using it and receiving its application by others. These children will grow into adulthood as mature people, expecting all others to behave as mature people, also. Those people who are not seeking maturity because they may feel they are already mature and do not need it, or are not seeking it for any number of other reasons, will be controlled or held in check so as not to exploit others. If everyone with whom the immature people come in contact control their own and the immature people's actions, the immature people will, in effect, be behaving as relatively-mature people. Their thoughts and feelings may not be those of a really mature person, but at least they will not be taking advantage of anyone. Through habit, learning from others, and with the coming of new generations, there will be a tendency to a more mature population. In being pressured to use their energies to pursue legitimate avenues for

91

the fulfillment of their potentials and the gaining of personal security, there will be more mature people in the world.

We want to create more people like the relatively-mature person, taking them from the immature, insecure person categories. These people will pressure others to maturity, and they will raise mature children. It is up to the present relatively-mature person to consolidate his thinking in regard to his own behavior, and to get those people surrounding him to think, feel, and, especially, act as maturely as he. The person who studies and accepts the concepts of this book will strive to become a relatively-mature person, and he will work conscientiously at utilizing the Mature Person-to-Person Philosophy.

As described, immature people exploit other immature people because, from it, they gain a feeling of self-confidence and personal security. It is a false security, however, because they have not really advanced themselves by their exploitations; they have merely attained a feeling of superiority in comparing themselves to the dominated ones. If an immature person's aggressive behavior is effectively curtailed by a relatively-mature person, and if he cannot find another person to exploit, he has been pressured to use his own potential in advancing himself. From his successes he will gain real self-confidence, personal security, and maturity. He will have no need or desire to exploit others.

It has been said by many, including leaders holding top positions in their respective countries, that the United States should not be involved in the war in Viet Nam, nor should it be bombing North Viet Nam. Those who feel this way, who believe that we should stop bombing North Viet Nam and should withdraw our troops from South Viet Nam, are resorting to immature thinking. They do not fully realize that we are contending with an insatiable aggressor. By retreating, we would be only inviting more aggression. In fact, any type of demonstration in this country, such as the burning of draft cards, peace marches, and a split in the thinking of our senators and other leaders, which raises doubt as to our foreign policy and unity of purpose, gives confidence and a sense of security to the enemy. They continue with their exploitation at even a faster pace. Just as immature are those leaders who are neutral or without a decided opinion as to our stand in Viet Nam. More immature are those who are directing, supporting, and condoning some of our present corrupt action in Viet Nam, the ineffective bombing and wasteful use of troops and supplies, and tolerating the transportation of supplies to the North Viet Namese from so-called non-aggressive nations. Most immature, of course, are the aggressors themselves.

It is true that the United States should not be fighting in Viet Nam, that is, not fighting in Viet Nam under the United States flag. The United States forces should be fighting in Viet Nam, and any other part of the world where there is exploitation of peoples, under the flag of the United Nations. Every other country of the world that believes in the dignity of man and freedom of the individual should be fighting as part of the United Nations, also.

Concerning the charge that the United States is an imperialist invader in Viet Nam, one should only examine the past performance of this country to dispel this notion. We have not attempted to place other peoples under our domination; in fact, we have given aid to most of the impoverished peoples of the world. We have tried to promote freedom. Exploitation has certainly not been our policy. Were it not for the desire and quick action of the United States to curtail the exploitation in South Viet Nam, the threat of world domination by Communism would be even greater than it is today. It is unfortunate that other countries have not come to the aid of South Viet Nam also, and more unfortunate that the United States and all the other countries of the world could not have supported the United Nations to have made it strong enough to stop the aggression there.

In considering the justification of our bombing of North Viet Nam, we have only to ask the intentions of the Communists. If they have as their goal to dominate the entire world, that which they have certainly expressed, then there should be no question that we are justified in bombing them, because the bombing will help us to preserve our freedom and our lives. We know that it has been the practice of the Communists to harass and attack relentlessly, in all areas of the world. Since the latter part of World War II they have made giant strides. No doubt, they are most successful in converting and controlling those people who are dissatisfied and unsettled, those who are immature, such as the people living under tyranny or in the undeveloped countries. Some have proposed the argument that it is a civil war in Viet Nam and that the United States has no business intervening in the internal affairs of that country. Whether or not it is a civil war is not important. If people are being exploited, as they are by the Communists, whether or not they are asking for aid, we, as a relatively-mature people, should give them the help that they need. Others have said that we should remain peaceful and learn to coexist with the Communists. The answer to this is very simple. We cannot coexist with someone who does not want to coexist with us. They might say they want to coexist with us, but it is only as long as it would take them to completely dominate us.

If there were decisive action by a strong United Nations in the very beginning of uprisings, they would be squelched, and there would be no wars. This means that the United Nations as a law-enforcing agency must be stronger than any other country, or combination of countries, intent upon the exploitation of other peoples. This means that every non-aggressive country must do its share in uniting with each other under the United Nations flag, and they must unselfishly and wholeheartedly support the law in immediately repelling an aggressor. All of this has been spelled out and tried but the reason for failure thus far, and the cause of the war in Viet Nam, is due to the immaturity and insecurity of all the people of the world. The people of the non-aggressor nations are immature and insecure in not having united in this common effort, and in tolerating mass-exploitation of themselves and others. The aggressors are without question immature in desiring and needing to exploit others in order to advance themselves.

We should bear in mind that our enemy in Viet Nam is Communism, the Russian Communists, the Chinese Communists, the North Viet Namese Communists, and all the other Communists of the world, who have as their doctrine to rule the entire world. Insofar as any Communist-dominated people and others might support the Communists, they are our enemies, too. However, there are many knowledgeable people living under Communism, Russian, Chinese, and others, who are our sympathizers and opposed to Communism. Also, the unknowledgeable and "brainwashed" would certainly not want Communism if they were given the opportunity to live and learn under a better cultural

94

system. Our real enemies, then, are in the Communist strongholds, from where the Communist leaders are dictating orders to the lesser Communists of the world; and these are in Russia and China. Looking at the world situation objectively, we, as members of the United Nations, should be fighting Russia and China, the instigators and supporters of the war in Viet Nam. More correctly, we should be fighting the Russian and Chinese Communists, not the masses of Russian and Chinese people—remembering that less than ten percent of the people in those countries are actually Communists.

It is an admitted fact, but not accepted by all, that the Communists want to rule the whole world. Their policy has been to gain victory through subversion, and not from all-out war. However, if they thought they could beat the United States, their strongest enemy, without too much difficulty, they would in all probability wage a war against us. Many people in the United States do not recognize, or do not want to recognize, the seriousness of the Communist threat to our country and our way of life. They would hesitate to go to war unless we were openly attacked, and some, not even then. Perhaps the greatest deterrent to an all-out war between the Communists and the free peoples of the world is the atomic bomb. If it were not for the fact that both sides, including leaders, would lose in a nuclear war, we might have had a confrontation with Russia years ago. It is surely regrettable that the people of the world did not act early enough to have prevented Communism from becoming as strong as it is today.

If, during and immediately following World War II, when the Communist expansion was at its greatest, there had been enough mature people in the world, the United Nations would have been made strong enough to have contained the Communists. Of course, the major difficulty at that time came as a result of unjust, unwise, and immaturely-made concessions to the Soviet Union and others. Since that time the Communists have grown extremely powerful, and their successes have given them a sense of self-confidence to continue with their exploitations. To expect them or the United States to disarm at this time, relinquishing their power to the United Nations, is resorting to immature and wishful thinking. This is similar to expecting immature, re-

95

bellious sons to give their immature father respect and power over them. In the first place, immature people do not give up their gains, and in the second place, the immature father, the United Nations, could not rule effectively knowing he was dependent upon his strong sons, Russia and the United States. Besides, it is incompatible for an aggressor to disarm, and folly for his enemy to disarm if there is no higher authority to protect him. That both would disarm at the same time, even if supervised, under the present circumstances without maturing, is illogical. Even if Russia and the United States could trust each other, they would both be fearful, and rightfully so, of the other pathologically aggressive countries in the world.

Had we been a mature world, Communism would not have originated or would have been squelched at its inception; and, most assuredly, immediately following World War II. The problem at that time was that the United Nations was in its infancy, and that Russia and China were considered to be our allies, and non-aggressor nations. It would have been difficult at that time, even if the people of the world had foreseen the Communist expansion, for them to have embarked upon a war with Russia and China immediately following a great war.

The sad part of all this is that, even if we now went to war with the Communist world, even if we had a nuclear war, managed to survive, and won, the same situation would exist after the war if we did not mature. Immature leaders would still be present on both sides. If we remained as immature people, as immature nations, we would be confronted with the same problems as exist now. In another generation or less, the same or other countries with immature leaders, bent upon the exploitation of peoples similar to what we see under Communism, would be trying to dominate other people. The only way to interrupt the vicious cycle of having wars is to interrupt the vicious cycle of having immature people in the world. The answer to having permanent peace is to produce more mature people and nations.

This is in opposition to the views of both the so-called "doves" and "hawks". The "doves" feel that we should stop the bombing of North Viet Nam and withdraw our troops from the South, whereas the "hawks" believe we should conquer North Viet Nam as rapidly as possible. Many of the "hawks" feel that we should threaten to use the atomic bomb—and, in fact, use it on the North Viet Namese if they do not stop infiltrating to South Viet Nam. Further, some advocate using the atomic bomb on the Chinese if they would come to the aid of the Viet Namese, and if they were beating us due to their superior manpower. They doubt that Russia would intervene, since they would have "too much to lose" in a nuclear war, in contrast to the Chinese.

If we attacked North Viet Nam, and especially if we resorted to atomic warfare, world opinion would most certainly be against us. A great many innocent people would be killed, especially if China entered the war. It could not be discounted that Russia would not defend North Viet Nam and China. In fact, it would be highly unlikely that they would not rally in the defense of China. If eventually we fought Russia, and if either side were in danger of being defeated, there would be the strong possibility that atomic bombs would be used.

We must remember that the North Viet Namese Communists are ultimately taking orders from the Russian Communists. The Communist-controlled people of North Viet Nam are being used by, and are fighting the battle for, the Russian Communists. If we won in North Viet Nam, and even in China, Russian Communists would continue to instigate subversive action in other parts of the world. At this moment our real enemy is the Russian Communists, the strongest of the world Communist movement. In a few years it may be the Chinese Communists, and it may prove true that they feel they do not have "too much to lose" in a nuclear confrontation with us.

For the United Nations to be an effective world-governing body the people of the world have to become mature enough to really desire and support it; and they have to send leaders to it who have maturity and wisdom, and whom they respect. To be effective, it must evolve into an independent and powerful body, more powerful than all the countries of the world. It must be able to act immediately and with authority, meting out the same justice to all peoples. The United Nations and the common good of the world will have to take top priority, over and above the common good of any individual country. Our present United Nations, not as strong as some of the countries whose actions it is trying to influence, cannot do as much as it would like to avert war. The two major powers, Russia and the United States, are in direct disagreement as to how people should live. So long as the Communists continue with their aggressive tactics, the United States has no choice but to resist them in Viet Nam, and in any other part of the world. All other relatively-mature countries should unite with us in doing the same. This may mean engaging in long-drawn-out and continuous wars, but it may avoid a nuclear holocaust, which nobody should want. Of course, it will be difficult for immature people, those who are impatient and desire immediate gratification, to accept such a policy. We should use this time to good advantage, maturing ourselves and the rest of the world.

We, the people of the free countries of the world, must become more mature individually and collectively. In this country we must work at interrupting pathological cultural trends which make us weaker both as individuals and as a nation. We have to guard against moral decline and dependence, and stop ourselves from heading in the direction of Socialism. We must become a strong and a secure people, which will be a contented people.

We have to work through example, negotiation, and pressure to show the Communists that man can live a meaningful life only in a free society. The Communist-controlled peoples, and especially the Communists themselves, have to grow more emotionally mature. They have to mature both individually and collectively. The leaders will have to stop their massive exploitations, and their entire culture will have to be changed to one in which they acknowledge the rights of fellow man. Their culture will have to change before their people, especially the children, will be able to become more emotionally mature. Their present culture is an impediment to their emotional, social, and spiritual growth much more so than ours, especially because of their lack of freedom and family unity. One might say that the Communists are more immature than we because of their restriction on full emotional development. We should derive no satisfaction from this statement, however. Instead, we have to reflect upon the awesome task that stands before us, that is, to change our own bad cultural trends and individual family patterns so that we become as mature as possible. We have to preserve world peace in opposition to the less mature Communist aggressors.

It is inconceivable that the Communists would voluntarily, or that they even could, change their ideas and give up what positions they now hold under their system. As another generation comes into being, with the children raised in nurseries and lacking in emotional development, educated only in their methods, it will be more difficult, and even impossible, for them to change. They will become more firmly entrenched in their pathological cultural ways.

On our side is the fact that man basically desires freedom and an opportunity to fulfill his potential. Yet, because this may be the case does not mean that truth will win out, and that there should be no concern that we will ever lose our freedom. Slavery has been in existence and accepted as a way of life for thousands of years, and it still exists. Eventually, there will be no slavery, but we may not see its complete demise for another thousand years. In the last analysis, even the Communists would want freedom and opportunity for themselves and their families.

It would be too much to hope for an upheaval of the entire Communist doctrine, especially with the present listless attitude of the rest of the world. To see a change for the good in the Communists, it will be necessary for all the non-Communists of the world to unite and oppose their actions. In thwarting their aggressions, we would be pressuring them to behave more maturely. Also, an attempt should be made to show their enslaved peoples our way of life. Last, but not least, a concerted effort should be made in educating, and making more mature and independent, the peoples that the Communists would plan to conquer. Through our immediate use of the Mature Person-to-Person Philosophy, our new generations of more mature people will be able to offset the more immature new generations of Communists. This is our answer to the "cold war", the Communists' use of subversion and all other tactics which they use for exploitation short of war. More important, just as the Communists are now making gains and winning because they are the aggressors and we are living in complacency, we will be taking a positive step toward dealing with them, and all immature people. We will be working toward containing their aggressions, thus forcing them to give their own people more freedom and opportunity for self-expression and individual fulfillment, that which they basically need and desire for themselves.

There has been more talk of late as to whether or not the United Nations should be maintained if it cannot avert wars. It should definitely be maintained. Because it is now stymied by the major powers does not mean that this condition will always exist. It may not now be able to avoid an all-out war between the major powers, but it can have a decided influence on all countries, even the major ones. By placing the problems of the world in open view for all the people to see, and by listening to the comments of everyone, pressure is placed upon the different countries and their leaders to exercise right reason and action. It gives the opportunity for all people to express their opinions, not only those who are the loudest and mightiest. It sets the stage for free discussion and negotiation. It sets the plan into action for a civilized people to use their minds, not only their hands, in the resolution of problems. Eventually, if the world has matured to the point of fully accepting the United Nations, it will be available as an efficient world governing body. Unless there is another world war, the transition of the United Nations, from its present state to that of the powerful organization it should be, will be a gradual one. Should there be World War III, should anyone survive, and if there is a predominance of relatively-mature peoples, it seems the United Nations will then rule supreme. If the people of all the different countries of the world mature enough to allow the United Nations to grow all-powerful, in the process not dominating each other and thus avoiding another world war, they will find less and less need to have their individual armaments. The countries may never disarm, but there will be no need to replenish their arms. Ultimately, there will be less and less need for the United Nations. When the people of the world mature to the point of achieving fulfillment of their own potentials, they will have no need to look at their neighbors resentfully and aggressively. They will have no need or desire to exploit others.

Nations, both large and small, should be expected and pressured to handle their own problems, both domestic and foreign,

100

insofar as it is possible. The large countries, and even the United Nations, should not interfere unless they are called upon. Of course, help should be provided by the relatively-mature nations if for some reason an exploited nation does not request it, yet obviously is in need of it. The object is to have each country become as self-sufficient as possible. One country may excel in farm produce, another in glassware, and a third in precision watches. Each country should strive for the amount of emotional, intellectual, and physical strength which is necessary to prevent immature, aggressive countries from attacking them. Every country will attain a certain pride and self-respect.

If a country, before the United Nations becomes powerful enough to immediately and effectively intercede, is exploited in any way by another, it has to take upon itself the responsibility for self-defense, and protection of its property and rights. Of course, it may seek, and should be granted, aid from all other relatively-mature nations. This has been the case with the United States helping South Viet Nam and, admittedly, itself too. As stated, even if a country, similar to an individual, does not request help, not believing that it is in need of it—due perhaps to not being advanced and sophisticated enough to know what is best for its people—it should be granted the aid that it really needs. Since the United Nations is not yet an effective higher authority, the attacked country, and any of its allies, will have to use their own good judgments as to how to best cope with the aggressor. They should not only think of themselves, but should also take into consideration the welfare of all the other peoples in the world. With the United States and Russia taking opposite sides in any dispute, there is always the danger of an all-out war. However, the Russian, and even the Chinese, leaders of the present generation should be as afraid of a nuclear war as our leaders. How the automaton-Communist leaders of the next generation will think about this is a different matter. There is indication they will think even less of human life than they do now, and they may show an utter disregard as to the consequences of a nuclear war. If the attacked country has not been provocative, it and its allies should ordinarily repel the aggressor immediately and with all their power. This applies to the United States, if it should be exploited by either China, or Russia, or anyone else. Of course, because of the large stakes involved, extra-good judgment has to be used in weighing the nature of the exploitation.

As a rule, to appease an aggressor merely adds fuel to his aggressive ambitions. In seeing that he is winning, his self-confidence is bolstered and he begins to feel definitely superior to his victim. The aggressive leaders of a country will attack all the more if they see that they will easily get away with it. The only time for a country to yield and allow itself to be exploited is when it is in danger of being overwhelmed, and it needs to stall for time to become stronger. As the aggressor gains strength in the sense of feeling more secure from his conquests, the exploited country should work to muster its own strength, especially its physical strength, so that it will be able to successfully thwart the aggressor. At the same time, through negotiation and pressure from the United Nations, other countries, and from within their own countries, war might be averted.

A weak country is going to provoke immature, aggressive countries to try to exploit it. Even a country which might be of the same strength as that of an aggressor will invite attack from the immature, competitive, and jealous aggressor. It is necessary for a country to be strong, and to have the aggressor know that it is strong and will use its strength, if it wants to be left alone to live in peace. It must appear to the aggressor that it would be foolhardy to try to exploit the country. An aggressor can be deluded into thinking it is superior to a particular country, and that it can successfully take advantage of it. Its superiority-feelings could be partially a result of previous successful exploitations with the same or other countries, and the particular country giving an appearance of being weak, although it may not be. In successfully repulsing any demands or attacks, the assailed country is doing the aggressor a favor in making its people turn to a mature and a rewarding type of behavior through the development of its resources. Of course, a thwarted aggressor will not turn to legitimate endeavors if it is given support by other aggressors, or if there are still other peoples that it might exploit. In order to have an aggressor seek peaceful pursuits, it is necessary for everyone to pressure it in that direction.

The relatively-mature nations, if much stronger than the aggressors, should try upon occasion, without actually retreating, to avoid a battle and stall for time in an attempt to negotiate. They will be people of more maturity, wisdom, and tolerance, and they should set the example for all others, including the enemy, to follow. With time and various pressures placed upon the aggressors, their—the aggressors'—actions might begin to reflect more emotional stability. They, or their progeny, may start to have a change of ideas. Although the aggressors might interpret this as a sign of weakness and gain self-confidence, furthering their exploitations, it is worth the effort to avert an actual conflict. They may gain momentum with their exploitations, but the relatively-mature nations, growing much stronger, are in no real danger of becoming overwhelmed by them.

In the case of the United States coping with the Communists, there seems to be no longer any danger that they could overwhelm us without being destroyed, too—if we maintain our superiority. We could lose our superiority, however, because of corruption and collapse within our country. If this country continues with its pathological cultural trends, condoning lack of discipline, dependency, laziness, moral decline, corruption, inadequate law enforcement, rioting, catering to the wealthy, unjustified labor strikes, bureaucracy, Socialism, and the stifling of people's opportunities for the utilization of their potentials in the search for security, there could, in fact, be internal weakening and collapse of the country. Whether or not the future generations of Communists might try to beat us in a war will depend upon our maturity, wisdom, and physical strength, and their maturity and wisdom. Had they believed that they could have conquered us without significant losses themselves, they, as aggressors, most probably would have tried to have done so by this time. We now have to repel their every aggressive action, all the while making ourselves overpoweringly stronger than they. We must surpass them not only militarily, but also with our maturity and wisdom, our arts and sciences, our government and way of life, and in all other areas, including space exploration. It is not that we should seek to advance ourselves based on comparing ourselves with them, but rather, to realize our potentials to the limit so that we can safeguard our existence and the existence of all other free peoples as dignified human beings. So long as they want to make us slaves we have to oppose them in every respect, no matter what they say or do to try to distract us, as in the way of proposing troop withdrawals and truce talks. We believe they are wrong in what they are doing, and we have to admit that we are really at war with all Communists. However, we do not want to fight an all-out war. Our strength should discourage them from attempting to fulfill their neurotic ambitions at this time. We have to believe, and let the Communists know, that we are not afraid of war, even nuclear war, and that we will fight to our deaths to preserve our way of life. We should not be intimidated by them. Only those people who are emotionally immature and insecure would say: "Better Red than dead."

The intention of the perpetrated act is more important than the act itself in determining how one should react to an aggressor. A minor act performed with malicious intent might serve as a prelude to what is coming. We already know that the Communists have as their intention to undermine, attack, and eventually destroy us as a free society. Whichever means they use to provoke us, we should take very seriously, and react with the thought in mind that their ultimate plan is to make us their slaves.

When people or countries are deliberately and openly aggressive, there is no problem in recognizing it, only in coping with it. Sometimes, however, one or both parties might be unconsciously motivated to immature, provocative, and aggressive behavior, which creates a more difficult situation to handle. Some aggressors rationalize their positions, and don't believe that they are the aggressors. They may feel that they were exploited previously, and that now they are retaliating with justification, or that they are prophylactically preventing further exploitation. In such instances, disinterested people might aid the aggressors in gaining some insight as to the true nature of their behavior. When the people of different countries are advancing their positions due to a realization of their potentials, they will have less resentment toward each other. If the adversaries are sincere in desiring the peaceful resolution of a problem, and if both are represented by mature and wise leadership, there should exist no real difficulties between them. If there is a question as to who is really the aggressor, all relatively-mature authority figures should pressure warring nations to stop fighting, and to attempt to view their differences in discussions.

In thwarting an aggressive nation, one should not exploit it. One should not humiliate it, which would be exploitative and immature behavior, but rather allow it to "save face." In humiliating and belittling an aggressor, which is often done unofficially through news media, it provokes it to retaliation in its search for self-worth and security. This is similar to the vengeful and immature "eye for an eye" type of philosophy. "Two wrongs do not make a right." Some submissiveness will do the aggressive nation no harm in motivating it to a healthier type of behavior. The goal is to pressure the aggressor so that it will direct its energies in a different direction, away from trying to exploit the same or any other weaker nation. This means that all other countries should repel the aggressor also, and that, ideally, all nations should aid each other if one of them is attacked. Such action will not allow the aggressor to behave in any other way except maturely. It will have to find legitimate opportunities for the self-expression of its people, from which they will realize their potentials and gain success, happiness, and security. The country will be able to excel in a certain area of endeavor in which it will be genuinely on an equal par, or even superior, to others. Its people will have a feeling of self-worth, and there will be no need for it to seek security, which would prove to be a false security, from the domination of others.

Not only should a nation strive for emotional and intellectual maturity in order to adequately cope with an aggressive nation in these particular areas, but also to contain its own physical strength. All leaders, those in this country, in China, in Russia, and in every other country in the world, although differing in certain values and principles, are similar psychodynamically. They all have the same needs, drives, and desires, and the motivating factors which have made them leaders are not so unlike. Even the people of a relatively-mature nation have to be on guard that some of their more immature leaders may not wrest too much of the physical strength from their over-all control and use it unwisely. The immature leaders of a relatively-mature nation could very readily provoke the immature leaders of an opposing nation to starting a world war. Of more consequence, because it is of a subtle nature and largely unknown to the public, are the immature leaders, making territorial and trade agreements between countries, and even selling goods to an enemy who frees its economy for the production of war materials, all for the personal gain of a few.

Just as dangerous a situation could result from immature leaders offering peace to their people, feeding their own and their people's insecurity feelings, and seeking personal gain for themselves. They would negotiate and give in to the demands of the aggressors at any cost. The immature, insecure people would tend to leap at the prospect of having immediate peace, immediate gratification, not recognizing that a harder-won peace might be the only way to a more stable and lasting peace. The relatively-mature people have to become more mature, knowledgeable, and active citizens, critical of their leaders' decisions, not following them blindly. They should pressure the leaders to explain their ideas and actions, and not be afraid to seek wiser and more effective leaders.

Much has been written regarding "just wars" and "unjust wars". Actually, as has been stated previously, wars are senseless and unnecessary. A war may be termed as "just" or righteous only when it is fought in self-defense, and that is only when one's own or another country is physically attacked by an aggressor nation and there is no immediate intervention by a mature higher authority. Without saying, the aggressor nation is immature in its action. The aggressive leaders are immature, and their followers are also immature in their having lived under their domination. The attacked nation and, especially, all the other peoples of the world are immature in that they have been unable to fortify themselves emotionally, intellectually, and physically, and have been unable to unify themselves in a common effort to have stopped the aggressors. Seeing that they have been attacked unjustly, they are now involved in a "just war" of defending themselves. However, everyone is immature in having permitted the war in the first place. When the entire population of the world matures, there will be no wars, and the problem of labeling wars as "just" or "unjust" will not exist. The world is in the process of maturing; and if most of the nations unite in common agreement to prevent wars, there will be no full-scale wars, only encounters in self-defense to repulse aggressors. These encounters might be termed "just" encounters. Ultimately, there should be no need for even these encounters, and people will be able to live in peace.

* * * *

We have discussed the Mature Person-to-Person Philosophy in this chapter. We have seen how it can be the answer to people getting along with people and the avoidance of war. It is a natural reaction for people to seek personal security, and for immature people to take advantage of one another in the search for this security. With people attaining personal security through the fulfillment of their potentials, it is no longer necessary or desirable for them to seek it from the exploitation of others. The Mature Person-to-Person Philosophy checks and channels people's aggressive energies so that they seek and work at legitimate opportunities.

Maturity was illustrated. The means of exploitation were discussed, as were the personalities of those who exploit. Pressure Psychotherapy and the Mature Person-to-Person Philosophy were described at great length. The Mature Person-to-Person Philosophy was discussed in reference to individuals, and then in regard to nations. United States involvement in Viet Nam, Communist aggression, and the role of the United Nations were examined. It was concluded that the world must grow more mature, which it can do through the utilization of the Mature Person-to-Person Philosophy, before there will be an end to all wars.

Chapter V

MATURE LEADERS

The government should be comprised of individuals, the individuals working together as a representative body with a purpose to serve individuals, including themselves. Too often a
person employed by the government, including a leader, does
not realize and does not grasp the full significance of the fact
that he also is an individual—a private citizen, like everyone else.
Due to his basic personality, the acquisition of political influence, and association with all others like him, he tends to
separate himself from the common man and elevates himself
into a position of rulership. One frequently hears a leader or
civil employee, no matter how lowly a job that he may hold,
refer to the public as "they", and not "we". One might hear:
"They (the public) ought to vote for this referendum," or "They
(the public) ought to give us a raise." These people should be
reminded that they are employees of the government—that is,
employees of the people; and they should have the interest of
the people they serve at heart. If they do not work in this
capacity to the best of their ability, they and the people who
tolerate them are behaving immaturely.

In this chapter we are speaking primarily of the leader in
government, but what will be said applies in general to all kinds
of leaders—to those in the military services, in the clergy, and
in all types of organizations in civil life. In the United States
we are supposedly self-governed, that is, our government is made
up of the people, for the people. This is what our country's
founders desired and what all free, mature people want. In
reality, however, the people of the United States do not rule
themselves. Due to their immaturity and insecurity, they unknowingly elect immature, insecure leaders who rule over them
instead of represent them. For the most part, the leaders are

not true representatives of the people serving for the common good of the majority of the people. They, with possibly some exceptions, because of their own insecurity feelings, are acting first in such a way to promote their own interest and security. Their immaturity and insecurity is in most instances the motivating factor in their seeking leadership positions associated with self-importance, fame, power, and money, in the first place. They are status-seekers par excellence, campaigning tirelessly for election as though they are entering a popularity contest, and looking for acceptance and security from as many people as possible.

It is basically because of the people themselves, due to their immaturity and insecurity, that the situation of being ruled, and of having rulers, exists. In the olden days there were the master and his servants, the lord and his vassals, the king and his subjects, and so on. Later came the dictators and more exploitation of the common people. Now the people are heading in the direction of strong Welfare States and Socialism, and of being dependent upon and ruled by the government. It is true that there was a larger gap between the rulers and the ruled than there exists today in a democratic government, where people have a voice in government. However, now, as in the days of old, both the governors and the governed are still immature and insecure. There is exploitation by immature people of immature people. This was discussed in more detail in Chapter I. Only will there be an ideal government, with the proper relationship between the leaders themselves and the people, when people have attained maturity and security. From the mature, secure ranks leaders will emerge to best represent everyone in a selfless manner, with the good of all the people foremost in their minds.

Unfortunately, too often the personality of the individual who aspires to a leadership position, and the methods that have to be taken today, are such that the person who ultimately gets to be a leader is one whom relatively-mature people do not want. His personality is such that he has always been motivated to think of himself first, and to compete, dominate, and surpass others. He feels that he "missed out" in childhood, and he has a "temper tantrum" if he doesn't get his own way. He is greedy and "pushy", and looks for more of everything for himself. He frequently overcompensates for his feelings of inadequacy and insecurity, and to the unsophisticated observer he appears confident and successful. He takes advantage of people, and may overwhelm a relatively-mature opponent who would have made a good leader but who was not recognized by the voters.

This type of person exists in all countries, in a democracy, under Communism, and in all other forms of government. The personalities of the leaders, whether they are Republicans, Democrats, Socialists, Communists, or tyrants, are very similar to each other. Their basic drives and needs and goals are very much the same. To achieve their goals, these leaders could turn to Communism, or any other means of exploitation. The differences between them are on a more superficial level. The leaders of a democratic country, due to their culture, spiritual training, and upbringing, may have more conscience and development of virtues, and more respect for life and fellow man. Due to freedom and the opportunity to achieve success and personal security, they have found less need to resort to exploitation, and the more crude and vicious techniques used when fighting for survival.

In the process of achieving his goal as leader, a person has had to make certain commitments to others so that he is even less objective about issues once he attains the leadership position. Because of his own feelings, his jealousy, resentment, greed, and prejudice, and because he is readily swayed by outside political influence, he is incapable of making valid judgments in situations which sometimes involve millions of people. With our system of government and elections, the elected officials are in most cases merely figureheads and puppets. There are immature men behind the scenes with money and power who are instrumental in getting a person elected and who, in turn, influence and receive favors from the official after he becomes elected. In the true sense of the word, the official is not a leader —not one who is representing all the people and working for the common good. He is representing his powerful constituents and working for their gain and his own gain, even enacting laws of personal benefit which might be to the detriment of most of the people. The appointment by the elected officials of friends and supporters to lucrative and influential positions adds "fuel to the fire", in that it forms a stronger union of more biased and less objective men ruling over the people. The wealthy and the lawmakers, the majority of them being lawyers, have gained control of the power in our democracy. They have enacted laws favorable to themselves first, and not for the common good.

People who are mature and secure will not expect favors and hand-outs from their leaders and the government. They will not have voted for leaders who believe in the practice of favoritism and patronage in the first place. They realize that a leader who owes people favors loses his objectivity. They know that the favorites are not chosen on their merit, and that the incentive for the favorite's competitor to set goals, to work, to succeed, and to gain personal security is lost in such instances. This constitutes less opportunity, less chance to exercise one's potential to the limit, and frustration and unhappiness for the competitor. Mature people understand that a leader who condones such practices is cheating the majority of the people in not giving them the most competent choice for their tax dollar. Of most importance, the leaders are supporting and nurturing the practice of exploitation by choosing their favorites, men who are invariably immature and prone to taking unfair advantage of others.

The well-known saying: "It is not so important what you know, but rather whom you know," is, unfortunately, true in our society. The reason that it is true is that immature people in leadership positions in all walks of life show favoritism. Such practice is certainly not conducive to getting our young people to work hard and to achieve on their own merit. Too many of our present leaders have been raised in families with abundance, and they prefer to follow the easy way of the past. Instead of doing their job to the best of their ability, they frequently spend most of their time getting voters indebted to them by doing them favors, and making "connections" with superiors, with their eyes set on their next political job "up the ladder".

People who are mature and secure realize that you rarely get anything for little or no effort. For what people are obtaining in the way of hand-outs by the government, such as social security, aid to education, Medicare, and others, they are paying dearly. Not only are the costs for the inefficient government ser-

111

vices astronomical, but there is an impingement by the government upon the freedom of the private citizen. Due to the immaturity and insecurity of the people, the leaders are offering the hand-outs in return for votes and their own security, and the masses are accepting them in their search for "more of everything" and security. As a result, a "monster" is created in the form of an overpowering state. This situation is bad because it curtails private enterprise and stifles one from exercising his potential to the limit. The leaders are indebted to their constituents who elected them, and in fear of displeasing those who are superior to them. They are not free to think and act for themselves, because they are fearful of those above them and of those beneath them with "high-level connections". They are indecisive and cannot assume responsibility. They do not want to say or do anything which will antagonize anyone and jeopardize their position. The people are restricted by governmental controls, and intimidated by their influential leaders. The result is a strong bureaucracy, Welfare State, and Socialism.

Just as the balance of power shifted in the direction of government creates an impingement upon people's rights, so, too, power in the hands of a few private citizens invariably results in an exploitation of people. If those who have achieved a degree of success and prosperity squelch others from attempting to gain the same, and do not want them to have the opportunity, there will be resentment and strife. What mature people want in the way of security is to be given the opportunity to exercise their potential to the fullest, and to seek success and happiness. From succeeding on one's own merit, an individual will add to his personal security. Not until the majority of the people mature emotionally, not want to exploit each other and not allow themselves to be exploited, will there be a balance between government and the governed. Not until people gain maturity and security for themselves will they be able to provide others with the same opportunity. Those provided with the opportunity will have to be mature, also, so that they will work and gain on their own merit, and not use the opportunity to take advantage of people. As mentioned previously, the ideal relationship between government and its people exists when there is a majority of strong, mature people from whose ranks strong, mature leaders are chosen as representatives.

There are those who have personality patterns similar to those of the leaders and who become the leaders' followers. Whether a political party is right or wrong, it will draw support from immature people who do not place the common good over their own gains. These people would never vote for a candidate of another party, even though the candidate of their own party might be far inferior. In the search for favors, or because they are "hero-worshippers" or status-seekers, these people associate closely with the leaders. They are basically striving for more personal security. Some of the subordinates identify with a leader and give strong support to his cause, even though they might be extremely resentful of him and would like to take over his position. In identifying with a potential winner and supporting him, immature people attain a feeling of success and security for themselves. Of course, they gain a feeling of security by being accepted as a valuable member of their party, the recipient of favors, and one with influence and "connections". If they feel that they are a part of the government, ruling over people, they may feel strong, superior, and even more secure. The security, basically, is a false security because they have not actually improved themselves as individuals. Without really evaluating the candidate's qualifications, or even caring if he is the best choice for the people, they will almost hysterically campaign for him in order to get him elected. So that they will succeed, they will favor a good "vote-getter"—for example, a candidate with a famous name, and one who "runs a hard race". Of course, these are not qualifications of a true leader.

A person in one leadership position need not be qualified for any other leadership position or a higher one in his particular field. Also, even though he may have been once qualified does not mean that he will always be the best to fill that certain position. Others may be present with more knowledge, enthusiasm, and newer ideas who could represent and serve the people better. In fact, after a leader has been away from his home environment for a length of time, as living at a nation's capitol while representing his state, he loses his "feel" for his people's problems. A person is not a good leader just because he can get a large number of people to follow him or vote for him, if the people are immature.

The job for which a person is being considered should be based upon his qualifications for that specific job. His intelligence, training, personality, maturity, and wisdom may be more suited to one position than another. Because a person is involved in politics from an early age, having experience in government, knowing the inner workings of bureaucracy, does not mean that he would be the best prepared for a higher position. To the contrary, a so-called professional politician's experience may be detrimental to promoting a more efficient government. The extent of a candidate's qualifications should be the determining factor as to the magnitude of the office which he seeks.

Quite often, men who have accumulated a great deal of wealth turn to politics and leadership positions. It might be that it is necessary to have a lot of money in order to enter politics with our present system of getting elected to office. Also, because men of wealth do not have to be concerned with earning a living, they have the time to contribute to office-seeking and public service. They usually, due to having lived better, having traveled more, having had a better education, having been in personal contact with other leaders, are more self-confident. They need not fear failure as much as the common man. Because they have the security related to material possessions, it is easier for them to do for others without the fear of being surpassed. It seems that most people believe a person who has been successful at accumulating a large sum of money will be one who will lead wisely. They do not consider that he may have inherited the money or achieved material success through neurotic motivation and the exploitation of others. The same motivating factors now may be turned toward his seeking fame and power, more personal security. Insecure people sometimes gain a feeling of security in knowing that a man of wealth, which is associated with power, is his leader. People without money may look in awe upon such a person. Similarly, it should be stated that a person may not prove to be a good leader just because he is poor. If he is poor and immature, he may be even more pathologically motivated to seek fame, power, and wealth at the expense of exploiting his fellow man.

Other factors besides money, quite frequently, influence people to vote for a particular candidate. There may be sentimental reasons; or the fact that the candidate is of the same religion, race, or nationality might serve as reason enough to vote for him. Immature voters and leaders do not vote for and appoint candidates according to their individual qualifications and merit. A person might be a father image or a brother image, for example, and a voter's own personality determines his choice for office. Of importance to some people are the candidate's imposing figure, his stature, and his distinguished or formidable appearance. They are impressed by one's white hair, piercing eyes, rimless glasses, or that he wears a vest; and by one's charm, forceful personality, stirring speeches and mannerisms, or that he smokes a pipe. All of the above are interpreted by many to signify eminence, respectability, venerability, stateliness, stability, trustworthiness, and wisdom.

Unfortunately, the glib-of-tongue, well-appearing, loud and boisterous politicians, depicting an air of confidence, become best known and are elected. The basic reason that voters elect such officials is that they believe they will derive the most benefit personally from their election. To think this way means that the voters are immature and insecure. Most people follow in the footsteps of their parents, friends, work associates, or church groups in supporting a candidate. With the advent of television, debates between candidates have become more popular, presumably so that their issues might be more clearly defined. These amount to nothing more than "beauty" and oratorical contests, and do not truly measure a man's wisdom and ability to make the best decisions for all. Due to neurotic motivation and overcompensation of his inadequacy-feelings, a candidate may appear as a very confident and capable person before an audience. To the television industry the political debates are a source of revenue, to the candidates they are a means of getting known quickly, and to the viewers they are a medium of gratification.

An ideal leader should be a person of wisdom. He should be one with emotional maturity and personal security. He should have been raised by mature parents in a healthy cultural environment, so that his emotional, intellectual, physical, and moral potentials have been realized to their fullest. He should be honest, without prejudices, and should possess the characteristics of a mature person. He should be emotionally stable, self-confident, and decisive, yet be flexible in the pursuit of a right judgment. From his and other people's experiences, from knowing past history, and from being able to listen and to deliberate over ideas and suggestions from others, he can make correct decisions. He has been able to give understanding and empathy to all involved with a problem. He has given objective study to everyone's views and, in the light of his own personality and knowledge, has wisely been able to arrive at a solution which is the best for everybody. Final decisions are his own responsibility.

As a rule, wisdom comes with age. It is true that many people grow old without really having gained very much from their many years of living. Also, an exceptional person may be very wise at a young age, but exceptional people are rare. It is through maturity, learning, and experience that one acquires wisdom, and this usually takes many years.

This is in opposition to electing young leaders as a rule, despite the argument that young people have more vigor, and newer and better ideas. If this is true, there is no urgency in most cases, and the person could keep his ideas until he grows older and more mature. "Why wait?", and "We want power now", might be the young people's rebuttal. Not wanting to wait for anything, and desiring immediate gratification, are signs of an immature person. Wanting to have power and influence over others without first proving that one is a responsible person in other areas is immature thinking. There is too much at stake to give one a leadership position so that he can prove his responsibility by trial and error. If one's ideas are good, they should stand the test of time, and they could even be improved upon before they would be put to use. That young people are more prone to action in contrast to the old is not necessarily an asset. All action does not constitute goodness and progress. Impetuous action can cause just as much, and even more, irreparable harm as no action.

116

In the same vein, this is in opposition to lowering the voting age—just as there should be opposition to a lowering of the draft age, if this is ever contemplated. The minimal age allowing anyone to engage in any type of activity should be such that the average person of that age can adequately perform the duties of the specific activity. It seems that those young people who are now favoring a voting age of eighteen are rebelling against their parents, all authority figures, and limits of all kind. They want to grow up faster and become adults so that they will have fewer restrictions, and more privileges and self-gratification.

These people argue that if they are old enough to fight and die for their country, they are old enough to vote. Actually, a person can be old enough to fight, but he may not be mature and wise enough to vote. Just as a child may be of an age to help his parents and himself with household chores, sharing in promoting the welfare of the family, a person may be old enough to serve his country and himself by being able to adequately follow orders and perform the duties of a soldier. The same person, however, may not be capable of making a right judgment in the election of a leader, just as the child may not be able to make important family decisions correctly. It is true that some fourteen-year-olds could vote very sensibly, whereas some people, no matter what age they attain, will never be able to make a sound judgment of any kind. The ideal solution to this problem, and to similar problems, is to have people take instructions and examinations determining their adequacy after they have reached an average minimal age. If it is found that the majority can pass the appropriate tests, the minimal age could then be lowered.

To be a true representative of people, a leader should be familiar with the problems, needs, and desires of the people he represents. He should be knowledgeable regarding other people's needs and problems also, including minority groups, and what they are doing about them. He should be wise enough to know what is really good and not good for his people. If a person is to lead a majority of people who are living in poverty, or are of the laboring class, or of the middle class, he should be one of those people, wiser than all of his kind, who has been elevated to represent them. It is true that a person does not have to have been a laborer to be a good labor leader, just as one does not have to suffer from an illness in order to be a good physician. However, all other things being equal, such as emotional maturity and intelligence, a person should be a better representative of laborers if, in fact, he were a laborer himself. In the same vein, all other things being equal, an independently wealthy person should be a better representative of independently wealthy people than someone who was born and raised in poverty. We should choose for a leader a person of any trade or profession or business, if that person best represents most of the people whom he is going to serve. It is a fallacy that lawyers, those who now serve as a majority to represent us, are best equipped to be leaders. The best leader, again stressing all other things being equal, is one who is typical of the majority of people whom he represents.

One who has lived in an environmental situation which he represents knows the "feel" of the people—again, all other things being equal. If he has worked hard in cultivating his capabilities, and has achieved family and job success on his own merit, he can better understand the problems confronting others who are in the process of doing the same. As mentioned, if the majority of the people are in the same category as he, then he would be the best representative of the people.

Quite often we see a man planning to run for a high government office frantically touring foreign countries on "fact-finding" missions, thus preparing himself as a "foreign expert". Actually, in his visits with the foreign leaders, he has seen and heard only what they have wanted him to know. He has not really learned anything about the foreign countries' people and their problems. He would have been better off to have spent all his time in one country and one place, living with the people and getting to know them, their needs, and their problems.

Politicians use various "gimmicks", such as visiting a certain disaster area or war zone, ostensibly to see the problem first-hand. Invariably, the real reason is for their personal gain, to be seen and to be known by more people, and to procure more votes. To give aid to people is only a secondary consideration. Many hire public relations professionals who influence the

118

ignorant public and do not present a true picture of the candidate. True leaders do not have to tell mature people who they are and what they have done. They should not have to expend large sums of money in campaigns for election. With our present immature leaders and immature population, those who spend the most money campaigning are the ones who become elected. Mature people keep informed as to a leader's accomplishments and reversals. If people were mature, the news media, radio, television, newspapers, and magazines would give equal, fair, and objective coverage regarding all prospective leader's qualifications and achievements. People, including those of the news media, would not be influenced by their own needs primarily, and would not support the candidate who would promise to do the most for them. They would have foremost concern for the common good.

A true leader is one who accepted his responsibilities, who displayed initiative, foresight, and courage, and who succeeded by the use of exercising his potential to the fullest. Because he possessed innate intelligence, emotional stability, strength of character, and a healthy motivation, he advanced himself and achieved excellence in his particular field of endeavor. He did not reach the top through neurotic motivation, from the subjugation of others, or by being supported and "pushed" by hysterical followers. He did not attain his high position by "playing politics", by threats, cajolery, or ingratiation, or by merely being appealing to the public and a popular vote-getter. He attained maturity and security for himself and wants to give others the opportunity to achieve the same. The possessor of the most desirable traits, he had stood out among his people. He proved that he was the best qualified to represent and serve them. The mature people, themselves blessed with similar characteristics, recognized his leadership potential, placed their trust in him, and encouraged and followed him. It was not necessary for anyone to train or groom him for his high office.

The mature leader has a keen desire to be of help to others. He wants to advance his people and country. He does not involve himself with favoritism or patronage. He does not seek personal gain from his leadership position, but rather is interested in doing the best job possible for the people whom he represents, and for the common good as a whole. His gain is the singular honor derived from promoting the welfare of mankind. He has already attained self-confidence and personal security from his achievements prior to his becoming a leader, and he does not have to prove himself adequate while being a leader, or seek gratification from his position. The mature leader does not consider politics as a profession. Any difference between his salary as a leader, which should be commensurate with his position, and any higher salary that he may have had prior to being elected, should be more than offset by the privilege vested in him to lead and advance his people. It is incompatible for an emotionally-mature leader to have any motivation other than altruism. He exercises the Mature Person-to-Person Philosophy in his every relationship.

The voters have to grow more mature emotionally and intellectually before they will be able to elect more emotionally and intellectually mature leaders. They have to be able to divorce their own feelings from a situation and look at a candidate objectively. Just as a candidate may have characteristics which are attractive to a voter, so, too, he may have certain traits which are a reminder of similar, more objectionable traits present in the voter or in someone the voter dislikes. The voter in this case could overlook the desirable qualities of the candidate. Each and every voter has to do some soul-searching, and forgo his own personal benefits and immediate gratification which might be derived from a particular candidate's election, in favor of choosing a candidate for the ultimate good of all.

A mature legislator would not be concerned whether a Democrat or a Republican is the sponsor of a bill. If it is a good bill, he will support it. He will know what is really good and not good for his people. Even though most of those whom he represents may be in favor of certain legislation, if he believes it would ultimately be bad for them, he will not vote for it just to please them. The more mature a person grows, the more he is apt to become an independent voter, and not a party voter. He will vote for the individual on his merit, not seeking personal gain from party affiliation. His primary concern will be the advancement of his community, his country, and the entire world. Ultimately, as people mature, there will be no political parties, and not a two or more party system, because all the people will agree upon what constitutes the best principles of government. As the people of the world mature, politics and politicians, as we know them today, will cease to exist.

It takes a very special person to become a true leader in the United Nations. Such a person is a representative of his people, but foremost he is a representative of all the people. He has to stand head and shoulders above all other leaders of the world. He has to rise above any personal emotions involving his own country. He should not have been chosen primarily because of his strong patriotism, or simply because of his previous arbitrative experiences. His goal is not to win decisions for his-country-right-or-wrong, but to make right judgments which will be of benefit to all the people of the world. He should be a man who is objective, mature, and wise, with no excessively strong attachments to the people of his country or any other country. He should be a person whose first interest is the advancement and well-being of all mankind.

Until there are enough mature people who can recognize the mature qualities of a true leader, and from whose ranks true leaders can be selected, a wise general rule to follow is to have a frequent turnover of elected officials and political parties in power. Our present immature leaders should not be allowed to become entrenched in the ways of favoritism, patronage, graft, and corruption. The people should strive to replace appointed officials with elected ones wherever possible. This applies to counsels, judges, postmasters, cabinet members, and many others. In too many instances these people are the puppets of those who appointed them. They do not qualify as leaders, they are not the best choice for all the people, and they do not serve for the common good. In gaining these positions by election, these people would be forced to achieve on their own merit, and to utilize their potential to the fullest. Even when there will be a greater number of more mature people in the future, a frequent rotation of leaders in office would enhance the efficiency of the government. There will be more mature people and more of a choice of good leaders. New leaders bring enthusiasm, new ideas, and progress to an office and administration.

* * * *

In this discussion concerning mature leaders, we have studied the relationship of government, its officials, and all the people. The personality, the role, and the behavior of government leaders were outlined. The reactions of the leaders' followers and the voters were examined. Explained was why certain types of immature candidates gain leadership positions, and why people vote these immature candidates into office. The criteria of an ideal leader were presented.

PART II
Working For A Permanent Peace

Chapter VI

MAN'S LIFE CYCLE

Since the beginning of mankind, there has been a constant struggle between men. Due to ignorance, false beliefs, distorted cultural views and value systems, but ultimately due to immaturity, men have accepted the idea of the inequality of men and have tried to dominate one another. A man has either truly felt the other person to be inferior to him, thus placing him in the capacity of a servant; or, due to his own basic inadequacy and insecurity feelings, he has attempted to take advantage of him in his search for personal security. With the increase in education of the world population, perhaps fewer people now believe and accept that there is a basic superiority of one human being over another, or that one person is born to be the slave of another. However, the exploitation of one another due to emotional immaturity is very much in evidence today, and seems to be on the increase. Living in a world environment in which there are immature people means living under constant stress. The immature people are forever imposing upon each other, each pressuring the other. They are attempting to take advantage of each other, and they find themselves continually having to repel each other.

We see the results of the constant tension between people in everyday life. It is seen in people suffering from severe mental illnesses where their personal security has been overwhelmed by the pressure of others. It is present between husbands and wives, parents and children, and between all authority figures and their subordinates. On one side are people trying to preserve and, even, extend their civil liberties, fighting for less censorship and more freedom of talk and action. On the other

125

side are people wanting to impose their will upon everyone else, subjecting them to a freedom-less state.

Constant pressure exists between labor and management. Workers seem not to want to give an honest day's work in return for a fair wage and good working conditions. They want less work, and more money and other benefits. Management seems not to want to give adequate wages and working conditions in return for good work. It desires more work from labor, and more than suitable profits for itself. Of course, it is true in many instances that both the laborers and management are satisfied with each other, but it is the labor union leaders who, in their search for personal gain, create unrest and dissatisfaction between them.

Pressure between people would be kept to a minimum and there would be little or no exploitation if they were mature and secure. If a person is successful in the achievement of life's goals, lifework, and marriage, he will be apt to succeed in the raising of mature children. He will have realized his potential in achieving the successes, and will have gained a feeling of self-confidence and security. He would not be looking for security at the expense of pressuring or exploiting others. Mature people live up to their word and work to the best of their ability without being pressured to do so.

In our society the ambitious, hardworking, and successful middle class of people, those who pay an unfair share in taxes, are forced, or pressured, through Welfare and other programs, to care for the lazy and unsuccessful lower class. It is the politicians, looking for personal gain in the way of votes from the majority, the lower class, who pass the hand-out legislation. It would be for the good of the lower-class people themselves and for the country as a whole if the politicians pressured them to "stand on their own two feet", to be like those who attained middle-class status. By not being given that which most of them do not really need, the people would be forced to utilize their own potentials. They would gain success, self-worth, personal security, and independence. They would advance in maturity and grow stronger.

People should undertake the responsibility of caring for their own needs, such as the acquisition of food, clothing, shelter, recreation, and the education and raising of their children. If they would, they and their children would not grow to be dependent people. Dependent people eventually become hostile, resentful, and rebellious toward those who have made them dependent. Although a person might feel that he gains security from receiving hand-outs, it is in reality a false security based upon the whim of the giver; and, also, he grows more insecure as he becomes more dependent. Worse still, people lose whatever initiative they may ever have had if they are cared for, and they become complacent and weak. We must remember that weak people are subject to exploitation.

Socialism, Communism, or any other type of government where there is too much state, agency, or dictatorial control is alien to the nature of man, and an impingement upon his rights to realize his potential to the fullest. It hinders his right to exercise his abilities and prove himself through his achievements, from which he gains self-worth and security. Without this, he loses a natural tendency of self-expression, which, when thwarted, causes a build-up of tension and frustration. He is prone to rebellious behavior. Any government which usurps man's right to mature is not good for the man, the country, or the whole world. It curtails the progress of man, the family unit, society, and civilization. The individual is not raised in an ideal family and cultural environment which would enable him to achieve emotional development to his capacity. Such a person lacks feeling, empathy and understanding for his fellow man.

A system of government is best—and it is the only one, if war is ever to be permanently prevented—which provides people with the opportunities to exercise their potentials in the attainment of personal security. More correctly, people do not and should not have to be given opportunities by the government per se, but they should have the freedom to seek, provide for themselves, and take advantage of opportunities. People need opportunities to prove to others and to themselves that they are adequate and valuable. They who are happiest in retirement and old age are those who are self-satisfied in having lived a useful and productive life. They had varied interests and experienced many achievements. They were well-adjusted during their younger years. In addition to career opportunities, active participation in worthwhile clubs and organizations serves in one's gaining a feeling of self-value and security. The more there are of different groups, peoples, and countries, the more there are opportunities for everyone to work for the realization of their potentials. This speaks against monopolies, consolidation of interests, and the idea of one-world dominion.

A system of free enterprise is the best one in which an individual can capitalize from incentive and hard work. He can advance to the limit of his capacity. His achievements, based on his own merit, will give him a feeling of adequacy and self-worth, and personal security. This cannot be taken away from him, as it could be if a person were receiving a sense of security from being dependent upon someone else.

One utilizing his potential successfully has no need or desire to seek success and security from the exploitation of others. When a person lives in a free society, he has the choice to discover his own abilities and to use them to his best interest. He has the freedom of deciding what his needs are, and of using his abilities in providing for his needs. This is in refutation to Marx's "from each according to his abilities, to each according to his needs"—where the State decides a person's abilities and needs, and does the taking and providing. With exceptions, taking from another is immature behavior in contrast to providing for oneself.

We have discussed how emotionally-immature peoples and their leaders are responsible for wars, and how not enough people now exist who have the relative emotional maturity, wisdom, and strength to prevent the immature, aggressive peoples from starting a war. It was shown how all the people of the world, including leaders, are emotionally immature and insecure, and how more and more immature, insecure people are being raised. To prevent wars, the trend of raising immature people will have to be reversed. In his path to permanent peace, each individual will have to work at making himself more mature, and in pressuring those around him to behave more maturely in their dealings with him and everyone else. The Mature Person-to-Person Philosophy will have to be exercised by everyone all of the time. Present cultural trends will have to be changed, and people will need freedom and opportunities so that they may utilize their potentials to the limit in the search for personal security.

Everyone, all of the time, should strive for the attainment of emotional maturity and peace. During adolescence, as soon as a person can comprehend the means of attaining the peace, he should study a formal course in peace and have reinforced the basic method of achieving mature behavior. It should be understood that aggression is a natural trait of all animals, including man, necessary for attaining personal security and self-preservation. Man's basic intelligence and capability for emotional development are such that he can control his basic aggressive tendencies. The more mature and secure a person, the less need he will have for aggressive behavior. People who are immature and insecure—those raised by immature and insecure parents—will use their aggression in the exploitation of others in the search for personal security and self-preservation. The people who have been raised to be more mature and secure, and who have achieved still more maturity and security on their own merit, will have less tendency to be aggressive and to exploit others in the search for security. The children of these relatively-mature people will also be more mature, self-satisfied, and less partial to aggressive behavior. Mature leaders will emerge from the ranks of the mature population. They will be able to resolve differences and disputes in a peaceful way, and wars will be avoided.

A war may prevent enslavement by an aggressor, but it is only a temporary victory if nothing is done to prevent the same aggressor or other aggressors from starting other wars. Aggression and violence must be controlled in the aggressors of the present, and controlled and prevented in those people who are not yet born. This is not to imply that people should not maintain the desire and ability to defend themselves. Also, it does not mean that people will lose the initiative, motivation, and creativeness which are necessary to advance and succeed. It means that people will progress according to their own potentials, and that they will not exploit others. They will not be neurotically motivated, but motivated and equipped intellectually, emotionally, and physically to attain success, personal security, and happiness. Then they will be in a position to desire the same degree of success for all other people.

Aggressive tendencies may be controlled in two ways: from within by the individual himself, and from outside sources. The children of relatively-mature parents will be raised without the frustration and hostility associated with deprivation and dependence, but with the feelings of security, understanding, and love for their fellow man. They will be raised to be virtuous, responsible, independent, and self-disciplined people. They, like their parents, and even more so, will be emotionally and intellectually capable of exercising their potentials to the limit, and achieving success, security, and happiness. They will not be neurotically motivated, and they will not have the need or desire to exploit and fight others in the search for these goals, as is the case with immature people. This is in keeping with the Mature Person-to-Person Philosophy.

Outside sources curtailing a person's aggressive tendencies will also involve the utilization of the Mature Person-to-Person Philosophy, which includes the setting of limits with children, and the enforcement of all rules and laws of those in authority. The application of the Mature Person-to-Person Philosophy will pressure an aggressor to channel his energies toward honest opportunities so that he will have to promote his capability as a person. Of course, freedom and opportunities will have to be available, otherwise the aggressor will try to turn to someone else to exploit. The Mature Person-to-Person Philosophy being exercised by everyone, plus providing legitimate opportunities in the quest for security, will turn the aggressor in the direction of peace. This new concept of aggression and its control is an optimistic one.

On the path to permanent peace, each individual of each generation needs to work toward the achievement of emotional maturity for himself and for everyone else. It is only when people attain emotional maturity that there will be peace throughout the world. Starting now, the people of the present older generation will have to utilize the Mature Person-to-Person Philosophy in their every relationship. They will have to strive for personal maturity, and deal with their peers and the younger generations in a mature manner; so that both the peers and the younger generations will have to deal with them, the older generation, in a mature way, too. The peers and the younger generations will not only learn through example, but will be pressured to reciprocate with similar mature behavior.

Starting now, the present younger generation has to use the Mature Person-to-Person Philosophy in its every relationship. Beginning in adolescence, when starting high school, the teenagers will have to make a forceful movement toward maturity in studying the formal course in peace. They will strive for personal maturity, and will pressure their peers and the other generations to react to them and to each other with similar mature behavior. There will exist a mutual learning experience by means of example and pressure exerted upon each other. The young people will seek mature goals in life, and exercise mature behavior in respect to their lifework and marriage. They, as relatively-mature parents, will raise more mature children. The more mature and secure the parents, the more mature and secure will be the children.

The children—that is, the next generation—from having had a mature relationship with their parents, will more naturally adapt to the utilization of the Mature Person-to-Person Philosophy. They will be more amenable to the Philosophy when it is exercised by others, and be better prepared in the execution of it themselves. They will use it automatically in every one of their relationships, starting from the time that they are very young. It should be easier for them, and progressively easier for the succeeding generations, to practice the Mature Person-to-Person Philosophy; because it will be part of their lives, incorporated within their new healthier culture, and there will be fewer emotionally-immature people in the world opposing them. They will act maturely in respect to their peers and their elders, and these others will be pressured to reciprocate with the same mature type of behavior. They, as their parents did before them, will take a formal course in peace when in high school. They should be even more successful than their parents in regard to life's goals, lifework, marriage, and the raising of mature children and leaders. The successes will provide them with self-confidence, personal security, and happiness. They should be even more mature and secure than their parents, even though the parents themselves have grown more mature and

131

secure in having been successful in the raising of mature children. (*See Illustration 2.*)

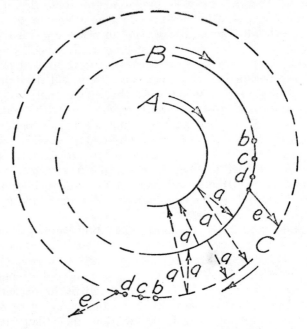

Illustration 2: Man's Life Cycle, and the Path to Emotional Maturity and Permanent Peace

A. Present older generation (about age 40 to old age). B. Present younger generation (birth to about age 40). C. Next generation. a. Influence of Mature Person-to-Person Philosophy by one generation upon another. b. In the beginning of high school the study of a formal course in Peace, and a movement toward maturity. c. Mature goals and successful career providing personal security. d. Successful choice of mate and marriage. e. Raising of mature children who will practice the Mature Person-to-Person Philosophy, and from whose ranks mature leaders will emerge.

It is the desire to raise more mature children. From their mature relationships with their parents, always knowing certain

132

boundaries while in the process of attaining independence, the children will grow up knowing what is expected of them. As the parents gradually give up their controls over the children, realizing that the children are accepting their responsibilities, the children will begin to exert their own controls over themselves, and become self-disciplined. The children will have no desire or need to rebel against their mature relationships with their parents, because they will have been treated fairly by them. They have respected their parents and identified themselves with them because the parents have been knowledgeable and strong, and the children have achieved a sense of personal security from them. The parents gave them love and guidance, and the opportunity for them to become independent. The children have been raised with a sense of responsibility and a sound value system.

Mature children, raised by mature parents, will be able to use their potentials to the limit. They will realize their emotional fulfillment as human beings, leaning toward love, understanding, the virtues, and the helping of their fellow men. They will be more objective and flexible concerning the opinions of others. These children will have been raised with less sibling rivalry, neurotic competitiveness, jealousy, prejudice, and bigotry. They will be less resentful and hostile, and have little desire or need to resort to aggression and the exploitation of others. They will have succeeded on their own merit, gaining personal security and happiness from the utilization of their own potentials.

It was mentioned earlier that, in order to raise more mature people, people who can realize emotional fulfillment, freedom and opportunities have to be provided. We have such an environment in a democracy, as in the United States, where a man can work for self-esteem. He can work for security and happiness for himself and his family. He can promote the family unit, the mainstay for the progress of civilization, which alone can cultivate an individual's emotional potential. It is in such an atmosphere that there is prime hope in advancing the Mature Person-to-Person Philosophy. In this country, and in all free countries, where there is the possibility to change bad cultural trends, there is the best chance to develop a nation of all mature people. At the same time that the free peoples of the world are working toward this end, all the other peoples should be gradually pressured and educated to the acceptance and practice of mature behavior.

Already discussed was that charity and dependency are not what people really need and should desire. If they were mature, and if they really understood all the implications of losing one's freedom and opportunities, they would want no part of government hand-outs. Actually, many of the recipients of these gifts become more irritated when they are reminded of what they do not have by what they receive. What they want, or should want, is an equal opportunity to exercise their initiative and capabilities, and to gain success and security. If they are lacking in initiative and motivation to want to work and succeed, to take advantage of opportunities that are provided for them, then they need extra help in this area. Also, they may require extra help in learning how to recognize and go about taking advantage of opportunities. Realistically, it may be that the people themselves will be unable to adapt and benefit from an opportunity-laden environment. If such is the case, they should be aided in the intelligent upbringing of their progeny. The offspring should be raised with the essential quality of desire to want to succeed. They should have the motivation and capability, and the will to work hard in order to be able to achieve success when the opportunities are available.

Aside from those people struggling for existence, it seems that too many people are preoccupied with personal pleasure, and they give little thought to the meaning of life and why they are on this earth. Barring religious factors, the more serious thinkers might agree that the main purpose of their lives is centered about working for personal accomplishments. The raising of children comes as a natural consequence, and that the children are his contribution to posterity will add to a person's feeling of accomplishment. Whatever successes one's children achieve will also add to one's feeling of accomplishment and self-worth. Accomplishments or successful endeavors serve to provide a person with self-confidence, and a feeling of self-value and personal security. Security is the ultimate goal and reason why man strives for achievement. It is conjoined with

134

emotional maturity. The search for security is an innate characteristic of the human being. It has really been the basic motivating force for the progress of mankind. Security is necessary in parents before they can transmit it to their children, and before the children can become mature. To be oriented primarily in the search for pleasure, and not in the direction of striving for security, implies that the person has not attained even the lowest level of maturity. Such a person is seeking immediate gratification, pleasure here and now. He cannot postpone gratification, and set goals for the future. He is insecure, yet is not concerned about working to become personally secure. He desires pleasure today.

With the American cultural trend heading in the direction of materialism and hedonism, very few people spend any appreciable amount of time in any type of meditation. Most of the people in our affluent society are living in what we will call a state of "hecticity". They are as on a treadmill, living a life of restlessness and excitement, never stopping or spending any amount of time by themselves. They do not review their past, or their goals in life, or if they are headed in the right direction. They do not capitalize from their own and other's mistakes, or modify or make new plans for the future according to the changing times. Many people have spent their entire lives in seeking comfort and entertainment for themselves, living as others around them have lived, even during their dying days not attributing any real or significant meaning to their having lived. There are too many selfish people in the world, concerned primarily with their own pleasure, not having any real consideration for others except for what benefit they might derive from them. It should be remembered, though, that seeking a moderate amount of material possessions and pleasure is normal behavior, as they are related to fulfilling one's potential, acquiring personal security, and deriving some joy out of life.

Ordinarily, a person should set his life's goals with the thought in mind that he will live to about age eighty, so that he will always be planning and working for something. He should not, as many do, work to a peak capacity until about age fifty, then live on his laurels and coast into retirement. It is true that much of the preparation and hard work for a successful career

135

might be performed by middle age, and that a natural follow-through and expansion take place in later years in which there are greater profits with less effort.

Living successfully and having good mental and emotional health means being able to adapt to the many varied situations of life. It means having sound goals, standards, and values, so that one's way of living is not uprooted, yet being flexible enough to adjust, to compromise, to "give and take". There are ideal times of one's life to do certain things. During those periods one is best equipped emotionally, physically, and intellectually to achieve certain goals and to obtain the maximum enjoyment from the achievements. For example, particular toys are enjoyed most by children of a particular age. Someone who wanted to own but who could not afford a convertible automobile in his twenties would not gain the same pleasure from owning one when fifty years of age. Attending school, marriage, or the raising of children are performed best by relatively young people. However, if, for any reason, a person could not pursue and experience certain goals at the ideal times of his life, he should without hesitation work for their realization at any time that he is able. It should be remembered that accomplishments give most people a purpose for living.

It should not be misinterpreted that it is wrong for children to have a higher standard of living than their parents. It is unhealthy only for the children to be given too much in the way of material gifts and pleasure without realizing the effort involved in obtaining these things. If they are handed everything for nothing, their sense of values will be distorted, they will feel that society owes them a living, and they will not have the desire and capability to achieve goals on their own merit. If they are raised in an atmosphere of affluence, but they are made to appreciate that they must fulfill their potentials as students and as family helpmates, it will ultimately be to their advantage and to everyone's advantage.

A child living in an environment of abundance need not waste valuable study time in helping support himself and his family. He can capitalize on being exposed to travel, and other cultural and educational opportunities. He will gain in knowledge, self-confidence, and in the art of dealing with people. He will make contact with successful people; he will "think big", and have higher expectations of himself. In the same light, children should not "look down on" their parents if, in comparison, they have grown bigger and healthier, and have gained better educations and more money. The improvement of generations is a natural sequence of events seen in the growth of a civilization.

There is a trend today in this country, with federal funds supporting it, for the establishment of day-care nurseries. So that mothers can work, centers are being founded where they can leave their young children for part of or even the entire day. As a result, many children are being deprived of a certain warmth from their mothers which is necessary for the attainment of full emotional development and emotional maturity. The deprived children will grow up to be selfish and excessively competitive, striving always for more for themselves, even at the expense of others. Of course, it is true that many of these mothers probably do not have much "to give" their children in the way of a mature relationship, anyway. In fact, in extreme cases some anxious mothers with pathological relationships with their children are doing their children a favor if they are able to be away from them for a few hours each day.

This is not to imply that all mothers should not engage in part-time work and other activities out of the home. Women who are fulfilling their potentials by adequately carrying the load of household and family duties in addition to part-time employment should be encouraged and commended. They will be more confident and secure wives and mothers in doing this, and their children will be raised as more secure children.

The unfortunate part of the day nurseries is that too many of the mothers who are out of the home are exactly the ones who should be there with their children. They should gain the help that they need in resolving their own problems so that they can cope with their husbands and children more effectively. They should be pressured to be as adequate wives and mothers as possible.

There could be many reasons why the mothers might welcome employment and want to get out of the house, away from their husbands and children. Some of the reasons may be real, some rationalized. The more pertinent might be: having a materialistic value system and living beyond one's means, desiring to shirk one's obligations in the proper raising of children, living incompatibly with one's husband, and selfishly wanting to fulfill one's own ambitions in the search for success, personal worth, and security, but without consideration for the needs of one's husband and children. Much of the fault may lie with a husband's fostering a competitiveness with his wife, she feeling that she has to work in order to keep up with him. His job and lack of money may have placed her in a position so that she had to work to supplement his income. He may be belittling, neglecting, and frustrating her so that she seeks gratification and security out of the home. On the other hand, it might be the wife who is unconsciously trying to belittle her husband by unnecessarily supplementing his income. She may be seeking favor from her children by acting as a martyr, and by giving them gifts which they do not really need.

Mothers should remember that a person gaining maturity must seek it in all areas. They should strive for the fulfillment of their emotional needs, as well as those in the physical, intellectual, spiritual, and social areas. They should seek a balance between the fulfillment of their husband's and their children's needs, and their own needs. They should not lose sight that men and women are different, each having their own individual and separate roles and functions as human beings. Their roles, goals, and manner of fulfillment of potentials should differ from each other. All people should recognize that the happy family unit is the best place for everyone, mother, father, or child, to fulfill his emotional potential.

In the search for a permanent world peace, concentration has to be centered upon the youth of the world. The youth will one day be parents and leaders, and the destiny of mankind will rest in their hands. Young people are flexible and subject to change; they can most readily interrupt the abnormal cycle of immature people breeding immature people. By the same token, young people are more unstable; they require example and direction to aid them in the setting of their goals. Statistics reveal that the population of young people in comparison to the older ones is steadily increasing. Also increasing is the incidence of crimes of all types, which is rising every year out of proportion to the population increase; and most of the crimes are now committed by those who are fifteen and sixteen years of age. To many, "The only sin is to get caught." This is the age group that requires immediate help, but it should be recognized that the prevention of such problems should begin in early childhood.

It is quite evident to those engaged in the study and treatment of youngsters that the parents are primarily responsible for their children's misbehavior and other difficulties. They, the parents, should be made to recognize this and to do something about correcting the situation. It should be the function of psychiatrists and those who are in authority position in schools, churches, courts, businesses, and the governments to pressure the children and the parents to bear their own responsibilities. If the children or adults misbehave or fall below par in any way, such that they become behavior or learning problems, alcoholics, addicts, psychiatric problems, or criminals, they should be given help by the professionals. However, the help that is given these people, and this cannot be overemphasized, should be in the form of pressure upon them to "stand on their own two feet," so that they will grow stronger and assume responsibility for their own actions. Promoting individual independence and maturity will help in the development of a healthy cultural trend. The greatest opposition to all of this is that those in authority positions, including parents and immature professionals, tend to make dependent people even more dependent; and they usurp the immature, dependent people's right to be responsible people.

Normally, the emotional maturity or emotional age of a child should be commensurate with his chronological age. Both should advance simultaneously. The parents, if mature, will relinquish their domination over the behavior and growth of their child in a gradual manner as they see that the child is assuming responsibility. If they are immature, they will want their child to advance even more than other children. Because the immature parents can naturally perform better than their child, and because they are fearful that their child might fail, this

139

being a reflection of themselves, they will tend to overprotect the child and do too much for him. They will, due to insecurity feelings, not being sure of their roles as parents, tend to not discipline as much as they should, and give too much in the way of privileges and material things. They do this so that they will be liked by the child and be thought of as being good and adequate parents.

The parents on the surface will appear to be strict disciplinarians, yet in analyzing the situation it will be discovered that they are extremely inconsistent, unfair, and poor disciplinarians. They may do a lot of yelling at their children. They sometimes ignore the children's confrontations, teasing episodes, and rebellious behavior, and at other times go overboard in punishing them to the point of hurting them. The disciplining is erratic, either at one extreme or the other. There is no discipline and "giving in" on one occasion, and too much of it on another. The parents are unsure and afraid of their own emotions and self-control, and they feel even more unsure as to how they should be dealing with their children. This causes confusion in the child's mind, his not knowing what is expected of him, and he feels the parents are unfair, ignorant, and weak people. To have weak and insecure parents makes the child feel insecure. The child will be afraid to act on his own, not knowing what the parents want of him. He will await further orders from them and he will be indecisive for fear that they will disapprove his decisions. He will not have learned to use his brain in the area of acquiring common sense.

The parents, seeing that their child is behaving immaturely, being indecisive, lacking in good judgment, and not acting his age in accepting responsibility, hold back and refuse his demands for more privileges. This will set the stage for the child to rebel and to be negativistic toward them and, later, toward all authority figures. The more the parents curtail the child's activities, the more he will strain to oppose them, much the same as a spirited horse fighting the tightening of his reins. The child in looking upon the parents as being emotionally weak and ignorant people will not identify with them. He will want to be different from them; he will want personal identity, individuality, independence and security—that which everyone seeks, but which he is not acquiring from his relationship with them. He will turn to goals and behavior which differ from his parent's way of life. He will be angry at his parents because they do not allow him to do what others his age are doing, which experiences would help him to mature. When he reaches adulthood, he will be resentful of the parents in finding himself not up to par with his peers. Because of his lack of maturity he will not be functioning as other relatively-mature adults. His achievements will not meet with his expectations. His parents have been basically responsible for his maturity lag.

Children should be given orders beginning when they can first understand "yes" from "no". Explanations should accompany the orders so that the baby can learn the reasons for things. The order-giving is gradually changed to giving guidance and advice as the child grows older and more intelligent. By the time the child enters into the adolescent period, he should be able to bear many responsibilities and make many of his own decisions. The parents by this time should be giving almost no orders, and there should be a gradual diminution of the guidance and advice-giving. Otherwise, if this practice should continue, the child will grow up to be a dependent, advice and decision-seeking adult. Starting before adolescence, the parents should be aiding their child in analyzing the different problems which are confronting him so that he learns to examine "both sides of the coin" in respect to any problem. They should gradually pressure him to try to solve his own problems. Eventually, the adolescent will learn to do this analysis himself, to make his own decisions, and to arrive at sound judgments by himself. In reaching adulthood he will have attained complete independence and emotional maturity. He will be able to utilize his potential to the limit. He will not be passive or aggressive. He will be satisfied with himself as an adult human being.

It was stated earlier that man needs a free government and opportunities in order to utilize his potential and attain emotional fulfillment and maturity. In addition, he needs freedom from neurotic blocks which impede his ability to function. A pathological parental relationship in his younger years may have an adverse effect upon a person, so that he will later be hampered in his emotional, intellectual, and social growth. He may develop such a severe conscience that he will impose unnecessarily harsh restrictions upon himself. Distorted cultural trends and false beliefs may contribute to his inability to function at his peak capacity. The lack of a warm family unit, existing in a pathological society, and living under a freedom-less government leads to a degeneration of the individual and the country. If people are raised so that they can grow in maturity, they will become creative and enhance themselves and the rest of the world. Those who are relatively immature, insecure, and unsuccessful have to be pressured to seek a realization of their potentials. The continuation of the advancement of civilization depends upon people being able to unfold themselves as individuals.

Before it can be said that a person possesses emotional maturity and wisdom, before it can be said that he has a full appreciation of life and its meaning, he should solemnly reflect on his position in the universe. He should give serious thought as to the purpose of the universe, of life, and why all of it is in existence. He should attempt to answer the questions: "What am I?" and "Why am I here?" A person should try to see himself in the broadest panorama of time and space imaginable. He should try to orient himself in respect to the beginning of time billions of years ago, to the onset and progress of civilization, to the present date, and to the unlimited future. He should try to place himself as one of three billion people, one living within a family group, as a minute part of a town, state, country, world, and innumerable galaxies.

In the past several years there have been many and varied projects instituted, some at great cost, for the purpose of attaining world peace. The Peace Corps, the hospital ship *Hope,* and the exchange of students and cultural programs between nations, are only a few of these. They are all good and serve the primary purpose of people helping one another. The people gain an understanding of each other and of the problems which confront them. The people on the receiving end learn that their benefactors are compassionate and trustworthy. They learn how to help themselves. Of course, there are always the dangers of being given too much, and of hostile-dependent relationships developing. Of extreme importance is that relatively-mature people be chosen to serve the people in need. Programs not carefully planned can cause more harm than good.

Every program of this type should be designed specifically for the particular people to whom it is to give aid. The purpose of the project, the personalities and the needs of the people giving and receiving, and the end result must be kept constantly in mind. All too frequently, organizations such as these snowball to the extent that an end-point is never reached and efforts are expended which are never appreciated. The ultimate goal of desiring to help others only to get started on the road to a more civilized world is not realized.

In participating in such ventures, the people are utilizing their potentials and are gaining a feeling of self-worth and personal security. It is only secure people who can offer help to others which is not neurotically motivated. Any personal gain beyond working for self-worth that a participant might receive is not considered mature behavior. For example, the givers should not feel superior to the others or seek any indebtedness from them. In most instances, an individual who enters such an endeavor is prepared to sacrifice for the sake of helping his fellow man, and any search for personal gain is minimal.

As stated, all of these programs are very useful, and it is consoling to see them in existence today during such world strife. However, they are not the entire answer to the avoidance of war. The needs of all the people cannot be satisfied by them. Resentment, exploitation, and immature behavior are ever present, even between the people who are giving as well as between those that are receiving. Favoritism, "politics", or corruption involve nearly everyone. It is only through the Mature Person-to-Person Philosophy, by people learning to deal maturely with each other, that there will eventually be peace in the world. Men of good will—that is, mature men of good will, of good intent—can have peace on this earth.

*　*　*　*

Discussed in this chapter was the fact that constant pressures and struggles between people have always existed. This condition will improve only when all the people grow more emotionally mature. The necessity for freedom, opportunity, responsibility, and the realization of one's potential were examined. Aggression and the Mature Person-to-Person Philosophy were discussed. Man's Life Cycle was illustrated.

It was explained how parents must favorably influence their children if the children are to grow into independent, mature, and secure adults. The detrimental aspects of government hand-outs and hedonism, and the benefits of seeking personal achievements and security, were mentioned. It was stated that there are different projects in action today in which world peace is being sought, but it will become a reality only when people learn to deal maturely with each other.

CHAPTER VII

BEGINNING IN ADOLESCENCE

A MOVEMENT TOWARD MATURITY

To prevent wars, the world needs mature individuals. It needs people with the emotional maturity, wisdom, and physical support that are necessary to control and thwart aggressive people bent upon exploitation and domination. Mature people will have no desire to compare themselves with others and to take advantage of others. They will work to their fullest capacity, utilizing their potential to the limit, in their search for success and personal security. They will try to make the world a better place for everyone in which to live. They will strive for emotional maturity in themselves and in others by working at dealing maturely with the others and forcing them to behave in the same manner. Mature individuals will exercise the Mature Person-to-Person Philosophy every minute of every day. They will pressure people to act maturely, no matter whether the immaturity is a result of their immediate family environment and upbringing, or cultural factors—even if handed down from previous generations. They will work at maturing themselves by learning to control their impulses, and learning to reason, so that they can more effectively deal with people and situations. The relatively-mature people will grow more mature, and the numbers of mature people in the general population will be increased. The most mature and wise people will be recognized and elevated into leadership positions by the mature population. It will not be, as it is now, that so many immature men will gain leadership positions because of their neurotic motivations, and because immature people support them. The mature leaders will lead the way to a permanent peace.

It is up to the adolescent to interrupt the vicious cycle in our

145

society of immature parents raising immature children. Every teenager is old enough and intelligent enough to begin changing the world. Beginning with the formal study of the quest for peace, during adolescence, a person should start to focus on the dignity and rights of the individual. He should demand fairness and equal justice for all the people of the world. It should be remembered that human beings are not basically superior or inferior to each other. The use of the Mature Person-to-Person Philosophy means giving the same love, respect, and justice to every person. It is loving each person, wanting to be fair with him, and pressuring him to grow more mature, secure, and happy. It is wanting him to not take advantage of you because you want to be dealt with fairly, too.

As free-thinking people, those who attain the so-called age of reason should begin to promote the welfare of the family unit. The emotionally healthy family serves as a culture medium for children and their parents in the achievement of their potentials. Likewise, those people who fulfill themselves as individuals advance the development of the family unit and, in addition, all social relationships, the entire society and civilization as a whole. With healthy families, mental illness and pathological cultural trends will be diminished. There will be fewer divorces, less juvenile delinquency, and a subsidence of crimes of all types. Through the utilization of the Mature Person-to-Person Philosophy, people and nations will be able to resolve differences of opinion and strive for a world serving the common good. There will be progressively more unity of purpose and agreement among peoples and, theoretically, the evolvement of a universal culture acceptable to most people.

As stated, it is those people who have been raised and live in a free society who develop most as individuals and who have the most opportunity to mature. They can do the most to improve themselves and the ills of their culture. In a country such as the United States, where everyone has many different avenues for self-fulfillment, it is easier for people to both exercise and respond to the Mature Person-to-Person Philosophy. Each individual can work at cultivating his own being to its utmost capacity, thus concentrating on growing more mature and personally secure all of the time. The person who is limited to mature action by mature people, not allowed to exploit others, will not find himself in a frustrating position, unable to move in any other direction. He will be forced to react, and in turn learn from habit to act, with a mature type of behavior in his every relationship. He will have been provided with ample opportunities to seek successes and security through accomplishments at work, in social life with various clubs and organizations, and with his family and home. If a person does not take advantage of these socially-acceptable opportunities, he will have to be pressured into it by all people who associate with him. He will be pushed to maturity and gain security from taking advantage of the opportunities. He will be taking advantage of the opportunities, and not of immature people. Most difficult, but of most importance, will be getting the people with rigid psychological defenses and little or no insight to exercise the Mature Person-to-Person Philosophy. For reasons of personal security, they will have much difficulty in admitting to themselves that they are immature and insecure, and they will balk at agreeing to the need for the Philosophy. Of course, one has to admit to being immature and insecure before he will work to mature himself. In a free country, there is a perfect situation for the development of a mature people and mature society which can then be extended to other peoples of the world. This is not to say that those living under more adverse conditions, perhaps with added cultural problems, cannot and should not similarly strive for maturity.

So long as man can achieve self-worth and personal security, as he can in a democracy, he will not seek other forms of government. In a democracy, the poor people are better educated and more satisfied. They would be less apt to follow in the footsteps of a dissatisfied, rebellious leader. Only the misfits would tend to look elsewhere for fulfillment of their needs and desires.

The young people will find that they will gain a feeling of self-confidence and adequacy from the successful use of the Mature Person-to-Person Philosophy. From their mature dealings and better relationships with people, they will gain successes and personal security. The self-confidence will be put to good use in encouraging a person to reach for higher goals, to work harder, and to make a better choice of career for life fulfillment.

He will strive for achievement at his utmost potential level. It will help one in his choice of mate and in the raising of mature children. In the practice of the Mature Person-to-Person Philosophy, love and sincere interest will be extended by parents to their children, as will be guidance and limits to misbehavior. The giving of love to their children will not imply that the parents are weak people, but that they themselves have been raised with deep feelings and a sense of security and strength. Being able to discipline their children also means that the parents are secure and strong, that they are knowledgeable and sure enough that they are doing the right thing. The children will grow up identified with their parents, with a good sense of values, and with deep feelings for their parents, siblings, and their fellow men. Their emotional potential as human beings will have been fulfilled, and from their strong, secure parents they will have gained personal security. They will have an understanding and a regard for other people. They will honor authority and the law, and they will strive to have more mature leadership. The successful use of the Mature Person-to-Person Philosophy will give self-satisfaction during one's old age for having lived a life of accomplishment, reward, and real meaning. Most important, from one's success in living, which will give one more self-confidence and personal security, a person will be better able to utilize the Mature Person-to-Person Philosophy, thus perpetuating and expanding the means by which there will always be a progressively more mature mankind.

People in high school, or the equivalent, invariably begin to focus upon their image and the impression they convey to others. Too often, principally due to the ideas of their parents and other adults, they concentrate upon their superficial qualities. They work at building their bodies and wearing attractive kinds of clothes in order to present a nice appearance. Their material possessions and status are of extreme importance to them. They may refer to a friend as: "He's that 1963 red convertible." More sophisticated young people may direct their energies at how they express themselves, their intelligence and education, and their emotional stability and reaction to people and events. They strive for an appreciation of music, ballet, literature, art, and sculpture. They scrutinize their actions, both physical and mental-emotional, and attempt to improve upon them. All that has been mentioned is worthwhile. However, what actually is of most value and deserves most attention is for a person to strive for wisdom and virtue, which encompass a fine intellect and emotional maturity. In the order of ascendancy, a person should work to cultivate his memory, his understanding, his correlation, his wisdom, and his virtues. He will then have attained a position of real creativeness. He has achieved his full potential, and now is seeking uniqueness.

It should be understood that you should not take advantage of others, and not allow others to take advantage of you. You should not permit an aggressor to exploit you from the start. An appeased aggressor, being immature and insecure, lacking basically in self-confidence but driven by neurotic motivation, will gain a sense of self-confidence from his victory over you which will spur him on to further domination. Winning gives him a sense of security which fans the flames of his neurotic desires. The security is a false security, however, because his victory has not made him a better man. He has not actually improved himself and advanced any as a mature person. His immature behavior has speeded his movement in the direction of becoming an even worse person. It is from comparing himself with you, the dominated one, that he feels he has gained in stature.

People who are immature and insecure tend to take advantage of you if you let them. They will compare themselves with you and will "look down on" you if they feel that they are superior to you in any way. They will belittle you, if they can, and they will feel secure from their being dominant over you. They may be so sensitive and suspicious that others are trying to take advantage of them that they feel they can trust no one. Feeling this way, they exploit first and all the more, believing it is better to exploit before being exploited. Dependent people may seek to take advantage of you by "pushing" themselves at you, for example, wanting you to do things for them. By the same token, if you are relatively immature, you may take advantage of an immature person by fostering his dependency upon you, by doing for him what he should be doing himself. The immature people who hold positions much higher than your own will be less apt to take advantage of you, except when dealing with you in particular areas in which they are competitive with you. They are usually concentrating upon exploiting people closer to their own level of functioning. Also, people in much lower positions than your own will be less likely to try to take advantage of you, simply because they feel they cannot get away with it. They may make an attempt if you give them the opportunity, and they have rationalized that they are on an equal level with you in at least that one area. Those who are most apt to take advantage of you are the immature people on a close par with you, who feel jealous of you, and who desire the self-satisfaction of believing they are better than you. Mature people of any age and at any level do not have any need or desire to exploit you. They already feel sufficiently secure.

People, including children, women, the infirm, and the elderly, should all be expected and pressured to handle their own problems insofar as it is possible. Others, even parents in the case of children, should not interfere unless they are called upon. Of course, help should be provided if it is seen that it is needed but cannot be requested. The object is to have every person assume his own responsibilities as much as possible, to have him learn how to cope with the adversities of life. When confronted by an anxious situation, one should stop to think objectively, even if only for a few minutes, about the problem and the other person's and one's own personalities before resorting to talk and action.

If an attacked person cannot avoid or prevent exploitation by others, he should take the responsibility, when able, to enlist the aid of a mature higher authority. In the case of dealing with a bully, a person should by himself attempt to avoid or thwart the attacks, resorting to any mature means short of physical violence. Physical violence is justifiable only in self-defense, when one is physically attacked—and only if a mature higher authority is not readily available to intervene. If one can stall for time while being attacked, fighting defensively while awaiting aid, he is obligated to avoid an all-out fight. If there is no possibility of any available help arriving in time before the attacked person would be seriously hurt physically, then the attacked, in self-defense, should strike back immediately with all his might. The aggressor will be surprised, and he even might be unprepared for this action—because he would not have been bullying in the first place if he did not think his opponent was weak, and that he could get away with it. To attempt to enlist the aid of an immature parent of the bully, or any other biased person, usually leads to futility. A bully's parents will be defensive about their child's behavior, will feel guilty in having been responsible for it, and will have little control over it. They may ignore requests for help, and seem not to care to curtail their child. In the case of the exploiter taking or destroying one's property, one is obligated to appeal for help from a mature higher authority, and not to resort to violence. In the last analysis, an aggressor in being squelched is being done a favor, although he may not appreciate it, for he is taught what is wrong behavior and is made to conform to mature and right action.

There are many obvious and also subtle ways in which immature people take advantage of one another. They may resort to insulting remarks, sarcasm, slander, and other forms of belittlement. They may have temper tantrums to gain their own way, and monopolize another person's property and time. There are some who are nosey, interfering always in other people's business. The selfish, forceful, and aggressive people will try to push themselves ahead of you. They may do favors and make someone feel obligated to them, and may keep someone in a dependent relationship. Some people make others feel that they, the others, would not be able to function and survive without their support. Other people rebel in not conforming to the standards of family and society in the manner of their speech, dress, and actions. There are those who procrastinate, refuse to work, or perform inadequate services. There are many other ways in which an immature person actively or passively imposes his will upon someone else. Everyone has seen examples of people "putting something over" or "walking all over" someone.

It is a known fact that certain people behave differently with different people. We have all seen people who put their so-called best foot forward and exhibit their best behavior only in certain relationships. There is observed a dominant-subordinate relationship between any two people, where one takes the lead. This is brought out more clearly when two friends are in the presence of others. In the presence of the dominant friend, the subordinate one will be reticent; when with others, without the dominant one, he may be apt to take over the leadership of the group. He will muster his energies and assume a more independent role. It is possible that the subordinate one is belittled and exploited by his friend. Of course, due to reverence for him by his subordinate, or because of excessive passivity on the part of the subordinate one, or perhaps for a number of other reasons, the dominant one may have been forced to accept the dominant position. Mature people behave maturely with all people. Admittedly, it is more difficult to act in a mature manner with some people, and under certain circumstances.

Educators usually pride themselves in being free and independent thinkers, searching always for the truth, and promoting unrestricted research. However, because the teachers themselves are unfamiliar with the dealings in the "cold, cruel world", because they feel it is beneath their dignity to discuss certain unpleasant subjects, because they are fearful, or for any other number of reasons, the students are not taught enough of the truth of everyday life. What students learn in school regarding business, politics, the practice of the professions, and other careers is idealistic. What they observe and experience after graduation is an eye-opener.

With exceptions, in our present-day civilized world people use "politics", legal loopholes, and other so-called shrewd business maneuvers in the exploitation of others. Years ago, they would beat or kill someone to achieve a similar end. It all amounts to exploitation, but of a different means, by immature people. It amounts to frustration and despair for the beaten person. To gain votes, politicians pass hand-out legislation, even though it deprives the people of initiative and freedom, and it weakens the country as a whole. Inequitable tax laws are promoted by the influential wealthy so that the burden of governmental expense falls upon the poorer people. The bureaucratic government is composed of incompetent workers whose positions are as sure as the amount of influence of their political friends. Bureaucracy, being as a monster, becomes uncontrolled, its mem-

152

bers too dependent and indebted to each other to carry on in any type of efficient manner. For the most part, success in our society is due to immature people with neurotic competitiveness, over-compensation, and aggressiveness dominating other immature people who permit it. Too few of our present-day successful people have achieved their goals on merit, and with concern for the common good foremost in their mind. In the same sense that mature people fulfill their potential and achieve success, it cannot be said that immature people are successful if they have acquired certain ends by neurotic means.

It is not the purpose here to dwell upon the injustices seen in the "cold, cruel world" on an adult level. Rather, it is the purpose to appeal to the student to become watchful and indignant at the wrongdoings experienced by him personally, and which are perpetrated by his parents, his teachers, other adults, his peers, and by himself. He should concentrate on his own relationships from day to day, and not on racial discrimination, or the war in Viet Nam. It is true that the latter are of utmost importance, but he should through personal experience first learn to deal maturely with his fellow man. Thus, he will form the habit of recognizing and dealing with right and wrong during his younger years, which he will carry over as a vital part of himself to later life. The manner in which each student conducts his personal life and deals with others will ultimately have a decided effect upon the culture and society. It is when he grows older that he and others like him, who have matured in the same manner, will have a profound and beneficial influence upon the world situation.

In their dealings with their parents and other adults, children are frequently criticized for their disrespect of them. However, oftentimes the adults, including mothers and fathers, do not merit the respect and honor they ask for or demand. Ignorant, immature, and insecure parents are ineffectual in their relationships with their children. They either do not know how to deal with them, or they are unsure of themselves and do not exercise discipline because they are afraid they will be disliked by the children and thought by others to be bad parents. The children have to learn that, just because their parents seem not to warrant their respect, all adults are not necessarily the same as their

153

parents. All people—men, women, and children—should merit respect from each other based upon their behavior, the manner in which they live their lives, and what they do with their lives. If people act maturely commensurate with their age, they deserve, demand, and receive respect. A person should not be considered to be inferior due to sex, young age, lack of intellectual endowment, emotional and physical infirmities, status, poverty, nationality, race, or religious affiliation. Age in itself should not warrant respect, neither from other adults, nor from younger people, and even children. Dishonest, immoral, and undisciplined parents should not expect their children to hold them in high regard. Parents who have not extended themselves to seek professional help for their own problems, thereby raising immature, dependent children with emotional conflicts and unfulfilled potentials, should not expect to be respected and honored by their children.

Unfortunately, most people measure another person according to his status in life, that is, his position and his wealth. The more strength and power in terms of money and influence that a man possesses, the more he is held in high esteem. The fact that he may have achieved his so-called success by exploitation, and that immature people are intimidated by his status, make him more prone to taking advantage of them. A person should be evaluated not so much for his achievements as for how he conducted himself in reaching them. He should be held in high esteem only for his having worked honorably to realize the fulfillment of his true potential.

Children should learn to take the initiative in discussing subjects with their parents involving themselves and the parents. They should attempt to confide in their parents, showing and proving to them that they are responsible people and can be trusted, and that their behavior warrants more privileges. It is through such action that they will become independent and mature people, because the parents will let up on their controls over them. If children should see that their parents, and others in positions of authority, are lax in the enforcement of discipline for themselves and for those under their care, they should bring this to their attention. If they believe their parents, and other adults, are materialistically oriented, or overprotective and fostering of dependencies, they should point this out to them. Mature parents raise mature children, but children, too, can do a great deal in pressuring their parents to a more mature type of behavior. All people should keep in mind that sincere, constructive criticism teaches one right from wrong, and it should not be misinterpreted as belittlement, exploitation, and impingement upon one's independence. People giving such criticism are not and should not be seeking personal gain, but are genuinely giving one aid and are aiming for the common good.

Parents setting effective restrictions for their children are in part utilizing the Mature Person-to-Person Philosophy. They are not letting the children take advantage of them through their misbehavior. Also, they are not taking advantage of their children by allowing them to misbehave. By not setting limits and by allowing them to misbehave, they would not be assuming their responsibilities for the care of their yet unwise children, who would be subject to hurting themselves. In not inundating their children with material things, and not overprotecting them, the parents again are in conformity with the Mature Person-to-Person Philosophy. By not earning what they receive, children grow up being deprived of a true sense of value for things. The parents have taken advantage of them by substituting material gifts for time and a mature relationship with them—that which the children really needed, and which mature parents would have given to them. Due to their own inadequacy and insecurity feelings, and believing that their children are incapable and inadequate, the parents tend to do too much for them. By being overprotected by their parents, children are raised as immature, dependent, indecisive people who find it very difficult to achieve any degree of success and happiness in the adult world. The parents have taken advantage of them in their own search for self-worth and personal security.

The adolescent should pressure his parents to change, when necessary, to become better parents, and to learn how better to deal with all their children. If necessary, he should force them to assume their responsibilities. In the case of any of their children having speech, reading, or other problems, particularly emotionally-related problems, the parents should be influenced to accept the responsibility for the correction of the problems.

155

The schools, the government, or any other agency or person, should be discouraged from usurping the parent's responsibilities and rights. As explained, the politicians, for personal gain, are only too eager to offer these hand-outs to the insecure parents who are seeking dependency and an unshouldering of the responsibilities of marriage and parenthood. In many instances the child's problem evolved due to familial, especially parental, problems. The parents should be made to participate in its correction and not be allowed to relinquish their responsibility to others. True, it will be the others who will provide the help that is needed, but the parents should be the directive force in desiring and seeking the remedial aid. If the parents are not pressured to take this responsibility, they may undo what the others have done to help the child.

Unfortunately, too many teachers show favoritism with certain students, and many students consider it an art to become adept at "apple polishing". This practice encourages young people to get by with the least amount of effort, and it minimizes the full significance of gaining knowledge and seeking the fulfillment of one's potential as a person. It discourages those who are not favorites from working hard and achieving according to merit. Oftentimes the children have seen this same type of behavior at home where they or their siblings were favored, and they have observed their parents practice it in their community, in social life, and in regard to their jobs. It is extended to government and every other area in our society, so that it has become a way of life. This is a weakness in our culture; it weakens the individual, the government, the country, and the world population. With favoritism the people are cheated and exploited in not having the best-qualified person represent and work with or for them, but in having someone's favorite occupy a particular position. It is up to the students to interrupt this pathological trend. They should expect only what they deserve from their teachers, and they should insist that the teachers be just in their actions. They, the students, should adopt the attitude to not expect anything for nothing, but to expect and receive reward and compensation for a commensurate amount of work and effort. This fair exchange of "give and take" should exist between pupil and teacher, employee and employer, the unions and management, between all people, and between governments. The teachers should be pressured to be dedicated to their jobs, and to display mature behavior in all their relationships.

Too many people now exist who do the least amount of work possible, not doing their fair share, expecting that others will do it for them. Adolescents should pressure their peers to study and act as mature people do. They should not condone laziness by doing the work for others. They should not tolerate disruptive behavior in the classroom which impedes their ability to learn. They should insist upon receiving what is rightfully theirs, and not allow anyone to cheat in examinations, or in any other way directly or indirectly to take advantage of them. When people advance by cheating, they exploit their fellow classmates. The standing in the class of those who do not cheat is passively lowered. The honest students are not given full recognition for their achievements by those not aware of the cheating.

In the case of sibling teasing, if the adolescents themselves tease, or if they see that their brothers and sisters tease, harassing the household, they should put a stop to it. If they see that their peers are trying to waste their time or appropriate their possessions, they should not allow it. By expecting their peers to perform according to their capacity, they are pressuring them to form good habits which will accompany them in adult years.

Young people should also pressure adults, waitresses, gasoline station attendants, store clerks, and all others with whom they come in contact, to perform adequate, not slip-shod, services. They should demand good products, and make people live up to their word. If they recognize immature behavior and exploitation in their parents, teachers, or any one else, and they cannot cope with it themselves, they should enlist the aid of a mature authority. All mature people should and will help each other in dealing with an immature person bent upon aggressive behavior. Not only should the young people pressure others to mature behavior, but it is of at least equal importance for them to set a good example of living as mature people themselves. Boys and girls should respect each other; they should live a moral life. They should have consideration for other people's property, time, and feelings. All young people should learn from an early age to deal fairly with each other. This will carry over to adult life.

Teenagers should make an effort, despite any attitudes of selfishness, rebelliousness, insecurity, excessive competitiveness or defeatism which were brought on by their immature parents, not to compare themselves with others. They should mind their own business and work to advance themselves. One sometimes hears one teenager say of another: "I don't want him to get ahead of me." They should not look to see what others are doing, or whether or not the others are working. Those who are guided by the actions and approvals of others never progress much further than the others. They spend most of their lives looking at the others, following in their footsteps. A person should strive to unfold himself as an individual, to realize his potential according to his initiative and ability. He should strive for full physical, intellectual, emotional, spiritual, and social development. He should concentrate not upon seeking material objects and pleasure, but upon the expression of himself and his relationship with people. Each adolescent should work all the time at behaving as maturely as possible, commensurate with his chronological age. A self-reliant person is a secure person, not afraid to oppose the strong will of another person, or of a majority, if he thinks he is right. He will have the necessary amount of emotional maturity, intellectual ability, and physical support to prevent immature people from exploiting him.

For a word of encouragement to those who may be lacking in personality, intellect, physical development, or appearance, those people can turn their deficit to an advantage. They can strive to cultivate any hidden talent that they may possess and achieve fulfillment of their potential in another area. As a rule, if a person works hard enough and long enough, he will be successful.

Occasionally, it is seen that people in high school who are successful—cheerleaders, football players, and others, for example— seem to become preoccupied with their own importance. They cannot stand success, as it were, and they try to live on their laurels, not striving for any more accomplishment for the rest of their lives. Some people, so that their teachers and classmates will not think they are stupid, display a "know-it-all" attitude. They are most probably overcompensating for basic inadequacy

158

feelings, and they do not remain silent long enough to give themselves a chance to listen and learn. Others, again due to basic inadequacy feelings, afraid of mistakes and failure, hardly open their mouths in class. If they could tolerate any accentuation of their feelings of inadequacy, and allow themselves to make mistakes, they would genuinely know a great deal more. It should be recognized that intelligent people learn from other's mistakes, and they do not waste their time going through every type of experience, good and bad, in order to learn. On the other hand, practical experience coupled with instruction from others is the best teacher.

Some people, due to rebelliousness and negativism directed at their parents and teachers, refuse to study, hurting themselves in the process. They seem to feel it is more important for them to oppose the adults than it is to advance themselves. They are really acting as slaves of the adults without realizing it, reacting to them rather than to their own needs and desires. If they were aware of this, it would aggravate them no end. They do not stop to think that they will have the same teacher for only one year, but that their entire future may be at stake if they do not apply themselves. Undisciplined children may want to only study those subjects which interest them and which are easy for them. They have not learned to persevere, to make the most of a trying situation, and to continue to work despite obstacles to further oneself. They should concentrate upon the fulfillment of one's potential, and not upon retaliating against their parents and others in authority. They should learn to at least tolerate their parents or the teacher until they can leave home or be promoted to the next grade. Students should realize that attending school and studying are similar to an adult's going to his job every day and working. It is their responsibility to work hard and do their best, even if it means the postponement of immediate pleasures and other sacrifices. It is of foremost importance for high school students to stay in school and to learn as much as it is possible. They should work for results and not just to "get things over with". People have to perform, achieve on their own merit, prove themselves to themselves and others, before they can really enjoy the feelings of self-respect, adequacy, and security. What one learns and gains in the fulfillment of his potential add to his self-confidence, self-worth, and personal security, but, unlike material possessions, cannot be taken away from the person. From developing good study habits and learning as much as possible, from accepting the responsibility of going to school and getting the most out of it, a person prepares himself for being able to accept more responsibility in the future. More responsibility means more fulfillment of one's potential, and the gaining of independence and personal security.

There is a trend now for our schools to be more permissive, to dispense with compulsory classroom attendance, and to not even give examinations and grades. The students have been accustomed to a permissive atmosphere at home, and they expect and pressure for the same at school. A common rationalization favoring the permissiveness states that the children should be allowed to think freely and not have their creativeness squelched. Actually, the giving of more unsupervised activity to these students is the result of insecure school authorities who cannot deny them. Privileges in regard to behavior are deserved and used to good advantage only by responsible and well-disciplined people. Most people need deadlines and a sense of urgency to do their work well and to its completion. In not having examinations, children are deprived of an incentive to study hard, to gain reward, to prove one's worth to oneself and others, and to gain personal security. Only those who are mature, well-motivated, and self-disciplined do not require supervision.

The responsibility of obtaining good grades and of behaving himself rests primarily with the child. It should be the duty of the parents and teachers to see to it that the child assumes this responsibility. To be promoted is the responsibility of the child. If he should fail, he should not blame the parents, the teacher, or anyone else. The schools should not recommend social promotions—that is, promotions given because the child will be embarrassed if he has to repeat a grade, due to his age or size. They should provide special classes for the child's instruction in such instances. If the child has the potential and is failing due to laziness, the embarrassment may provide him with the necessary stimulus to do some work. If emotional factors are responsible for his learning difficulty, the proper treatment should be sought. The promotions should be given based only on performance, and not on potential. The child should be pressured to perform according to his potential. Otherwise, he and others like him will be done a disservice in believing that they "have things coming to them", and that they "deserve something for nothing". They will think they can succeed with little or no effort in this world. They will lean toward desiring a Welfare State and Socialism.

Many boys have the mistaken belief that emotional maturity means being exceedingly masculine and aggressive. Girls in many instances believe that the more they are feminine and dependent, the more they are emotionally mature. They see adults concentrating upon these traits, and they equate emotional maturity with adulthood. Teenagers frequently resort to smoking, drinking, sexual indiscretions, and other activities, in order to be like adults. Unfortunately, they are learning bad habits from immature adults, who themselves do not know how to behave. Being immature, the young people will compare themselves and compete with their peers, not wanting to be outdone, attempting to surpass them in the race to adulthood. It should be recognized that not all adults are mature, and that any person regardless of age can be mature for his age and sex. There is an average amount of emotional maturity for each sixteen-year-old boy and for each sixteen-year-old girl. A sixteen-year-old may have the emotional maturity which is average for an eighteen-year-old. Of course, he may be extremely immature, and may be functioning at the level of a twelve-year-old. Both boys and girls should strive to maintain their own sexual identities. They should make an effort to attain independence and individuality. They should both work to fulfill their potentials, not to exploit each other or anyone else.

In striving for popularity, many young people follow the crowd to be accepted, and resort to bizarre activities to be recognized and approved by their peers. The main reason that a particular person is popular is that he does something for someone else, that is, he fulfills a need for another person. The need may be praise, entertainment, help with his work, companionship, feeling important by association, or any number of other things, but they all amount to the other person's desires being satisfied and his coming to feel more like a total and secure person. This other person, and still others like him, whose needs are fulfilled by the particular person, will seek him out, and he will find himself to be popular. Those who are popular have the ability to be interesting to others. They know how to remove the barriers between each other and make people comfortable. They are not demanding or critical, nor do they have high expectations of people. They do and say what the others want to see and hear.

In the case of studying or working, a good general rule to follow is to do the most difficult tasks first if they are familiar to one. The easier tasks can be left to be done later, as one tires from working. If the tasks are new and unfamiliar, one should do the easiest first. From the experience of working with the easiest, one will learn to attack with facility the more difficult tasks which are to follow. It is generally the case that those who are orderly in regard to their personal habits, punctual, clean, careful of their clothes, and the like, are usually organized in their thinking and do the best in their studies.

Some recreation is necessary. If a student feels he should study rather than attend a special school function, under normal circumstances he should plan to attend and enjoy himself. Should he choose to study instead, he will invariably waste time deliberating over the decision, work at half speed during the function, and end up not being rejuvenated and ready to get back to work after it is over. Had he made the decision to attend, he would study doubly hard before the event and after it was over, knowing that he would be going to it.

It should be stressed that cheating, lying, not studying, dropping out of school, immorality, over-indulgences, lack of self-discipline, and not trying to fulfill one's potential in every area are all signs of weakness. These characteristics, multiplied a number of times in our population, cause a decadent society. Due to his upbringing, a person may have basic feelings of inadequacy, inferiority, and insecurity, plus other attitudes, which will make him function below par and appear to be weak. A person may also appear weak because of indecisiveness, small stature, lack of social poise, or seemingly low intellectual ability. People with these traits invite exploitation by immature people. As mentioned in Chapter I, a decadent society is an immature and a weak society, and it invites domination from aggressors.

The important thing is that something can be done about all of this. Each and every person can strive for and achieve individual excellence, and gain success, security, strength, and happiness according to his capacity. He can prevent exploitation.

If we are living in a modern world and we want to be modern, we should progress in every area of functioning the same way as we have with our scientific achievements. We should strive to advance in the humanities and in the way of our individual and collective maturity. We should work to remove any emotional and cultural factors prohibiting us from gaining maturity. It is the purpose of practicing the Mature Person-to-Person Philosophy that we might prevent our destruction from our intellectual achievements.

The more mature the young people become, the more successful they will be in school, and in choosing and carrying out their careers. The more mature and successful the young men and women are before they marry, the more chance they will have of a successful marriage. Each other's maturity will be enhanced from the marriage, and they will raise mature children.

*   *   *   *

In summary, we must start a definitive movement beginning in adolescence for people to strive for more emotional maturity in themselves and in others. Their children and future generations will grow progressively more mature. Of crucial importance is to have the children apply the Mature Person-to-Person Philosophy in regard to their own experiences, so that it will become a way of life with them. They will learn to deal with all immature, exploitative behavior, including that of people promoting violence and war. Various modes of mature and immature action with examples were presented. Behavior with respect to parents, teachers, peers, and the self was particularly stressed.

Chapter VIII

LIFE'S GOALS AND LIFEWORK

As alluded to in previous chapters, man must formulate definite objectives during his lifetime in order that he may have a meaningful purpose for living. Without clearly-defined goals, a person's energies are diverted aimlessly; he is not utilizing his potential to the limit; and he becomes frustrated in his attempts to achieve success, personal security, and happiness. Without success, he loses confidence in himself and tries even less to prevail in any new ventures. Without self-confidence, and with feelings of inferiority and inadequacy accentuated by his failures, he will be indecisive, functioning at a level beneath his capacity; and he will tend to experience even more failures. He will grow more and more insecure. He might become depressed and even lose his desire to go on living.

Man's success in determining and carrying out his goals, especially his career and his marriage, will help him and his children in the gaining of maturity. On the other hand, a poor choice of a career and of a partner in marriage, with poor planning as to the raising of a family, will lead to failure and dissatisfaction. Discontented parents cannot have a mutually-beneficial relationship with each other; they take out their frustrations on each other and those surrounding them, and their children's well-being is bound to suffer. With the achievement of maturity, security, and happiness, parents and their children will have less frustration and hostility, and there will be less need to exploit others in the search for security. There will be less need for neurotic competitive and aggressive behavior, the person's energies instead being used rewardingly in the development of his innate capacity. He will gain success and real security based on his own merit. It will be easier for him to apply the Mature Person-to-Person Philosophy.

The more immature that a person may be, the more he will fail with his goals in life. He has maintained a feeling of always having been deprived, of having missed something, and of needing more of everything. He will have set unrealistic goals in the first place, perhaps with too high expectations; he will have difficulty in the attainment of them; and even if he has attained them, he will never be satisfied with what he has accomplished.

A person's maturity and his attitude toward goals are related to parental influence and are determined in early childhood. It is not so important what the parents tell their children in regard to which goals to pursue, as it is what they expect of the children, and what the children learn by example in the way of life of their parents. From restricting a child's misbehavior and punishing him when he does wrong, pressure is bestowed upon him to choose more favorable goals. One is exercising the Mature Person-to-Person Philosophy in this respect in not allowing the child to take advantage of you and others with his wrong-doing. By praising and rewarding a child when he does well, the child tends to work for even better goals.

In the younger years, motivation is due to pleasing a person who is significant, such as a parent, and receiving praise from the respected person. The praise and approval makes the child feel worthwhile, and from this he gains confidence in himself, and a sense of personal security. He will try all the more to perform and to succeed. He will learn to follow this pattern of setting attainable goals, and of receiving reward in the form of self-satisfaction and security from his doing well. In later life, the person's motivations come from his quest for more personal security. Finally, the mature man is motivated by his desire to help mankind and to make the world a better place because he lived in it. This is the motivation of a true leader.

Goal fulfillment, or success, is an invaluable tool, and the only means by which a person can gain self-confidence and security. One person cannot give another person self-confidence. It might be true that a given person may make a decision and act if he receives moral support from a highly-respected other person. However, in the last analysis he will have gained a feeling of self-worth and security only from his own successful perform-ance. It is ideal and mature behavior for a person to have sufficient motivation to utilize his potential to the limit in his search for self-excellence and security. He should not have goals which have been displaced upon him from his parents. He should not be acting only because he is comparing himself to others and competing with them. He should not always be watching those around him to see if they are working. By set-ting his own sights according to his own interests and abilities, and by working hard for himself in insuring the fruition of his own decisions, he will have more chance of total success, and the rewards will be very much greater. Mentioned at the be-ginning of this paragraph was that a person can gain self-confi-dence and security only from his own successes. It should be said that, in infancy and early childhood, a person grows secure if he has mature, secure parents. It is during and after early child-hood, for the remainder of his life, that he gains more security only if he succeeds on his own merit. Successes and security enable a person to function at his optimal level, and they spur him onward to more self-confidence, new ventures, more suc-cesses, and more security.

If children are raised in a family in which there is a lack of love and security, and confusion about goals in life, they will have difficulty in identifying with their parents. The parents will not have had their own lives planned as mature men and women, fathers and mothers; and their children will not have the proper guidance and a good example to follow. The chil-dren, just like their parents, will be confronted with the prob-lem of not having a meaningful existence, and of not establish-ing any type of effective goals. They will turn to interests out-side of the home, readily seeking acceptance by their peer groups with the accompanied security, and they will identify with each other in sharing similar dress, music, dance, and other traits. Just as they rebelled against their parents, they will con-tinue to dissent as a group. Group goals replace the inadequate individual goals, the person still not having set his sights accord-ing to his own interests and abilities. He will have a poor chance of securing lasting success and happiness for himself.

An individual needs to live under a government where there

is freedom and opportunity in order to make and fulfill goals which utilize the extent of his capabilities. He needs a cultural environment where prejudice and bigotry, and similar other factors, are not present, serving to preclude a sound thinking ability. The person should have sufficient maturity so that he is able to forgo immediate pleasure and look to the future for his reward. He should be able to sacrifice and work to his capacity, overcoming, circumventing, or adapting to obstacles in the pursuit of his goals. This means he needs strength, perseverance, and flexibility of character. Strength in all areas of functioning—physical, intellectual, emotional, spiritual, and social—will aid a person in the achievement of his goals. He should not be dependent upon others. This means that the others should not have been overprotective, but have let him and made him do for himself. This makes for self-reliance and motivation so that one will want to strive for things in life, strive to learn, and to obtain an education. Parents and other adults should provide only the guidance that a child needs, and not any more. He should have full realization that he himself is ultimately responsible for his own direction and whatever success he achieves in life, even though, in his upbringing and in the present, he has been greatly influenced by others.

Neurotically-motivated goals are not mature goals. A person may want to succeed only in order to outdo others, to try to make himself feel secure. He might be always reacting to someone else's actions, being always in competition with others, and not really living to fulfill his own needs and desires. An example is a child not learning due to negativistic behavior directed at his parents. He is reacting to them, hurting them, at the expense of really hurting himself in not living his life successfully. A person's motives should not be based on comparing himself with others and of being jealous of others. This is the motivation of an immature person. He attempts to "hold down" someone else, by belittlement, or by placing obstacles in front of him, or at least wishing the other person bad fortune, so that he himself will feel "above" the person, superior and secure. As explained previously, this is a false sense of security. Immature people are excessively competitive, and they are influenced only to act for their personal gain. By the accumulation of money, position, and power, they search for more and more of what they interpret as being security. They want to surpass others, gain control over them, and feel dominant. They have to be forced via the Mature Person-to-Person Philosophy to use their aggressiveness in the development of their own potential, and to leave other people alone.

Immature people, on the one hand, may overcompensate in their efforts to succeed and feel adequate. On the other hand, they may fail to put forth maximum effort, the reason being that it would be frightening to them that they would have "nothing left" if they had put forth all their effort and still failed. They would prefer to believe that they could have succeeded if they "really wanted to." A person may not put forth maximum effort because his goal may not seem important enough to warrant a great amount of work. Those raised where everything has been done for them have not really learned how to put forth any real effort, and work is too painful to them. Some people may feel that they are not deserving of success, and they may, in fact, never quite succeed. These, and others, require psychotherapy.

Whether or not an individual can set wise goals for himself depends to a large extent upon his sense of values. Values are determined primarily by parental influence and guidance and, as the child grows older, by the schools he attends, religious teachings, and by what he observes and learns from other people. Unfortunately, too many people are concerned with material possessions today, and there is a cultural trend toward materialism in this country and throughout the world. This is easy to understand because materialism is equated to pleasure, comfort, success, and security; and immature, insecure people are excessively preoccupied with making themselves feel more secure. Of course, not to have enough money presents people with problems; but what is considered to be enough is related to a person's maturity. Also, it should be remembered that the acquisition of wealth, or success, can be associated with maturity and the fulfillment of one's potential.

A common complaint nowadays is that the teenagers lack an adequate value system, and that there is a subsequent increase in juvenile delinquency. It is said that they are lacking in moral and ethical values, and are primarily interested in what gives pleasure, such as automobiles, music, dancing, and sex. They listen to musical records constantly, and even carry transistor radios on their persons so that they have music all of the time. They want a steady boy friend or girl friend, which makes them feel acceptable and adequate, and provides security. These children in school are told that they should study hard, and that in later life they will be rewarded for their efforts. Yet, at home, from their parents, and from other adults in the business and political world, they learn that the road to success, really material success, is through cheating, connivance, and doing the least amount of work necessary. There is little wonder that they are confused as to proper values and what direction they should take in life.

The young people of today almost hysterically support and follow entertainers with no talent, such as singing groups, while not appreciating highly-skilled musicians, circus entertainers, and others. There seems to be no equality in the salaries of entertainers as a whole, as compared to those engaged in the professions and in technical research. Again, however, it is the adults who are setting a bad example for their children to follow. Out of proportion are the fees for professional services based upon a percentage of the total amount of money involved. For example, an attorney may charge his clients one-third of the cost of a transaction. In another transaction involving ten times more money, but invariably not ten times more work or more proficiency, he still draws a one-third fee for his services. In the case of an accident, for example, the distortion in values lies in the attorney's collecting more money, not commensurate with his own effort and skill, but based on more elaborate doctors' reports, the client's disability, his length of time out of work, and other factors. The same applies to real estate sales where a realtor makes considerably more for the sale of an expensive house as compared to a smaller one, which does not involve more ingenuity or a proportionate amount of increase in work.

A false sense of values exists when people are "keeping up with the Joneses", comparing themselves with others, and are not mindful of only realizing their own potentials. They are preoccupied with the type of car their neighbor drives, the house in which he lives, the influential people that he knows, and whether or not he has traveled to Europe or the Caribbean.

By falling into the tide of materialism and status-consciousness, one has lost sight of the important qualities of a person. One has lost sight of his own attributes, of his own individuality. Superficial qualities are taken on by the person—those qualities which are easily observable and admired by immature people. People appraise each other by their material possessions, and not by their virtues, talents, strength of character, emotional stability, and how they conduct themselves in business and private life. These people never know their real selves, as they live only so that others will admire them and "look up" to them.

Some people turn toward intellectualism in their striving for security. They may achieve self-value and acceptance from others by cultivating their learning ability and being thought of as being "brilliant", or they may use their knowledge as a means to acquiring material possessions. Too many of our young people attend college principally because they know they will receive a higher income in later years. Some become pseudointellectuals and agnostics in their search for success and security. Perhaps most people reach their death-beds without having satisfactorily evaluated their positions in life, not really having known themselves, and not having had realistic goals. They have striven for a false security without realizing it by having "kept up with the Joneses".

Already mentioned was how many people in their search for security travel along the avenues of materialism and intellectualism. To a lesser extent, there are people who strive for excellence in exercising their potentials in areas such as physical, emotional, religious, and social development. Becoming expert in any of these areas and acquiring prestige, fame, and fortune bring security to an individual. However, a person is immature if he achieves excellence in even more than one area if he has neglected one of the other areas of his total development. A mature person has a balance of interests and does not ignore any aspect of his total self.

Our young people should be made to realize that, the more they develop their intellects and their other areas of functioning, the more they will enjoy their lives. The more they fulfill the potential of their minds, emotions, and bodies, giving full expression of their innate capacities, the better they will meet the challenges of the world. They will gain success and security, and understanding of themselves and others. They will achieve a better conception of their role in infinite time and space, and will therefore appreciate their lives all the more.

A person who has feelings of inferiority and inadequacy in the first place, will have these feelings accentuated if he lacks an education. Just to go to college to be able to earn a bigger salary, to gain more possessions, to gather material things that have already been handed to them by their parents, seems not to be a satisfactory answer to a lot of young people. Fortunately, they are searching for a deeper meaning to life and why it is worth living.

Those people who have healthy religious beliefs tend to be more mature. They are able to forgo personal and immediate gratification, and are able to think of someone else rather than always think only of themselves. They have faith in themselves and are able to have it in others. They have more conscience, and better morals and ethics. They have a better feeling for their role in the universe.

Today's youth should be taught by example not to study only to receive good grades. Studying and attending school, unlike a job where there is generally more supervision, requires self-discipline. When disinterested in a subject and not motivated to learn, one can daydream and waste time no matter how much he is pressured to produce. The prime interest should be to understand, to correlate, to create, and to advance in all areas of knowledge. The more knowledge a person accumulates, the more independent he will feel. He will have a more realistic sense of values, having an appreciation of the work involved in his having acquired the knowledge. He will be more successful in his job. It will lead him to a fulfillment of his potential, and to the achievement of personal security and happiness. He will learn how to cope with his problems better, and how to get along better with his fellow human beings. He will feel self-confident and secure in his position in life, and he will raise his children to become more mature adults.

It seems that certain factors contribute to a person's motivation to want to succeed. Deprivation during infancy and childhood, and even in later life, and discomfort and dissatisfaction with his lot in life tend to influence a person in his want for security. People living in a temperate climate seem to progress more, possibly because they are not handicapped by heat or cold and the concomitant time and energy which is expended to survive. Strife and a sense of urgency, a threat to one's security, propel one to drive ahead and to create. If there are too many adverse conditions, and too much time for work is needed to survive, one can only hope to be able to adapt to his environment and not produce anything new. It is human nature for a person not to put forth his maximum performance when times are good, he has plenty and is living in comfort, and things are going well for him. On the contrary, when business and times are not good, there being a threat to his security, a person will work harder and perform a much better service.

A person has to feel that he is worth something, that what he is doing is worthwhile in his eyes and in the eyes of others, in order to feel secure and happy. This search for security and happiness provides him with the initiative to set important goals and strive for their fulfillment. In general, with the exception of mature leaders, those who put forth their maximum effort and work the hardest are those who are working for themselves to advance themselves. The opposite holds true, also, where people usually do not work as hard as they can when they work for others. The reason for this is that an insecure person working for another unconsciously does not want to contribute to the advancement of that other person. He himself feels he does not have enough of everything, that he is lacking and inadequate, and he feels that he needs to receive, and not work and give to another. In comparing himself with the other person, the other person is seen as growing stronger, and the insecure person does not put forth maximum effort in order to curtail the other person's progress. The insecure person may feel the stronger person is a threat to him, or he may be plainly jealous of him. It is true that some insecure people do their best for others for the praise they receive, but the praise serves to add to their own personal advancement, self-worth, and security. They may identify with and support their employer, gaining security from the association, yet not having to bear the employer's responsibilities. We see that the people who are happiest in old age are those who have a goal for which they are working even at the time of their death.

Too frequently we hear even a person in his late teens say: "I don't know what I want to be, what I want to do." This indecision and lack of goals is a sign of immaturity. The important thing he should realize is that if he does not set his own goals, goals will be set for him by others who actually are imposing their will upon him. By having his decision made for him, his dependency and his pattern of being indecisive are being fostered. By making his own decision in regard to a goal, even if it is a poor one, by working at it with all his effort, he can make it a right decision for himself and he can succeed. The above is what frequently happens when a person had been in a quandary as to what course to follow, and later he says that "everything worked out for the best." Just to hope and wait and see if "everything will work out for the best" is not a mature attitude. It implies doubt and distrust in one's ability to see to it that he will succeed. A person has to display confidence that he is as competent and conscientious as the next man before those surrounding him will have faith in him and give total support. A mature person "takes the bull by the horns" and directs all his energies toward making things work out according to his plan. Only results are important, not just going through the motions, a great deal of time spent, or a good "college try". To have come close to succeeding and to have fought a hard fight are not good enough. It is the final accomplishment which counts. If maximum effort has not produced favorable results, one must re-examine oneself and the circumstances.

Some people act impulsively without thinking. At the opposite extreme are the "dreamers", those who are always thinking but who never do anything, due to fear, lack of self-confidence, and a feeling of insecurity. Ideal is the mature person, the one who thinks things over carefully and who has the courage, the security, to act and to work steadily at achieving his goals. He is not one who, if he strikes a stumbling block, feels that the "grass is greener on the other side of the fence" and jumps to an entirely different endeavor. His goals have been set by himself as a result of his interest, aptitude, motivation, education, and training; and he is progressing on his own merit, using his potential to the limit. Having the proper preparation, strength, and perseverance, he is able to have a "never give up" attitude. Although sometimes feeling downtrodden and beaten, he is able to produce the needed extra spurt of energy to turn the tide and to keep on fighting with renewed effort. He does not accept second best. However, if he should encounter a stumbling block, if it is a case of inefficiency of progress to attempt to continue in the same direction and a stalemate develops, and if it is impossible to resolve the problem, he will look about and evaluate the situation. He will seek an opportunity in a closely-allied area, perhaps merely a new approach, and then continue to surge ahead in a direction similar to his original goal. (*See Illustration 3.*)

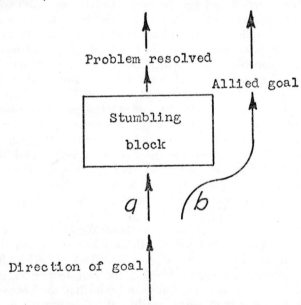

Illustration 3: Life's Stumbling Blocks

The mature person takes either course a or b.

174

One should learn to recognize an opportunity from one's own and other's experiences so that, when it arrives, one can take advantage of it. This means becoming thoroughly familiar and well versed in as many areas as possible. If you are not aware of an opportunity you will, of course, "miss the boat." Too many people do not recognize an opportunity until it is too late. Opportunities may present themselves by chance; but, if not, one should work at creating the opportunities for oneself. This can be done by preparing oneself emotionally, intellectually, physically, and socially to an advanced degree, cultivating oneself and one's relationships, and the situations which surround oneself. Once an opportunity is recognized as such, one needs security and self-confidence to be able to act on it. Because one is reasonably sure that he has made a right decision, he will now work to make the opportunity a successful one for himself. The person does the best that he knows how at the time that he does it.

It is easy for people to make up their mind about wanting something, after someone else has come to the conclusion it is worth having. After the other party makes up his mind, the first passive, indecisive party can more easily make up his mind, too —having gained the reassurance from the other party that the thing is worth having. The first party has been indecisive, and now reacts to the second party's actions. Insecure people, even though they may have superior qualities, frequently are left behind others with less talent. Instead of advancing themselves according to their capabilities, "saying nothing and sawing wood," they spend most of their lives looking at what others are doing. They are easily discouraged by those who are also insecure and doing nothing. They worry about everything, which amounts to having a great many unresolved and anticipated problems. They are indecisive, and even after having reached a decision, they are not sure that it is the right one. A person has to bait his hook and throw his line in the water before he can expect to catch any fish. He has to try before he can hope to succeed.

175

Basically, immature, insecure people cannot make decisions, keep promises, or "make good" their word. They rationalize that external changes in events make them change in regard to their obligations. It takes a mature, secure person to make a good judgment and, more important, to be able to follow through in making it succeed without being influenced to changing his mind by outside sources.

An intelligent person does not expect to learn everything by himself, or from his own experiences only. He is receptive to everything new, and learns from history and from the experiences of others. He correlates everything that he learns with that which he already knows, sifting out what he feels is unimportant, and formulating his own ideas about things. He continually organizes, consolidates, and expands his thinking and his activities. He learns not to let himself become submerged with trivialities. He in this way alleviates stress while performing more efficiently at his peak capacity. His primary concern is to do his work accurately and with speed. He attacks his most difficult tasks first unless, from the easier tasks, he can gain a familiarity which will aid him in the resolution of the most difficult tasks.

By associating with creative people, and by being attuned to what is going on in the world, a person himself will tend to be creative. As he thinks and acts creatively, he is stimulated to even more creativity. Unconscious material begins to emerge, and the person is operating at the peak of his potential. One draw-back to working with creative people, as in research, for example, is that a subordinate may be unintentionally squelched by superiors and tradition.

In regard to choice of career, a person who is interested in something will usually work his best at it and be most apt to succeed in it. For the most part, one becomes interested in that area for which he has some aptitude. Success in one's work is probably the greatest source of security that a person may draw upon in making himself feel personally secure. He spends almost one-half of his wakeful hours at work, and the work should offer enjoyment, satisfaction, and fulfillment of the greater part of his needs. A job that presents a challenge to a person, and in which the person is successful, serves as even more of a victory to him, and he gains immeasurable self-confidence and security from it. He feels he is doing something useful, and he feels valuable to himself and to others.

A father's security in a job gives a feeling of security to his children. The fact that the father can be depended upon to bring home money for food and other essentials is reassuring to a child. Of course, unless there is some problem regarding employment, the fact that the father provides for his family is generally taken for granted by his children. More important than the above is that a father who is insecure in his position feels inadequate, and he is unable to discipline and guide his children with any degree of authority. He cannot set a good example of his being knowledgeable and self-confident, and he cannot relay the feeling of having high expectations of his children. The children become unsure of their own ability, and they also feel inadequate and insecure. The father faces constant frustration at work, but he may "take out" his aggressive feelings on his wife and children. This is because he can get away with it. A temper-tantrum at home will not get him fired from his job. The reason for the problem lies in the father's immaturity and insecurity, his not having prepared himself better in every way for his career, his not having made a better choice as to his type of work, and his not adapting and doing a good job. Now, to remedy the situation, he should strive to learn his job better and utilize the Mature Person-to-Person Philosophy. By use of the latter he can direct his aggressive feelings in a mature manner where they belong—at his boss, fellow employees, competitors, customers, and others who might be trying to take advantage of him; and he, of them.

There is a tendency for children, providing there is a good relationship between them and their parents, to have the same likes and dislikes, the same interests, the same goals as their parents. It is a natural reaction for the parents, because of the lack of time and their own interests, to have their children follow in their footsteps. However, parents should expose the children to as many kinds of sports, cultural media, job opportunities, and other activities as is possible. They should be shown art studios, factories, farms, police stations, courtrooms, jails, hospitals, and other institutions in action. If the child shows a special interest or talent in a certain area, he should be encouraged to participate in it even more. From his interest and participation he will derive pleasure, perseverance, skill, knowledge, self-confidence, and a healthy respect for others, among other things. Whatever the child undertakes, he should be made to give it a fair trial period, and not to quit it in too short a period of time. The child will learn that it is worthwhile to forgo immediate gratification and to work hard instead, because in the future he will gain a much greater amount of pleasure when he finally realizes his goals. He will learn how to set and work for goals as a mature person.

How secure a person feels will determine what he will attempt, and for what type of job he may strive. If he feels insecure, having been influenced by his parents, for example, who were raised during an economic depression, he might lean toward a government job which would offer more security to him. The most secure people might tend toward private enterprise, with its concomitant risks. They are self-confident that they have the potential to succeed. They are willing to face the risks because, with success, the rewards are greater.

For those people who have intelligence, emotional stability, initiative, good judgment, and perseverance, the odds are in their favor that they will succeed in their endeavors. From their successful accomplishments they will gain experience and more self-confidence, so that they will want to attempt even more. However, immature people might be hurt by any success or good fortune. It may serve to magnify their self-importance, and they may exploit others all the more. They might become preoccupied with their newly-acquired material things, and have even more difficulty in evaluating people as to their virtuous qualities, instead of only for their possessions. It should be recognized that intelligence, physical appearance, and some other factors that contribute to one's gaining success are inborn characteristics; but virtues or moral excellence, which determine the means by which one attains the success and are of most importance, are acquired traits, and can more readily be improved.

Girls, as well as boys, should strive to obtain a higher education and to learn as much as possible. Attractive girls—probably more true than with boys—have a tendency to not unfold themselves and realize their potential. Their plain sisters, on the other hand, are pressured to cultivate all their attributes. To have many friends and to be an interesting person, they learn that they have to read and know about a great many subjects. To have interests in common with others, they have to concentrate in sharing experiences. With modern developments in which today's housewives and mothers have more time on their hands, there should be more formal preparation for out-of-the-home activities. In addition to their homes and children, modern women gain a feeling of success and satisfaction from part-time careers, civic activities, and the like. It is in feeling valuable from being a good wife and mother, and feeling useful either at a job or in a community organization, that a woman gains a feeling of self-confidence and security which is transmitted to her children. She is able with a formal education to relate better to her husband, and to understand more about his type of work and its associated problems, thus creating an atmosphere of mutual interest and compatibility. The secondary schools and colleges should provide a more varied type of curriculum, geared to a girl's becoming a knowledgeable wife and mother and a participant in civic affairs. In today's schools, girls are given the same courses as boys, and after competing with them for a number of years the girls are expected to settle down in marriage and take on the new role as helpmate. An exceptional girl should be given the opportunity to pursue any course of study and career, because she should be able to accomplish a great deal more than the average person.

Too often we see workers in all types of fields who do not show any pride in their work. It seems that, the more lowly a position—one not requiring too much intelligence—the less conscientiousness one finds in the worker. Of course, there are exceptions, perhaps seen mostly in those people who have not attained their true potentials, or in others who have acquired high positions not based upon merit. Therefore, there may be waitresses and janitors who are a great deal more conscientious than nurses and engineers. Attributes of success, such as intelligence, initiative, perseverance, and the like, which were essential in the person's having achieved his position in the first place, generally measure how well the person will perform on the job. A scientist, for example, has to have more qualifications than a plumber to achieve his position, and he will more than likely work more conscientiously at his job than the plumber will at his. From the above, then, it is deduced that, as a rule, one should not judge the working ability of a plumber by using the same standards as that for a scientist. Rather, comparisons as to workmanship should be made only between people in the same field. Emotionally-mature individuals, whether or not they lack intelligence or any other qualities, will seek and attain the best possible career that their ability and circumstances will allow. They will then work with conscientiousness and pride commensurate with the type of position they hold.

An employer should be primarily concerned that his worker is doing a competent job, and not that he graduated from an elite college, that he is of a certain nationality, or that he once suffered from a "nervous breakdown". He should set a good example for his workers. He should insist upon vacations for himself and his workers which will serve to relieve work pressures and the boredom of home routine. Holidays provide relaxation and entertainment, so that a person will return to his job with a spirit of rejuvenation.

Ideally, to ensure success and happiness, a person should exercise the Mature Person-to-Person Philosophy in his every relationship. He should acquire as much knowledge about everything as is possible. He should work for the development of self-confidence and security so that he can make decisions and act upon them. He should love everyone; because all human beings in this world are, in a broad sense, of one family. And they, just as he, are trying to survive in the best possible way. However, it is not wrong to dislike another person's traits, his thoughts and actions. Everyone should be aware that it is human nature to want and to need love and security. Last but not least, to ensure success and happiness, a person should strive to curtail his exploitative drives and forgo his need for immediate gratification, but learn to relax and enjoy himself for the little time that he has on this earth. (*See Illustration 4.*)

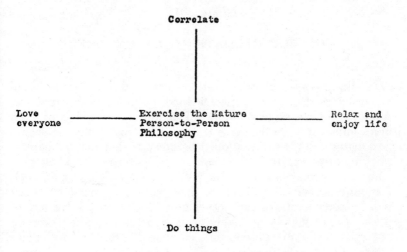

Illustration 4: Guide For Living

CHAPTER IX

CHOICE OF MATE AND MARRIAGE

In the previous chapter it was discussed how a successful career gives a person self-confidence, security, and happiness. A successful marriage provides all of the above and is of even more importance in that it is the basis for the raising of secure and mature children. Mentioned before was that mature parents raise mature children. The more mature the man and woman who enter a marriage contract (this is true with any contract), the more successful and happy they will be in marriage. They will be considerate of each other and be able to resolve any of the problems which inevitably arise. Separation and divorce do not exist when the parents are emotionally mature, and there are no juvenile delinquency and other emotionally-related problems when both the parents and children are mature.

The reason a man and woman are attracted to each other is that they fulfill each other's emotional needs. The most apparent need, it seems, is the need for sexual satisfaction. To seek gratification primarily, especially immediate gratification, is a sign of emotional immaturity. There seems to be a lesser need for sexual gratification in the more mature individuals, although this should not be confused with those disinterested in sex, which is pathological. In animals the fulfillment of the sexual urge and the preparation for the young are instinctual, and necessary for species preservation. In humans, too, the need for sexual fulfillment serves to preserve our existence in the world.

In man and woman, the sexual drive is controlled by the emotions, and also by reason. Humans are gratified not merely by the climax or orgasm involved in the sexual act, but also, and even more so, by the fact that they are accepted by a mate. They feel a sense of closeness and self-value by having been accepted as a sexual partner, and their security is strengthened.

The man and woman may at first be attracted to each other

physically. Soon, personality factors, intelligence, and other traits in each other might be admired and desired by the other person. The more desirable that the traits seem to a person, which sometimes may even be lacking in himself, the more he may feel the need to have the other person in close association with him. Holding the other person in high esteem, and uniting with that other person in close relationship and marriage, gives one support and a sense of personal security. The fact that still others may admire the same traits that you admire in your partner will reinforce your feeling of security. Being complimented by a spouse who is highly respected also gives one a sense of self-worth and security. In addition, comparing himself with a partner who might be lacking in some area gives an immature person a sense of feeling adequate.

In the ideal union between a man and a woman, there should be a balance between them, so that they complement each other. Each boy and each man, each girl and each woman, possesses, or should possess, an average amount of emotional maturity for his or her own chronological age and sex. The characteristics and maturity of a male should not be measured in terms of the characteristics and maturity of a female, and vice versa. Under ordinary circumstances a man has the edge over a woman just because he is physically stronger. If a man and woman of the same age, background, intellectual ability, and a seemingly similar amount of emotional immaturity were trying to exploit each other, the man would undoubtedly win if there were no higher authority present. All things being equal, an immature man may or may not be able to take advantage of another comparable man; yet, because of the strength factor, he may very readily dominate a more intelligent woman with a seemingly similar or even greater level of emotional maturity. By the same token, an immature woman may or may not be able to exploit another comparable woman, yet, by behaving very passively and weakly, she may be able to have her own way in making a more intelligent and mature man believe that he is even stronger than he is from comparing himself to her. There may be many pathological variations, for example, where the man may be the more passive one and the woman more dominant; however, we are referring to the mature man and woman in an ideal marriage, fulfilling each other's needs in their relationship with each other.

There are different types of needs in males and females, and in individual males and individual females. It would help young people to be aware of some of their own needs and the needs of others so that they could look more objectively at a prospective marital partner and not become involved with one who would ultimately prove to be a poor choice. A person could analyze the significance of his needs, which could alter his ideas and influence his entire concept of marriage. Once a person becomes emotionally involved with another, he cannot view clearly the factors which were important to him in forming the relationship in the first place.

Mentioned already have been the mutual needs for sexual gratification and personal security. Insecure people generally seek a partner who is secure, that is, one who is strong physically, intellectually, and emotionally. However, an insecure, immature person may also seek a weaker person, one whom he or she can dominate, and thereby gain a feeling of superiority and security. An insecure husband may do everything for his wife and make her dependent upon him in order to feel strong and secure. As stated previously, this proves to be a false sense of security. Problems arise in a marriage where a spouse is not the same personality that a partner anticipated before the marriage. For example, the insecure wife may become unhappy and frustrated because she finds her husband not strong enough for her to depend upon as much as she would like. She may even find him to be as dependent as her children, and he may resent and be jealous of the time she spends with them. As a rule, weak people dislike to see undesirable traits, such as weakness, in those near to them, because it reminds them of their own weaknesses. Sometimes it is difficult to recognize weakness in a man, in that he may find it necessary to overcompensate by acting especially manly and strong. Also, a woman may be considered to be very feminine, but in reality she is the "clinging vine" type and extremely dependent. A woman is by no means masculine if she has realized her intellectual, emotional, and physical potentials, and if she is independent, mature, and secure. In the same vein, a man is not weak or effeminate if he

184

is sensitive, understanding, and considerate of others.

An immature person will blame his spouse for his own mistakes, not wanting his feelings of adequacy and security to be insulted. Some men with the potential to be the dominant one in a marriage take the passive role when the wife, sometimes more insecure than the man, but overcompensating, takes the reins of the household, doing all the disciplining of the children and making all the decisions. If an insecure wife finds herself married to an insecure man she may oppose his every move, trying to remain the stronger, for fear that he will take advantage of her any time that he has the opportunity. She will compare him to other men and drive him to work harder. Both the husband and wife will find themselves attempting to outdo each other by belittling each other's worth and fighting each other, trying to build up oneself and feel secure. They are seeking recognition and respect from each other, and would want the other to fulfill their need of security. Each wants the other to "give", not to "take", but neither one can "give" due to feelings of insecurity. It should be emphasized that the two people are unaware of what is really taking place in their relationship, and much of what is said and done is not deliberate. They can take out their frustrations on each other because they know they can get away with it, that is, know what their partner will tolerate.

An immature husband and wife may be looking to their spouse for the something they missed, but of which they are unaware, from their own mother and father. Abnormal attachments may still exist with their own parents and siblings, and they may not be able to relate freely with each other. They may be in search for acceptance, recognition, love, understanding, and security to an extraordinary degree. They expect their spouse to be also a mother or a father to them. The reason why a girl married a particular man may be that he resembled her father, which meant security to her; and a boy may have married a mother-image because of extreme dependence upon his own mother. Still present from childhood days may be sibling rivalry, competitiveness, and resentment for the opposite sex, which now becomes directed at the spouse.

With the coming of children, mature parents, who have been

able to "give and take" with each other, are now able to "give" to their children. The children are not intruders, as is the case in a household with immature parents, demanding something in the way of love and security from their parents who have very little of it themselves. Mature parents should be able to fulfill the emotional needs of their children, and the children, in turn, should be raised so as to fulfill the emotional needs of the parents. Parents should not displace their neurotic desires to their children and seek vicarious pleasure from their behavior. They should not overprotect or neglect to limit them in order to be favored over their spouse. They should not exploit their children in other ways.

Immature, insecure, and anxious parents cannot give their children a mature, secure, and anxiety-free relationship. They give an immature type of love, and set inconsistent, inadequate limits, due to ignorance, or immaturity and insecurity. Their anxiety makes the children feel insecure. The children do not have mature parents with whom to identify and a mature relationship to which they can respond. Immature parents raise emotionally-deprived children, and this continues the cycle of immature people in the world.

An immature husband is allowed by his immature wife to influence and intimidate her so that she becomes even more emotionally unstable. She will feel belittled and may experience an awakening of her basic inferiority and inadequacy feelings. She may depreciate herself because of her apparent deficiencies as a wife and mother to where she may even bcome depressed, all of this "adding fuel to the fire" so that she will be functioning even more below par. Depending upon a person's predisposition, she may be so overwhelmed that she will suffer a psychosis. On the other hand she may react in an opposite way. Not being affected emotionally in the same manner, due to a different personality background, yet still unable to cope with her husband's attacks, she may rebel by doing slipshod housework and being "too tired" for sexual relations. She may seek acceptance, pleasure, and security from other sources, such as work, her children, or another man. No doubt the children are going to suffer from such a situation. The children will sense their mother's inadequacies, and they will tend to take advantage of her and not respect her in just the same way as their father. They will feel insecure with their disunited parents and visibly weak mother. They will feel even more insecure with their parents' disharmonious rules of discipline and the consequent lack of boundaries as to how they are supposed to behave.

By the same token, an immature wife is allowed by her immature husband to influence, irritate, and nag him so that he becomes even more emotionally unstable. He will feel belittled by her and have even more difficulties in performing up to par as a husband and father, and on the job. He might "internalize" his problems and suffer from headaches or peptic ulcers. Again, according to his basic personality structure, he may react differently and attempt to "escape" his wife's abuse and look for security from drinking alcoholic beverages or seeking out other women. In this instance, too, the children will suffer. They will "look down on" their father, not respond to his disciplinary measures, if there are any, and tend to be rebellious and negativistic toward him. They will be disrespectful and rebellious with all authority figures, the teachers, the police, and others, in later life. They will be raised as insecure people.

As described earlier, for the most part people are attracted to each other and marry because there is a mutual fulfillment of emotional needs. Also, it has been said that man and woman have characteristics common to their own sex, and there is an average norm of maturity for each of them. Man and woman unite in what we shall call the Railroad Track or Parallel Track Concept of Marriage, where they complement each other. There are normally bonds or "railroad ties" between the husband and wife as they continue their parallel ways through life. These bonds are their possible similar backgrounds, interests, likes and dislikes, ideas, beliefs, their mutually-shared friends and experiences, their children, other common concerns, and those traits in each other which fulfill the emotional needs of the other. Ideally, if both husband and wife are relatively mature individuals, they will continue on their separate parallel ways, complementing each other, and providing their children with the mature relationship that they need to grow into mature individuals.

If both husband and wife are immature, it is possible with the coming of children that the relationship between them, between the father and mother, may become too close in certain areas. It may become so close that they may almost function as one to the detriment of the children. They will be depriving their children of what they require to mature. They are not living their lives as mature individuals along parallel paths. This type of marital bond will produce immature and even schizophrenic children. We shall call this the Unparallel Track Concept of the Origin of Schizophrenia. Potentially pathological factors in the parents' basic personalities interact so that there is a pathological complementary union of the two personalities. There are formed pathological bonds or "railroad ties" between the mother and the father. Their personalities have united so that they cannot "give" in the way of a mature relationship to their children, even as much as they potentially could have given had they not met each other. Instead of enhancing each other's emotional potential, as mature mates would do, they drain each other of what little they had basically. A pathological relationship then is formed between the parents' pathological personalities and their infant child. As is the case in any parent-child relationship, the relationship between the mother and child is the more intense and significant one in the early development of the child's personality. However, both the parents' personalities will contribute in the formation of a pathological personality in their child. Different factors in the lives of the parents may affect the pathological intensity of their personalities so that they might influence their child more strongly at certain times, or they focus on certain of their children and others might be spared. A parent's pathological needs may be fulfilled from an intense relationship with one child, and the other children may not be so influenced. Also, certain normal periods in the child's development, such as toilet training, might demand a more intense relationship with the parents, and the child's personality will become more abnormal at such a particular period of his life. The child will be predisposed to manifest emotional illness and schizophrenia if he continues to be in contact with his parents, or if his personality comes under stress from other pathological personalities or situations where there is an overwhelming threat to his personal security, even years later.

At the other extreme—again, if both parents are immature—with the coming of children the relationship between the parents may become too distant. They may remain together in apparent harmony, or they may even separate and divorce. The father, for example, may be withdrawn for any number of reasons. Pathological bonds or "railroad ties" will exist between the spouses; and a very intense pathological relationship may develop between the mother and one of her children. The children are deprived of the mature parental relationship they require to mature. This, again, will produce immature children with the predisposition to many different types of emotional problems, including psychosis. The children of such marriages will grow up to have potentially pathological factors in their personalities, which could become operative and transmitted when they themselves marry and have children. (*See Illustration 5.*)

The man, as a husband and father, has as his job to be the chief provider for his family. He should not relinquish any of his rights and obligations and should not impinge upon the rights and obligations of his wife. The woman, too, as a wife and mother, has a job to perform as the chief housekeeper. She should not relinquish any of her rights and obligations, and should not impinge upon the rights and obligations of her husband. Both the husband and wife should exercise the Mature Person-to-Person Philosophy in respect to each other and to their children, and the children should be trained to exercise it with their parents and everyone else.

Most women have been raised so that they have identified with their own mothers. They look forward to getting married and fulfilling their role as a woman by having children. A man, too, under normal conditions identifies with his father and desires a family and the perpetuation of his kind. Marriage and the establishment of the family unit are the basis for the progress of civilization. The raising of mature children, boys and girls, presupposes one man and one woman, not a group of people such as seen in communal nurseries. The father and mother of a child can best draw out that child's potential and nurture him to grow into a mature individual. The mature parent-child relationship is essential in order for the child to be raised to recognize the dignity of man, in order for him to have

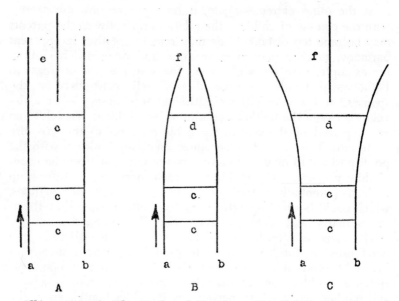

Illustration 5: The Railroad Track or Parallel Track Concept of Marriage, and the Unparallel Track Concept of the Origin of Schizophrenia

A. A marriage with relatively mature husband and wife. B and C. Marriages with immature husbands and wives. a. Husband's path in marriage. b. Wife's path in marriage. c. Normal bonds or "railroad ties" between husband and wife. d. Pathological bends or "railroad ties" between husband and wife. e. Mature children. f. Immature and potentially psychotic children. Not illustrated are other pathological variations.

love, compassion, and respect for his fellow man. Such a person will grow up to not want to hurt another human being, let alone kill him, unless it is in defense of his life or the life of one who cannot protect himself. No nursery or communal arrangement can truly replace the parents.

Ideally, a man and woman should use common sense in addition to their emotions in choosing each other as mates. They should have as many interests in common as is possible. There will be enough problems and differences later in their married life. They should have an understanding as to the number of children they will desire, where and how they will live, and what they expect out of life. A person's entire life will be influenced by the mate that he chooses very early in his life, and the importance of his selection cannot be overemphasized. For example, an insecure woman will gain security from a relatively mature husband. She will not only feel secure from being in his presence, but he will deal with her so that she will gain self-confidence and independence. He will help her to exercise her potential, to do things and to feel useful. On the other hand, her marriage to an immature man will bring out her basic inadequacy feelings, and she will feel even more insecure.

The more mature and secure the married couple, the better they will be able to adapt to any changes in their married life. Immature, insecure people will have difficulty in resolving their problems; but also they will have trouble in adapting to their successes. For example, a wife may not be able to adjust to her husband's job promotion and a higher standard of living without "looking down on" others. He, in turn, if he advances in his schooling or job, may feel that she is too beneath his level, and he may take advantage of her all the more. He may feel stronger and more secure in his new position, and believe that he no longer needs her support. The wife, on the other hand, may begin to feel inadequate and insecure, and may even become depressed in no longer feeling needed by the husband. Of course, the wife's basic inadequacy feelings and feelings of insecurity stemmed from childhood and her relationship with her parents, and now they have been awakened by her husband's change in attitude toward her. Therefore, it would be beneficial for these people to advance and change together, the wife either learning something new or becoming involved in community affairs, sharing their new interests with each other. They would in this way both gain success and personal security, and continue to complement each other and fulfill each other's needs.

As stated before, immature people sometimes might hold back their feelings, all their love. The reason for this is that, if they gave all their love, it could still be rejected. They would feel they had failed, that their love was not good enough; and their failure would be a threat to their feelings of adequacy and security. Also, their immature partner would realize this, and dominate his mate that he now sees as being even weaker and more vulnerable. They might even separate from each other. An immature person feels more comfortable in being loved more than he believes he loves the other person. This explains why in some cases a man or woman does not allow himself or herself to fall in love unless they are certain of the love of the other person. Also, it explains the reason in some instances for impotence and frigidity in males and females. A total attempt at providing sexual satisfaction and having the immature mate reguard it as a failure is demoralizing, so it is learned unconsciously not to put forth with best effort. Of course, a mature mate would be pleased with the immature one's performance, and would help the mate in his or her fulfillment of emotional potential. In the case of two relatively mature mates, their sexual relationship should be a mutually satisfying one and should enhance their emotional and social relationship.

Sexual intercourse before marriage and not with one's spouse is not mature behavior. Those who are single and engage in sexual relationships, and adulterers, are not acting like mature adults. They are deriving the pleasure associated with marriage without bearing the responsibilities of it. There are privileges awarded a person as he or she attains a certain age, but there are also concomitant responsibilities. Just as a holder of an important job or of a high office is awarded more prestige, benefits, and pay, he also has to assume more responsibility. In the present day a person has to reach a certain chronological age in order to drive an automobile, drink alcoholic beverages, marry, and vote. As in the case of obtaining a driver's license, he should be given instruction and have to pass examinations in order to gain the privileges and the responsibilities of drinking, voting, and marrying. The instructions and tests would help to better determine if a person is mature, adequate and capable of shouldering the responsibilities which accompany the privileges. Such a procedure would pressure a person to more preparation in a particular area, and more mature behavior. As it is now, there are too many mistakes caused by immature people which fall upon the shoulders of others, sometimes those of future generations, to try to rectify. More attention should be paid to the prevention of mistakes, and the trial-and-error type of social relationships at the expense of partners and children and others should not be tolerated.

The higher the esteem a person has of himself—and this should not be confused with one who is conceited—the more highly he will think of others. He will treat people with dignity. A person who enters marriage in a condition of chasteness will recognize and appreciate the virtues of his or her mate, and the mate, in turn, will respect the spouse's strength of character. The introduction to sexual experiences before marriage—and this applies to both males and females—brings coarseness to an individual. Being immature, these people will compare their spouses sexually with their previous partners. The opportunity for the full acquisition of a certain emotional warmth for another human being, between husband and wife, which can only be cultivated in a marital relationship, becomes lost forever. Lost is the opportunity for the possibility of attainment of complete emotional fulfillment and maturity. Lost is the opportunity to give to their children as warm and as mature a relationship as they once had the capacity to give, and the children will be deprived of full emotional development. If these are lost, it will be up to the next generation to capitalize on their parent's mistakes.

This certain warmth and trust between the man and woman as husband and wife, and then between them and their children, never fully develops when they have been unchaste. Their children will have been deprived of the optimal emotional climate necessary for them to realize their fullest emotional potential. In this sense, there is a sacred obligation to one's lineage that one has done his best in promoting excellence in his own offspring. This excellence in their children is never realized, the certain warmth and trust necessary for the ideal emotional climate not having been fully developed because of the coarseness of the parents. Lost to the children has been the opportunity to attain the ultimate in maturity, and love and feeling for their fellow man. The more mature the love that a husband and wife have for each other, the more that they have experienced fulfillment of their emotional potentials, the more chance will their children have for the fulfillment of their own emotional potentials.

Those who are preoccupied with sex and who indulge in premarital sexual relations and adultery are selfish, and they are seeking immediate gratification, acceptance, and security. They feel personally secure in their being desired and approved by the other, being given love, and by giving pleasure and proving themselves sexually adequate. To alleviate her guilt feelings and to maintain her self-respect and personal security, a woman may give the excuse that she "fell in love", or "it just happened" that she engaged in sexual intercourse. Security can also be obtained by the immature person's hurting and exploiting another sexually, thereby being dominant in comparison. The sexual act itself may serve as a release of tension and aggressive feelings. A man may force a woman into having sexual relations with him and even make her pregnant intentionally. He may complain that she does not love him if she does not yield to his advances, yet in reality he does not have true love for her in insisting upon sexual intercourse if she has reservations about it. A woman may use sex to seduce a man, or deprive him of it by feigning illness, for example. Those that are unfaithful to their spouses are seeking personal security from their relationships with others, such as gaining "understanding" which the spouse does not give, or gaining conquests and proving oneself to be a "man" or a "woman". They sometimes rationalize their actions by saying they are involved in a "sophisticated" extra-marital love affair. As explained previously, all these people are immature, and this is as a result of an inadequate relationship with their parents when they were growing up. They are looking for a certain "something more", that which they feel they missed during their childhood. Actually, they missed a mature love and acceptance, a mature relationship with their parents. Now they feel they are missing something which, in reality, they are missing—adequacy, maturity, independence, and security.

Premarital sexual relations and adultery are an insult to one's integrity. In addition, marital unfaithfulness is exploitation of one's spouse and, of course, immature behavior. It has an effect upon one's image and influences one's relationships with his children and others. On a practical level, such behavior can be responsible for the loss of all of one's family, social, and business gains. Infidelity is seen in an immature person whose excessive demands for love and security are unmet in his marriage, and he looks for it elsewhere. Needless to say, no one person will ever satisfy him. Unfortunately, because the incidence of infidelity and divorce is rising, and it is seen more in prominent people today, the younger generation might be prone to interpret this as being a desirable part of our culture, and fashionable.

The more mature and intelligent a man and a woman are, and the more suitable the "railroad ties" between them, the better they will be able to adjust to each other, and the more successful they will be in their marriage. They will be able to communicate with each other, understand each other's feelings and actions, and resolve the differences which arise between them. Some people are, of course, much more suited for marriage than others. Therefore, some should have to work much harder at making it successful. Unfortunately, those who are least suited for it generally have the least insight into the fact that they are unsuited, and they have the least motivation and ability to work at improving it. As implied previously, young people should be educated intellectually and emotionally before embarking upon marriage. After they marry, when problems arise, they should receive help in dealing with each other and with their children. They should not be allowed to rush to the divorce court, but instead be pressured to gain maturity and responsibility. The preservation of the family unit and fulfillment of their children's emotional potentials are at stake, and so is the future of mankind.

Both the husband and the wife who separate from each other or divorce each other, perhaps one partner more so than the other, are emotionally immature. They lack self-discipline, emotional control, and good judgment. They may have married too young, prematurely, or made a poor judgment as to their choice of mate. More important, due to immaturity, they have been unable to seek and capitalize from the help that they need to have preserved the marriage. They have not been able to adapt to each other and to receive proper fulfillment from each other.

Too frequently, one hears as grounds for divorce that a person is married to a "nagging wife" or an overly critical husband.

Just to blame the other person is not the answer. If a spouse is dealing with his or her mate in the above manner, it means that the mate is immature in allowing it, and the mate is just as much at fault that the problem exists. To complain, for example, that "my wife doesn't understand me", and to search for the "understanding" in another woman, implies that the husband has not been mature enough to have brought out his wife's potential. He has not helped her to gain the desire to learn to analyze and understand his feelings and actions.

It seems that the one most important reason why marriages fail is that people marry for fear of losing each other. This is further proof of the immaturity and insecurity of our present-day population. In analyzing these people, one usually finds that either the man or woman was fearful of not being accepted by the other, therefore overcompensating in giving of himself or herself, and in return receiving affection and acceptance from the partner. It is really one immature person pushing himself upon another, winning over the other, and the other person allowing himself to be overwhelmed because he is immature, too. After the initial attraction to each other, the more immature, insecure party, confronted with the dread of impending rejection—which rejection would accentuate his basic insecurity feelings—devotes more time and energy to cementing the relationship. This idea of "playing hard to get" is used as a trick by either spouse in winning over the other; that is, the one person may show apparent disinterest in the other, and the other person reacts to attain acceptance. These immature people cannot tolerate the threat of not being valuable and desired. Also contributing here is the fact that something or someone is desired more if it seems to be unattainable. Of course, both persons are immature in such a relationship and, unfortunately, they enter into a lifetime agreement based upon an untenable foundation. The more immature and insecure a person, the more apt that he or she will be swept into such an unhappy marital situation.

Common sense tells us that the contract of marriage is the most important contract of a person's life. Married people should realize that, in marrying, they have assumed a grave responsibility toward another human being, their mate. When children

196

arrive, the responsibility to the spouse increases, and there is now additional responsibility to the children. One frequently observes those who are immature giving love and attention to their families, thereby gaining the personal happiness and security which accompanies this, but only so long as there is not an impingement upon their own time and comfort. In marriage one cannot be selfish and think of oneself first, and allow innocent children, the result of one's actions, to suffer. A parent, no matter how immature, should be made to realize that he has to forgo immediate gratification for himself—that his car, his golf game, and his other personal pleasures have to take a "back seat" to his family. This does not mean that an immature spouse should be allowed to deny his mate any personal enjoyment in married life, and that marriage should be a life of sacrifice to the spouse and children. Mature husbands and wives are able to find a balance between their personal lives, which includes their jobs and social lives, and their devotion to their mate and children. For the reasons discussed, it seems logical to pressure married people to more mature behavior. Permission to marry should be granted only by examination and after serious deliberation.

* * * *

In this chapter we have covered the importance of marriage and the choice of marital partners. Some important psychodynamic features concerning the man-woman relationship were discussed. How males and females attract and complement each other, and some of the problems and reactions between each other were studied. The Railroad Track or Parallel Track Concept of Marriage, and the Unparallel Track Concept of the Origin of Schizophrenia were introduced.

It was explained that extra-marital sexual relations and divorce were displays of immature people. The Mature Person-to-Person Philosophy should be exercised to the limit by every man and woman, every spouse and parent, all of the time.

197

CHAPTER X

RAISING OF CHILDREN
TO BECOME MATURE INDIVIDUALS

To raise mature individuals, thereby preventing mental illness in our families and a perverted cultural trend in our society, is the main object of our labor. The mature individuals will be able to utilize the Mature Person-to-Person Philosophy more readily. They will choose from their ranks mature leaders who will exercise the Mature Person-to-Person Philosophy to the maximum degree, and prevent wars. The more mature people there are in the world, the less they will have to work at utilizing the Mature Person-to-Person Philosophy. It will be an easier life for them, not always having to be on guard that a person is immature and that he is going to try to take advantage of them. The immature person will be in contact with more and more mature people, who will be pressuring him to act in a mature way.

The Mature Person-to-Person Philosophy should be exercised between the husband and wife, and between them and their children. The children will learn from experience to use it with their parents and between themselves, and in every one of their other relationships in the present and future. They will be raised by their relatively mature parents as mature, secure people, having realized their full emotional and intellectual potentials. They will have received a mature relationship from their parents, and there will have been minimal sibling rivalry for the parents' attention and approval. They will be in good control of their aggressive tendencies, and in acceptance of outside controls from their parents, others in authority, and the law of the land. They will be receptive of the Mature Person-to-Person Philosophy. They will be secure and strong enough in every area of functioning so that they will not allow themselves and others

198

to be exploited by immature people. Their use of the Mature Person-to-Person Philosophy will be reinforced when they study it in the formal course in peace which they will take in high school.

The children will be raised to be adults without excessive aggression, resentment, and hatred, but with love and feeling for their fellow man. They will be unselfish. They will have understanding and empathy for another human being, and have the wisdom to negotiate differences between each other—knowing that might does not make one right. They will lean more toward morals and ethics and virtues. They will want to help one another and advance the lot of mankind. Each child's potential as a human being will have been nurtured from birth by parental feelings which will have been reciprocated. The more that the mother and father are mature, secure, and "giving" of themselves, the more love and warmth will the child acquire, and be able to "give" in return. The emotional potential of the child will have been stimulated to the fullest, which will influence his having positive feelings toward his siblings and other people. From having this capacity and from his dealings with people, he will be able to acquire even more feeling, empathy, and understanding in later years. He will seek the finer things in life.

People transmit their own problems in human relations to their children. In addition to the major problems, such as divorce, juvenile delinquency, crime, and mental illness, there are the more subtle, but extremely important, problems of undesirable personality characteristics, attitudes, habits, and values. There is also the all-important factor of parents raising children so that they will be subject to tension and stress in later life. They will have been raised to feel insecure, anxious, and competitive, so that predisposed organ-systems of their body will be placed under stress. This can result in a person's developing illnesses such as peptic ulcer, rheumatoid arthritis, and even coronary occlusion and cancer.

All the people in this world, including leaders, in some way, to some degree, are insecure. The infant begins to feel insecure from the time he begins to realize that his comfort and discomfort, such as a full stomach or a feeling of hunger, or being dry and warm versus feeling wet and cold, are dependent upon someone else. He begins to gain security and trust in his mother when he sees that he can depend upon her. Her own security and consequent lack of anxiety make him feel secure. Her love for him becomes reciprocated. His love for and trust in his mother is then extended to his father, siblings, and others, especially if these people are mature and no adverse circumstances arise when he is growing up. He will become more secure as he is raised in a stable environment, and begins to recognize his acceptance and self-worth. As the child grows older, even through adulthood, he will gain security from his accomplishments.

Mentioned was that a mother's lack of anxiety made her baby feel secure. On the other hand, an anxious mother makes an infant anxious and insecure. A mentally average or above-average baby is alert and sensitive, keen and perceptive to outside stimuli, even within the first few weeks of his life. The more intelligent the baby, the more sensitive and perceptive he will be to his environment. To the insecure, anxious mother, it will seem that her baby cries and spits up more often, and demands more attention, than the ordinary baby. This insecure, anxious mother will wonder if something is wrong with the baby, or if there is something wrong with her or the way she is caring for the baby because he is reacting in this manner. She will become even more anxious and unsure of herself. The baby now, being aware and sensitive to all stimuli, will react in being anxious, and may fuss, wet more often, and become colicky. He will grow to be irritable and angry for being uncomfortable, and he will begin to feel that he cannot rely upon his mother to keep him free of discomfort. This in turn creates more anxiety in the mother, and the vicious circle continues where anxiety and insecurity and immaturity are perpetuated. Hereditary predisposition and cultural factors will exaggerate these personality traits. The more anxious the mother becomes, the more anxious and insecure will grow the baby. He will cling to her, making her feel smothered, and more anxious. As the child grows older there will be inconsistent disciplining, overprotection, and an over-all pathological relationship between the anxious mother and the now-anxious child. The child will become more demanding and threatening to the mother, testing her frequently, which will cause her to have even more anxiety and guilt; and she will feel even more unsure that she is raising her child correctly. The presence of the father and the child's siblings, with their own personality problems, all interacting with each other, will add to the child's becoming immature and insecure. It is natural for the mother rather than the father to be closer to the baby, but it cannot be overemphasized that the father can be more responsible than the mother for the baby's anxiety and insecurity. He can be indirectly to blame by creating anxiety and insecurity in his wife due to his immature relationship with her. A below-average or lethargic baby may be ignored by his mother, so that he is not provided with enough stimulation to mature to his capacity. When he grows older, if the same slow development persists, an anxious mother will be responsible for creating anxiety and insecurity in him.

This book will help people to become more mature, secure, and less-anxious parents. They will be better prepared in the raising of their children, starting with their first child. As it is now, most parents mature themselves in the raising of their children, and they generally tend to do a better job with each succeeding child.

It should be understood that immature, insecure parents are responsible for nurturing their child's aggressive and violent tendencies. As stated in Chapter VI, aggression is a natural trait of all people, necessary for the attainment of personal security and self-preservation. All babies are born with the capacity to be extremely aggressive and violent, but not one is destined to resort to extremely aggressive and violent behavior during his lifetime. The development of aggression can be curtailed and prevented. A person's environment from birth can be such that he can unfold to his utmost capacity as a human being, so that there is little or no need for the extreme growth of his innate aggressive tendencies. If he gains the feeling of personal security from his parents, aggression will be at a minimum. His aggressive energies can be used in the realization of his potential in the search for his fulfillment as an individual. He will have no need or desire to advance himself due to comparing himself with others, and by being aggressive and exploitative with others.

He will have been raised by his mature, secure parents to be mature and secure. He will achieve even more maturity and security from succeeding on his own merit, and he will not be seeking security from the exploitation of others.

In previous chapters it was stated that, in order to realize one's own potential, one must have opportunities under a free government. In addition, unhealthy cultural trends which stunt a person's ability to think and feel for himself have to be changed. Preconceived judgment must be replaced by objectivity. To fulfill one's potential, one must be free from overprotection and domination by others. Also, emotional conflicts and neurotic motivations blocking a person from utilizing his ability have to be eliminated, or at least modified, through psychotherapy. Of great importance is to attempt to prevent in childhood these emotional conflicts and pathological motivations.

The children of today are raised by immature parents in such a manner that they are overprotected, "spoiled" in the sense of being given too much in the way of material things—and not disciplined. As a result, they lack independence, initiative, and self-discipline. The government, really the greedy politicians who are seeking votes and personal gain from their leadership positions, is dealing with the people in the very same way. People raised by immature parents, under such a government, do not desire or are incapable of studying and working, all of which contributes to nationwide poverty and a lack of progress.

Just as some people are less suited to marriage, there are people who are less suited to being good parents. Perhaps, most often, the suitability to marriage and parenthood coincide in the same person, and this is based chiefly upon the parents' emotional maturity. Just as in each grown-up there is a norm for emotional maturity, a child can be considered to be mature or immature according to an average for his chronological age. For example, a five-year-old boy may be having frequent temper-tantrums, such as those seen most often in two-year-olds. Mature children, like mature adults, unless they have reason to the contrary, will respect other people, both adults and children. However, immature children find it difficult to respect even the adults. Age itself is not enough for the children to respect a person, and the adults have to earn the children's respect by behaving in a mature way. Husbands and wives who merit the respect of each other usually merit the respect of their children. They are relatively mature people, and invariably they turn out to be good parents.

Immature, insecure parents are selfish, and they cannot give love, adequate limits, and independence to their children. They cannot complement each other, and they cannot "give" to each other and to the children. In fact, they are looking for more of everything for themselves. Sibling rivalry develops to an extraordinary degree where the children are vying with each other to obtain love and approval from their parents who cannot "give". The children also seek more in the way of material things, more toys or a larger piece of cake, and they complain that their brother or sister is getting more than they. The parents' favoring one child over another exaggerates the rivalry. This is frequently seen where the parents may dote upon a newborn to the neglect of the other children, when really the older children could derive more from the attention than the baby. Children missing their parents' attention and recognition, their love and acceptance, develop a feeling of rejection, worthlessness, and insecurity. Actually, no amount of time given by an insecure parent is satisfactory for the proper emotional growth of a child; in fact, an intense relationship with an insecure parent will only tend to make the child feel more insecure.

In trying to prove themselves adequate, the children become overly competitive, jealous, and resentful of each other. To an extreme degree they grow hateful and aggressive with one another, and they attempt to exploit each other and other people. They tease each other to retaliate and dominate the other, to feel superior and secure; but for the most part the teasing is unconsciously directed at their parents. They want to gain their parents' attention, receive punishment because of guilt feelings, or "get even" with them for their not being able to "give" a mature relationship—all related to the search for security. They become rebellious and negativistic with the parents, seeing them as weak people from whom they cannot receive security, and do not conform to the parents' way of living or to society in general. They grow up as resentful and selfish people, caring only for themselves, always feeling that they missed something

203

in childhood, and seeking in their every relationship only to "take" from others and not to "give".

From childhood, when they tried to gain favor, love and security from their "non-giving" parents, they establish an ingratiating pattern of behavior in which they attempt to "apple polish" their teachers, bosses, and others who can do them some good. From vying with and taking advantage of their siblings in order to be recognized by their parents, they adopt a behavior which is excessively competitive and exploitative in dealing with their classmates, fellow workers, and anyone else that they can dominate. They constantly compare themselves with others in "keeping up with the Joneses". When they themselves marry and have children, if nothing were done so that they changed, their own children may acquire similar personality traits.

An important point in producing mature individuals and leaders is the fine transition which takes place in early life when the child changes from one who takes orders and is completely dependent to one who accepts responsibility and achieves gradual independence. How such a successful transition takes place involves a number of factors. To the infant and preschool child, the parents need to offer love and acceptance. In order to do this the parents have to be mature and secure themselves, so that they are able to "give" of themselves. They have to possess a certain warmth which will serve to nurture their child's emotional growth. The child's inherent traits will attain the fullest degree of maturation. He will feel secure, so that he will not be afraid to accept responsibility, and he will have developed intellectually and in other areas so that he will be able to succeed at new things.

Another important factor is for the parents to be able to set consistent limits; which means, first, that they have to be in agreement with each other as to disciplinary measures and other major matters. This again requires mature, secure parents who are sure of themselves, and who will not be afraid that their child will dislike them and make them feel that they are inadequate parents when they impose restrictions. Actually, the child will gain a feeling of security from knowing his boundaries and realizing that his parents are understanding, fair, and strong, and that they know what to do in their dealings with him. Behavior such as this is a reflection of secure parents, and secure parents raise secure children. The children are able to accept love, reward, and punishment from their parents. They then become capable of giving love to the parents, and their siblings. They learn to "give and take" with all people. They develop a self-discipline and a responsibility for their actions. They have learned to trust and love their parents, siblings, and others. Brotherly love will extend itself to loving, respecting, and working compatibly with one another outside of the family. There will be no malicious and evil intent for others.

As the children grow older, they want to identify with their respective parents in becoming independent like them; and the parents, being mature individuals, do not want the children to remain dependent upon them. As mentioned earlier, immature parents gain a sense of importance from feeling necessary to their children. They foster a dependency relationship with them, overprotecting them. The overprotection causes the children to feel dominated and stifled, and they become prone to rebellious and explosive behavior. It is natural for an individual to express himself, to realize his potential as a human being. Being dominated, the children might become neurotically motivated and want to out-do their parents. As they grow older, they become hostile and aggressive toward the parents for not having prepared them for the failures and frustrations of life, and they tend to dominate and exploit others when they find themselves unable to compete with them on even terms.

As the relatively mature child advances in physical, intellectual and emotional development, he normally wants to undertake more to do for himself. Born of mature, secure parents, and mature himself, he does not compare himself with others and compete with them. Rather, he is secure enough and interested in utilizing his own potential and advancing himself. The parents should, through example and instruction, get the child to realize what is expected of him—things which are not beyond his capability. Frustrating assignments, severe criticism, and belittlement from the parents might deter the child from attempting anything on his own. In admiring his parents, and in achieving success, and in receiving praise from them, the child will gain self-confidence and security, and he will look forward with enthusiasm to doing new and more challenging things. He will be functioning intellectually and emotionally at his peak potential, which will ensure more success. Success breeds self-confidence and whets the appetite for more attempts at succeeding. He has gained the desire to take on more and more responsibility.

For example, a boy will observe his father's routine of shaving, washing, dressing, and eating, and of getting to work on time. He will be expected to maintain his own schedule, to get himself ready and to school on time. He should learn how and when to do his homework and chores. He should be pressured to plan and work out things for himself. It should be his responsibility to keep lists of things which have to be done, and to see to it that they are carried out to completion without having to be reminded and supervised. In the beginning he will have to be helped, reminded, and prodded to tend to his duties. As he grows older, however, he should be left alone to accomplish these things, and praised for his successful performance of them. It is important here for the parents not to continue doing too much for the child, not to tell him what to play and what to wear, when to get ready and when to leave. The parents should not shield him from any appropriate punishment if he fails to produce according to his ability. He may enjoy being told what to do and being catered to as a child, but he will meet with disappointment when he realizes as an immature adult that he is not up to par compared to his self-reliant peers. He, like all immature people, will not work and accept responsibility if someone else is available and ready to think and work for him. He will be quick to "lean on" someone, as it will be the easiest thing for him to do. He will always seek the easiest way of not thinking and doing for himself. Most people can perform very adequately if given the opportunity, or if it is necessary for them to do so.

If a child has too much done for him by the parents, he will not only be irresponsible, but he will rebel against being given any orders, and he will grow hostile at being dependent. He will feel and be inadequate because he has not learned. An immature child rebels if he feels that someone such as a parent or teacher is attempting to force him to work and study. If he feels

206

that he is working and studying for himself, rather than for others, he may try to work even beyond his capacity. A relatively mature child, on the other hand, would work to the best of his ability even if he felt pressured to do so. He would feel loved and accepted, and he would seek to please, gaining personal security from his successes. He would work to his capacity to prove himself to be adequate to others and to himself. He would grow up to be a responsible person.

Apropos of this, it is interesting that large numbers of parents are taking evening courses in modern mathematics, which their children are now studying in school. They explain that they are interested to know what their children are learning. However, the real reason in most instances seems to be their wanting to help their children with their schoolwork. They feel important and personally secure in doing this, but in the process they are fostering the dependency of the children.

Also in the same vein, in analyzing children afflicted with the so-called school phobias in which they ostensibly have a fear of the school, it is invariably uncovered that the children really are suffering from anxiety and fear relative to leaving their home and mother. The mothers, extremely insecure themselves, have overprotected their children and made them fearful and insecure. The more insecure the mother, the more the child will seek her and attach himself to her. The mother on the one hand will be pleased by her child's need of her, yet on the other will be annoyed and feel drained because of the little that she has to "give" to the child. In both overprotecting and rejecting the child, the mother is fostering even more dependency. As she sees the child fearful and inept, her own inadequacy feelings and feelings of insecurity are even more aroused, and she wants to help her child even more, overprotecting him all the more. This forms a vicious circle which can be interrupted only when the mother begins to feel more personally secure.

Similarly, an immature, insecure father may find that his child is seeking what seems to be an extraordinary amount of attention from him. The child may be afraid to wander too far from the house, and he may have nightmares and want to crawl into bed with the father. Really, the child is looking for personal security which would come from a mature relationship with his father. It should be understood that these problems, such as school phobias and nightmares, are not necessarily specifically related to the father or the mother. In most instances, both parents are immature and insecure, and they both contribute to their children's immaturity and insecurity, and the concomitant problems.

Parents should not give their children more toys, clothes, or choice of food than they need. Of course, immature children will have insatiable needs, and their immature parents will tend to provide them with too much in the material sense because they have too little to "give" in the emotional sense. Also, the parents may be fearful that the children will not like them if they are deprived of what other children possess. They are afraid that their offspring will not grow up to be good and successful children. To really help their children, the parents should not over-indulge them, and not be quick to replace their clothes and toys which are destroyed due to carelessness. The responsibility of caring for personal belongings, and of doing homework and chores, should be that of the children. A child will not learn to be a responsible person if his parents buy him a newspaper delivery job, drive him from door to door to deliver the papers when it rains, and handle his accounts for him.

A child will gain self-satisfaction from his gradual attainment of responsibility and independence. If he should perform poorly, such as being late for school, he should be made to realize it is not ordinarily the fault of the mother, and that any punishment inflicted upon him is the result of his own making. Having known the penalty for not conforming, and not caring enough to avoid the penalty, he should now suffer the consequences. Also, it is not the school that he should blame for his being punished; for it is he himself who is responsible for his misdeed, and the school is merely the instrument for the punishment. It is the same as being arrested for driving through a stop sign and wrongly blaming the police officer and judge for being fined. They are the instruments of the law, and it is the responsibility of the driver to obey the rules and avoid being punished. Of course, the punishment should be proportionate to the violation.

In order to get their child to obey and conform, a parent should not have to make compromises, give favors, or pay the child. There are certain rules of the household to which the child should be expected to adhere. There are certain chores which he should perform. As stated before, children feel secure from knowing there are rules, and that their parents are knowledgeable and secure enough to enforce them.

Parents may wonder why their children have learned only how to "take", and not to "give". Even many of the more mature parents, who have been capable of giving love and understanding to their infants and children so that a reciprocal relationship of love and of "give" and "take" ensues, err when the children grow older. Through giving allowances, really bribes, to the child, a practice seen in almost all American families, they give to the child the impression that he is being paid to conform, that he is one to be catered to, that people owe him a living. He is being paid for merely living his family life in a routine fashion. The children expect the same in later life from others, and especially from the government in the way of hand-outs. They feel that their government and the world owe them something. They have not learned to appreciate the real value of anything if they have been given things for nothing without having had to work for them. They adopt the policy to expend the least amount of energy necessary, because there will always be someone else present to work and care for them.

Parents usually rationalize the giving of allowances in saying that the children will learn the value of the dollar and how to manage their money. Actually, by receiving money continuously, they look for ways in which to spend it and not to save it. It is immature parents who would be more apt to give allowances to their immature, demanding children. Many will do as their neighbors do without thinking much about it. The real reason that parents give the allowances is that they may have some doubt that they are good parents. They may not be devoting enough time to the children, or they may not really be able to give them a warm relationship. The parents may want to impress them with the money they have, wanting to be admired and liked by them. They are substituting money for a mature relationship.

In general, the father brings home the money, the mother does the housework, and the children should be expected to contribute their share without pay by doing well in school, conforming socially, and helping the father and mother with certain household chores. The chores should be performed in the spirit of the parents and children working together for the common good of the family. The child's education, his clothes and lunches, music instructions, reasonable entertainment expenses, and the like, should be paid for by the parents. These items are all part of the proper raising of children, and the parents should not make the children feel indebted to them for providing these services. For special occasions, where the child may require money of his own, he can draw from his personal savings given to him for birthdays and other holidays. When he grows older, he can earn more money from small jobs outside of the home.

Immature, insecure parents are indecisive and unsure of their ideas and actions, and they do not set effective limits in regard to behavior for their children. The children quickly sense that the parents are uncertain as to what to allow and not allow them to do. The realization of this causes anxiety and insecurity in the children. They test the parents constantly to see if the parents will give in to their demands, which they so frequently do. The parents sometimes permit a certain thing, then refuse to give permission another time. Worse still, some parents refuse a child's request, then, after continued urging by the child, they give in. Such action causes confusion, frustration, anger, and hostility in the child. The child does not learn what is right and what is wrong behavior, what is mature and what is exploitative behavior. The child blames the parents for seeming to be overly strict, whereas he would only have himself to blame if he were being punished for breaking set rules. Not being sure of themselves as to how to deal with their children, and trying to exercise what they read and hear about child behavior, the parents seem almost afraid to react normally to their own feelings. They would, in fact, be more effective in dealing with their children if they followed their feelings and common sense.

It is important to begin setting effective limits as soon as the child is able to understand what one wants and does not want him to do. This is before the age of one. If there is no effective discipline the first ten years of a child's life, and then it is attempted, both the disciplinarian and the child cannot expect to have an easy time of utilizing and accepting it. The disciplinarian will find it difficult to change, and the child will balk at conforming, especially with the same disciplinarian. The parents should be knowledgeable as to the setting of limits. Equally as important, they should be strong enough emotionally and physically, or have the physical support, to enforce any needed punishment.

With inadequate parents, the child will react to the weak, seemingly-ignorant parents with both love and contempt, sometimes with pity, consciously and unconsciously dissatisfied that the parents are not a stronger source of security to him. The child will rebel against the parents, and eventually against his teachers and all authority figures. As an adult, he will rebel and exploit any weak person, just as he did originally with his parents. He will have a temper-tantrum, so to speak, in order to attain something which he feels he cannot do without. Chiefly due to ineffective disciplining as a child, he will be pathologically motivated as an adult to achieve "at any cost" and will exploit everyone with whom he comes in contact.

It does not mean that a parent, in setting limits for his child, dislikes the child and is taking advantage of him. It does mean that the parent is not allowing the child to take advantage of him, and that the parent likes the child enough to want him to behave in a mature manner. The child, in his acceptance of the limits imposed by his parents, will in later life respect all authority figures and the limits imposed by them. It should be stressed that if the parents do not set adequate controls, the children will rebel against them and all people in positions of authority. Of course, the children's acceptance of limits pre-supposes that both the parents and all the other authority figures are mature and earn the respect of the young people. The acceptance of limits will enhance the acceptance of laws of the schools, communities, countries, and of the world. Children gain a sense of security from knowing that strong, knowledgeable parents and others in authority are available to restrict them, keep them from getting hurt, and help them to behave maturely.

In setting an effective limit, a parent should think over the restriction he is to place upon the child, explain the punishment if the child disobeys, and follow through with the punishment if the child does in fact not obey. For example, if he has thought it over and has decided that he does not want his child to climb on top of the kitchen table, or else he will spank him, the parent should explain this to him, and spank the child if he does get on the table. This does not mean merely tapping the child on his rear, as the child will have won out in his search for attention—something which might have prompted his action in the first place. It means causing a discomfort, but not maliciously, that is mental, emotional, and physical, which the child does not care to experience again. The punishment, a discomfort replacing a pleasurable feeling, may be in the form of reprimand, deprivation, isolation, or spanking. All of these are really self-defensive measures used to protect oneself or one's property from the child's exploitative behavior. Some children will seek even a severe beating in order to gain attention from a parent. Here the answer is for the parents to try to give the children a mature relationship. It is not true what so many parents say, that "some children just do not respond to any amount of love or punishment." Of course, punishment is only truly effective when given in conjunction with love. Invariably, a secure parent, one who can give love and attention to his child, can administer punishment when it is warranted, but finds less need to do so. On the other hand, an insecure parent finds his child misbehaving more, but due to not being sure if he is right and wanting to be liked, he finds himself unable to administer adequate punishment. If there is no doubt as to setting the limit in the first place, there should be no doubt as to inflicting the punishment if the child disobeys. Limits which are imposed from the beginning are quite readily accepted. Those which are laid down after a period of time of no restrictions are usually opposed, and accepted only resentfully.

Unknowledgeable and insecure parents invariably tell their children to do something half a dozen times before their wishes are obeyed. They will at first speak softly, and even not check, but hope that their orders have been carried out. If they follow through and are stern with the sixth command, they will usually have a good result. One wonders why the parents do not speak sternly the first time when they have seen on countless occasions that the children respond best to the sternness. Children and adults alike tend to rebel to repeated demands, especially when they already know what they should be doing. A relatively-mature person will become annoyed by the continuous reminders, but he will carry out the orders anyway. An immature person will be angered at the one harping at him, as he will feel it is an attack upon his intelligence and independence. It will make him feel belittled and insecure.

Frequently it is heard from the mothers of undisciplined, "spoiled" children that a child "wants to do everything the way he wants it when he wants it." "He wants to do only what he wants to do." "He always wants his own way." "He will not accept correction." "He just won't take orders." They sometimes proudly refer to the child as being "strong-willed", having "a mind of his own", being "aggressive", or having "initiative". They may say that he has "too much energy", "a very active mind", or "a great imagination", when really the child is extremely anxious, trying to prove himself, and in search of personal security. The child is erroneously thought to be independent, when in actuality he is found to be very dependent. Invariably, he is rebellious and negativistic toward the mother in the home, but timid and insecure in public. The mother may believe that she is overly strict with the child, but in reality she is inconsistent in disciplining him, and most of her efforts amount to her merely nagging and yelling at him. Actually, such a child's first concern is immediate gratification for himself. He may not want to attend school or church, or he may refuse medical or dental aid, because it is not pleasurable and involves some discomfort to him. He will not be able to see the future rewards, and resists to such a degree that insecure parents might let him have his own way in order to be not disliked by him. It is reasonable to believe that the parents should know more than their children about such matters, and they should force the children to comply. Otherwise, the children will grow up to be rigid, stubborn, and unyielding, and make excessive demands upon other people. They will be inconsiderate of others. There would be fewer behavior problems in later years, less defiance of authority, and less aggression and exploitation. Children rebel only against immature authority; they quickly learn that they cannot rebel against mature authority. As they mature, they find themselves not wanting to even try to rebel against mature authority. Parents, teachers, and others who are more immature than their children cannot hope to be effective in disciplining them.

The parents should set the rules for the household. No matter how old the children, if they live in the same house, they should be expected to conform to the rules. Actually, if the parents are relatively mature, there should be few problems between them and the children even when the children are older. In the case of immature parents, if the children have attained the average age of self-sustenance and they do not wish to abide by the parents' rules, they should be told to live elsewhere. The problem here is due to the fact that the parents have been responsible for the raising of the immature children who are rebellious to their commands. They may be overprotective, excessively demanding, and unreasonable in their requests of the children. The children may be reacting with similar excessive demands and unreasonableness, and they are rebellious and negativistic with the parents. The ironical part of all of this is that the children are dependent and inept, and they do not really want to leave their parents even though they are constantly fighting for more freedom. The parents continually complain of their children's transgressions, and they may be telling them to leave, yet they are unable to follow through in letting the children go live elsewhere. They are unwilling to give up their overprotectingness and the dependency relationship.

Just as young people should live elsewhere if they do not wish to abide by their parents' rules, they should transfer or move if they do not want to follow the rules of their college or university, church, or government. The only other alternative is dignified protestation and an attempt at re-education of their superiors, if they believe that their ideas are more correct than those of the superiors. If they completely and violently oppose the rules set down by an institution, they should leave and try to establish their own institution. Of course, that they could be successful at doing this would be highly unlikely. Mature people can exchange ideas in a peaceful manner and arrive at answers which will advance both parties.

Children are frequently attention-seekers at home and in

school, misbehaving and interrupting the routine, so that they will be noticed, feel that they are worth something, and feel secure. A child may tease and exploit his parents indirectly through teasing his siblings, as stated previously, or he may tease his mother "to get a rise out of her"—that is, to irritate her and gain her attention, and to feel important or elevated in position. The child may interfere with the mother's telephone conversation, or create a disturbance when in a grocery store, knowing that the mother during those times may feel to be at a disadvantage to reprimand and punish him. The child may climb on the mother's lap when she is dressed in her best clothes, or may waste his mother's time, especially when mother is busy or in a hurry. Even if he succeeds with his teasing, however, he will feel insecure for having such an inadequate parent whom he can manipulate and overwhelm. He may become confronted with symptoms of personal insecurity such as anxiety, hyperactivity, more misbehavior, withdrawal, daydreaming, short attention-span, and learning difficulty. The child's symptoms will create more anxiety in both the parents and the child. There will be an intensification of the pathological relationship which already exists between the child and his parents.

Teasing is immature behavior in which a child seeks to feel secure from his having successfully taken advantage of another. It is only in his comparing himself to the teased one that he is superior, however, and in reality he has not advanced himself from the teasing. Children tease for a number of reasons, but they all amount to attempting to build up the self and to feel secure. Generally, those children who are teased by older children will turn to teasing younger ones when given the opportunity. Teasing sets a bad example for children, as it is the forerunner of people taking advantage of people in later life. It should not be allowed by parents. The parents, in not permitting the teasing, in being strong and secure in enforcing limits, are a source of security to the children. The parents should intercede and pressure the teaser to direct his aggressive energies to the fulfillment of his potential. They should not let the teaser turn to others to tease. Also, they should not permit the teased child to turn to others to tease, but they should pressure him to deal with the teaser by himself, or to seek help from them or others. All relatively-mature people will readily give aid. By not being quick to shield a teased child unless he is in obvious immediate need, but by separating the teaser and the teased until they want to try to get along with each other again, both can gain responsibility in learning how to handle their own problems. Both will grow more mature. They will become more secure from the parents' having shown security, and from their having been successful in dealing with each other. This is in keeping with the Mature Person-to-Person Philosophy.

Ideally, both the mother and father should share in being the chief disciplinarians of their children. The church, schools, police, government, or anyone else, should not usurp the parents' roles as the chief disciplinarians. It should not be made too easy for the parents to relinquish their responsibility for the management of the children. They should be pressured to seek professional help for any mental and emotional problems if it seems that they are in need of it.

If both the mother and father are mature, one will not look to the other to reprimand their child, but will handle the disciplining as the need arises. They will be in general agreement as to policies regarding their child's behavior, and will not permit the child to turn one against the other. In the case of immature parents, it might occur that one of them may countermand a spouse's limit in order to gain the child's favor. If both parents are immature and insecure, they will be quick to criticize each other's lack of discipline of their child. They promote their own feeling of adequacy from belittling the other. The child invariably feels insecure, and he is raised as an anxious, fearful, and confused person.

Usually, one parent is weaker than the other, and the stronger one is forced into assuming a dominant role as the principal disciplinarian. An immature, insecure father may over-compensate in being assertive on his job, and have a let-down at home to the extent that he leaves all the decisions and disciplining to his wife. It may be that both the father and the children may be very timid and compliant at work and in school, but behave in a dominating and disruptive fashion when in the home. It is sometimes seen that the mother tends to ignore her child's "trivial" exploitations of her because she is exasperated, and unsure how to handle the child. A mother may resent her husband's weakness in disciplining the children, belittle him before them, and make it all the more difficult for him to be respected by them and to discipline them. If the mother is not handling the job of disciplining properly, the father may overcompensate in this area and be looked upon by the children, and even by the mother, as an ogre. The father might complain that he is afraid to discipline his child for fear of hurting him. The mother may prevent the father from imposing any disciplinary measures. She may overprotect the child, and set even fewer restrictions than previously.

As mentioned earlier, the immature parents are in a constant struggle competing with each other, trying to outdo each other to be better by comparison, and to feel valuable and secure. They are vying with each other to be favored by their children. In feeling inadequate as a parent and in wanting to be liked by the children, a parent may let up on the setting of limits and disciplining, bribe the children with material gifts, and tend to overprotect them. On the surface, and especially to the children, such a parent appears to be a good parent, and he gains a sense of security from this. Occasionally, both parents, being unsure of themselves, become truly overly-strict and uncompromising in dealing with their children. In trying to be adequate parents and not make any mistakes, they overcompensate and become perfectionistic. This only breeds more rebelliousness and negativism in the children. The parents may dominate and belittle the children so much that they grow up to be insecure and dependent. At the other extreme the most immature parents, due to rigid psychological defenses and little or no insight as to their patterns of behavior, completely reject their children and do not discipline them at all.

The answer to this aspect of disciplining is for both the mother and father to try to act as maturely as possible, and to complement each other in the combined roles of being chief disciplinarians. They should be in agreement as to schedules, proper behavior, punishment, and other features in the raising of their children. The behavior of the parents should be exemplary for the sake of the children. One parent should not step in and take over the reprimanding of a child from another parent, as this practice is degrading to the first parent, and the children will try even more to take advantage of him. Each one should bear his own responsibility and not take advantage of the other by looking to the other to handle his or her problems. Each should support and pressure the other to enforce his or her own disciplinary measures by refusing to take on the spouse's responsibility. This, of course, is the Mature Person-to-Person Philosophy in action. Both the mother and father will gain self-confidence and security from their success in setting limits and properly disciplining their children, and in seeing them raised as mature and secure individuals.

Occasionally, it is seen that an insecure parent has been unable to set adequate limits for a particular child, and as a result of this failure the parent develops feelings of anxiety, frustration, and hostility toward the child. Even more hostility and dislike for the child develop as the child's behavior becomes "spoiled" and obnoxious. Now, it is relatively easy for the parent to favor the child's siblings. When the child sees that he is being rejected, he will fight all the more for recognition and acceptance, resorting to even more attention-getting misbehavior. He will invariably succeed at being noticed, because the parent has been unable to set adequate limits to any misbehavior in the first place. The parent becomes even more anxious and insecure as to how to deal with the child. He may feel that he is a bad parent. The child will develop into being an immature and insecure person if this parent-child relationship is not altered.

In setting the limits of behavior, and in punishing a child when he disobeys, the parent must guard against an attitude of constant belittlement of the child. To an immature parent, the child's continual misbehavior will seem to be a continual act of exploitation directed at him. In effect, this may prove to be the case. It would then be a usual reaction for the parent to feel hostile in relation to the child and retaliatory in regard to everything that the child may do. To avoid this, it is necessary for the parent to deal with every act of misbehavior separately. A constant grudge should not be held against the child. A build-up of anger and resentment brought about because of many preceding, unresolved incidents should be guarded against. The parent should deal appropriately with every incident as it occurs. He can then wipe the slate clean, so to speak, and maintain an over-all atmosphere of affection and acceptance of the child. Only when the child misbehaves does the parent punish—which admittedly is belittlement, but belittlement of the child's act of misbehavior and not of the child himself. If the parent does not deal with each provoking incident as it arises, or sometimes leaves it for the spouse or someone else to handle, he will find himself continually belittling and exploiting the child. He, of course, will be acting immaturely, and he will be raising an immature, insecure child.

If parents are so immature that they are obviously failing in the management of their children, they should gain help from a higher authority to control the children. Frequently, the parents who are struggling and losing the control of their rebellious offspring will turn against all other authority. They will oppose and even undermine the efforts of the police and the courts. They will side with their children even though they can barely tolerate them, possibly so that the others will not succeed and prove the parents as being inadequate disciplinarians. Perhaps the parents, in protecting their youngsters, are really protecting themselves, in that they feel the children's misbehavior is a reflection of their own personalities. In the last analysis they do want the children to like them, and they do want to be thought of as good parents. Having successful children would make them successful parents, and make them feel more secure.

It should be stressed that children who are limited in their behavior are not limited in their ability to be creative. Many insecure parents tend to rationalize that they must give their children freedom, even to the extent that they can do whatever they wish, if they are ever going to realize their creative potential. Of course, the parents may truly believe this, but basically, they are not strong enough emotionally, not sure of themselves, so that they might prevent the children from misbehaving. Actually, it is when the children do misbehave, when they are confused as to what is right and wrong behavior, and insecure due to the parents' apparent ignorance and weakness, that they become anxious, inattentive, and befuddled. They are then in a state in which they cannot think clearly, function up to par, fulfill their potential, and be creative. It is true that, when a government, parents, or other authority, or when a person himself due to emotional problems, imposes severe restrictions, one is incapable of functioning at a peak capacity. However, this is different from a parent's not allowing a child to take advantage of him. Children who are not permitted to misbehave are being done a favor. They will have the opportunity to grow up to be mature and secure, to realize their potential, and to become truly creative and unique individuals.

The number of children that parents can raise to become mature individuals depends upon the maturity of the parents. Emotionally-stable parents can raise one to any number of mature children. Of course, it may prove more difficult to raise one or a great many children, as compared to a family of three or four. It should be stated, also, that the parents of one or of a great many children, excluding religious or similar motivating factors, may be very insecure, basically. They may feel it might be easier to handle one child, or they may seek security from a great many children. They may feel more secure and cared-for being surrounded by a crowd of loved ones. Some may be fearful that one or two children could be physically or mentally handicapped, or could die, and that at least some of their children out of a large number might grow to be successful. Some may hope that at least one of their children will succeed where they themselves have failed. Parents who plan to have only one child may feel psychologically and financially incapable of raising more than the one.

Immature parents will find difficulty in raising any number of children, and the children themselves will have to work extremely hard to attain maturity. An only child may benefit from the fact that his immature parents do not have to "give"—that is, give a mature relationship, love and effective discipline, of which they have little—to other children. However, he will suffer because he will be the focus of all their pathological influence. By the same token, a large number of children will benefit from the fact that there will be a dilution of their parents' pathological influence on them. However, they will suffer because the parents have to distribute among all the children that which they have very little to "give".

Most people working with children who have emotional problems will probably agree that adopted children have disproportionately more problems than others. Invariably, it is found that the adoptive parents of these children are more insecure and anxious than they no doubt would be had they their own children. They feel more tense in the handling of someone else's baby. The reason for this seems to be that their basic feelings of insecurity and inadequacy are accentuated by their not having been able to have children of their own. They are generally at an older and more inflexible age when they do get around to adopting. They may have only one child or, at most, two, and the children are usually of different parents and of different appearance and temperament. If older, the children may have had unhappy experiences living in previous homes prior to being adopted. These and other factors place both the adoptive parents and the adopted children at a disadvantage. These new parents are placed under pressure to prove themselves to be adequate parents. They have to answer to the adoption agency, their relatives and friends, and themselves. They tend to dote upon the first child, which promotes sibling rivalry. They are afraid that they will be disliked by the children, so they overprotect, give too much in the way of material gifts, and do not discipline effectively. They may even fear that the children might be taken away from them. Considering everything, it takes more mature people to properly raise adopted children than it does to raise their own.

Just as adopted children have more emotional problems, all children not raised by their true mother and father are at a disadvantage in being more prone to immaturity and emotional difficulties. This applies to illegitimate children, and those of divorced parents, or of families where a mother or father died when the children were still at a young age. This is not to say that there are not innumerable foster parents who are much more suitable as parents than the children's true parents. Also, it does not mean that countless children do not have it much better living with foster parents than if they had their true parents. All things being equal, children raised by true parents have an advantage over being raised by foster parents. True parents have the most potential to bring out their children's potentials. The children who lose their parents must adapt and compensate as well as they are able, so that they can grow up to be mature, secure individuals.

Due to divorces, children being raised in nurseries, both parents working, jobs requiring fathers to travel and be away from home, private schools, summer camps, nursing homes, and other factors, the present-day family is spending less and less time together. Due to emotional conflicts and the inability to communicate on a mature level, there is a trend to even less togetherness in the family circle. We frequently see children requesting to have their friends accompany them on family trips or vacations because they do not feel comfortable in the presence of only their family. They have not learned to communicate with their parents and siblings. There is competition, not a spirit of love and helpfulness, between the siblings. The children are not satisfied with the family relationship, in that they show a preference for being with those whom they feel understand them better. Of course, for children to be too closely attached to the family and home, without outside friendships and interests, is just as bad a situation. The problem of present-day family disunity is due to inadequate relationships between immature parents and their children. By the time the children become older, the pattern has already been set, and the parents then err in allowing the older children to disrupt family harmony even more.

Children on the whole feel more secure when they have a daily routine to follow, and they are organized as to their short-term and long-term goals. Although a certain amount of flexibility is necessary, for the most part a child accomplishes more and has more peace of mind from having set rules by which to abide. Good habits and an orderly routine help to train a person to have a clear-thinking and logical mind. A child should have a sufficient amount of restful sleep and should get to bed at an early hour. Older siblings should be permitted to stay up later in keeping with their having more responsibilities and more privileges. To eliminate delays and conflicts, the children should bathe and prepare for bedtime immediately after supper, then do homework, review, and read until it is time to go to bed. No television, radio, or other similar activities should be allowed on the evenings preceding schooldays. Upon awakening by themselves, they should wash, dress, and eat immediately. It is not necessary for children to be awakened by parents and alarm clocks if they are getting the proper amount of sleep. The responsibility of preparation for school and getting to school on time should be placed upon the shoulders of the youngster. After school the child might be involved in extra-curricular activities, but he should spend some time out-of-doors. Depending upon the age of the child, recreation and homework will occupy his time before supper. Regular trips to the library and reading for pleasure should be a part of his schedule.

The mother and father separately should talk to each child individually every day, even if only for a few minutes, so that the children will learn to confide their feelings and not have to continually vie with their siblings for their parents' love and attention. It is the quality and not the quantity of the time spent with the children which is of most importance. The emotional maturity of the parents and the mature relationship which they give to the children is of prime significance. From their parental relationships, the children will learn from example and instruction what the parents expect of them. They will assume the responsibility of planning and carrying out an orderly and rewarding daily routine.

Today there is too much adult supervision and organized play for the children, such as Little League Baseball, so that the children are deprived of the freedom to plan for themselves, to take the initiative, and to learn how to get along with one another, that is, to "give and take". Too much organized activity does not allow the children to think, meditate, and individuate. Frequently the children are the victims of their parents' displaced neurotic desires, encouraging competitiveness and aggression in the children. The children do not play for enjoyment or to perfect their playing ability—that is, their physical potential; but to best their opponents and gain favor from their parents. The parents, driven by neurotic motivation, not looking only to realize their own potentials, show their children through example to compare themselves with others, and pressure them to be competitive and to out-do their peers. As stated before, this competitiveness is an extension of extreme sibling rivalry brought about by immature, insecure parents who cannot "give". Tempering sibling rivalry will in later life lessen "keeping up with the Joneses", "holding someone else down to build oneself up", and aggressive and exploitative behavior.

It is not necessary for adults to constantly amuse children. The trend nowadays to build expensive youth recreational centers where they are not needed is, again, in keeping with the children receiving too much for little or no effort in return. The problem here lies in the fact that the communities which can most afford these centers are those in which the children least need them. Children who have been raised by mature parents will be kept busy working for their high goals, and they will have little time to spend in such centers, anyway. The object is to provide areas of recreation wherever necessary, such as in cities, but to pressure the children to take the initiative to entertain themselves.

There is a current, so-called modern trend for children to call their parents and other adults by their first names. Some of these parents say that this does not bother them—in fact, that it is a sign of closeness between them and their children. One could safely guess that most of them really are annoyed by this practice. It should not be tolerated. Such familiarity denotes disrespect for, and belittlement of, the adults. A parent cannot be both a "pal" and a good parent to a child. There is a marked difference between a parent being a "pal" and a mature father or mother.

In not being properly motivated to study and work, but in being pressured to do so by immature, lazy, and ignorant parents, children tend to rebel. A mother who spends most of her time watching television, and a father who plays cards or golf during all of his leisure time, should not expect that their child will study hard because they tell him it is the right thing to do. When a child observes that his parents work unselfishly, diligently, and perseveringly, he will be more apt to follow their direction. It will not be likely that he will quit music lessons after taking them for one month, or give up in despair because of a difficult school assignment. He will not seek only that which comes easily and which is pleasurable to him. He will learn to defer immediate gratification, to be patient and persevering, and

224

to work hard for the greater rewards which he will reap in the future. He will not be afraid to try something new, and he will work at it to its completion. He will not shun the least amount of discomfort and frustration, but he will put forth effort in an attempt to adapt, to overcome problems, and to succeed.

Parents should continue to strive to attain their own goals. Not having achieved them, they invariably project their unfulfilled desires upon their children. If the parents are dissatisfied with their roles in life, if they feel that they are failing in the home and on the job, they will become too engrossed in the lives of their children. They will be disheartened by every one of their children's reversals, and annoyed by the children's insignificant antics. If they were successful themselves, they would not tend to live their children's lives. The children would be allowed to grow more independently, and not be subjected to their parents' pathological influences.

It must be emphasized that children should be expected to conform generally to the standard patterns of behavior set by the population. They should be expected to behave properly in the home, the school, and the social environment. They should be expected to perform to the limit of their capacity in school, just as adults should perform in the same way at work. Children should learn to play fairly, so that in later life they will deal fairly in their businesses. Mature children will have learned to "give and take", to share fairly with each other. Through their parents' expectations, example and instruction, through their mature relationship with them, and in their search for more personal security, the children will have become motivated to study and work hard, and to succeed on their own merit. It has been mentioned that it is not enough for parents to merely lecture children as to what they should do and how they should behave. In working hard themselves, and in guiding their children when necessary, the parents pave the way for the children to take the initiative, seek achievement, and fulfill their potentials. In the process the children will gain confidence, responsibility, independence, maturity, and personal security.

As stated in Chapter I, immature people who are neurotically motivated do contribute to the progress of civilization in their sporadic endeavors. In the process of proving themselves adequate to significant persons, they overcompensate and become successful. Due to their immature parents, deprivation, and excessive sibling rivalry with resulting competitiveness, among other things, they may in their search for "more of everything" during their lifetime succeed in achieving a great amount of education, money, power, or fame. However, they invariably succeed at the expense of others. They are never truly happy and satisfied, and they never feel that their goals are fulfilled. They do not ever feel really secure. A great deal of harm is done from their example of exploitation of immature people—harm which far outweighs what they contribute to the advancement of civilization. They may contribute in a materialistic sense, but their actions are detrimental to the generations which follow them in the humanistic sense. It is the more mature people of the world who are responsible for the uninterrupted and lasting progress of civilization. Each individual gains true self-satisfaction and personal security only when he sets and fulfills his own goals, not comparing himself with others, but developing his own potential to the fullest.

The importance of the family unit cannot be overly stressed. It is through the close relationships of marriage and family life that people have advanced to the present stage of development without destroying each other. The family has been responsible for the maturation of man's emotions. The ability for man to have feelings, both positive and negative, plus his capacity to reason, have been essential for the establishment of a social order. Whether man was motivated by positive feelings in his search for survival and security for himself and his loved ones, or whether he was motivated by negative feelings in trying to best his rival and in the process gain a similar security for himself and those close to him, he still contributed some to the advancement of civilization. It is only through the mature, loyal family unit that unselfish children will be raised and the human race will continue to fully mature.

From being raised by mature, secure parents, children will feel secure, and have feelings and compassion for other people. Their family environment, due to their parents' having been chaste prior to marriage, and faithful as spouses and parents, will have been conducive for the realization of full emotional

226

development. Their parents, self-satisfied because they have gained success in their careers and marriage, and fulfillment of their potentials, had been able to "give" of themselves to each other, and to the children. The children will not have grown up having the feeling of having "missed out" in childhood, and looking always "for more", always "taking" and not "giving". They will not have felt rejected by their parents, and will not have developed feelings of selfishness, jealousy, and resentfulness. They will have had a mature relationship with their siblings, sharing feelings of love and helpfulness for each other, and not a neurotic competitiveness. They will be self-satisfied with having been able to achieve their potentials, and in having attained fulfillment and maturity in all areas of functioning. They will gain more security from their successes, and have little or no need or desire to exploit others in the search for security. Their family unit will have been a stable and a happy one. They will have had a close relationship with their parents, siblings, grandparents and other relatives. They will have acquired deep feelings for the members of their family, which will be extended to their friends and to all people.

* * * *

To summarize, we have seen that parents transmit their own problems to their offspring; and that they can, if they concentrate upon correcting the problems, raise less aggressive and more mature, secure, and successful children. "Non-giving" parents, overprotection, teasing, and disciplining were discussed at some length in reference to a child's developing responsibility and gradual independence. The importance of the family unit was stressed. The pattern of behavior and daily routine of children were studied in regard to the achievement of responsibility, and the planning and attainment of mature goals.

In conclusion, we, all the people of the world, have to "grow up"—that is, attain emotional maturity—before it is too late. We have to grow emotionally as well as physically and intellectually, and become complete men and women, mature and strong in every area of functioning. We must raise a world of people who are personally secure and self-disciplined, and who have a purpose to living which is more than only seeking self-gratification.

Just as we would not allow a child to play with a loaded gun, we should not be at rest knowing that immature people are now in control of nuclear devices capable of destroying the world.

Parents must raise mature children and prevent mental illness in their family, since the family unit is the mainstay in a civilized society. Parents who strive for maturity in themselves will raise children to be mature, to be virtuous, understanding of themselves and others, and charitable. The children will grow to be amenable to the Mature Person-to-Person Philosophy. Being raised by relatively-mature parents to be personally secure, they will have a minimal tendency for the development of aggressive and violent behavior. Gaining success, personal security, and happiness from a realization of one's potential, the people will have little need or desire to exploit others. They will be self-disciplined, and they will be able to avoid and change pathological cultural trends. They will be strong enough intellectually, emotionally, and physically to practice the Mature Person-to-Person Philosophy, and thus mature more people. From the mature population more mature leaders will emerge, and they will lead the way to a permanent peace.

SUGGESTED EXAMINATION QUESTIONS

Chapter I
1. Describe some characteristics of immature people.
2. Discuss dependence in reference to parents and children, government and adults.
3. Discuss the effects of lack of discipline.
4. Give 3 reasons why man may not be able to utilize his potential to the fullest.
5. Give 10 examples of immaturity in people.

Chapter II
6. Give 2 excuses sometimes given as to why wars are necessary. Discuss.
7. Describe how all people are similar.
8. In which way are cultural factors important in regard to war?
9. Discuss the relationship between immature people.
10. Discuss the Immature People Concept of the Origin of War.

Chapter III
11. Why is Communism a threat to peace?
12. Describe life under Communism.
13. Are the Communists really interested in the welfare of people? Explain.
14. Compare opportunities under Communism in contrast to those in a free country.
15. Name 5 reasons why people become Communists.

Chapter IV
16. Explain the concept of maturity as defined in this book and give examples.
17. Illustrate and explain exploitation among people.
18. Describe Pressure Psychotherapy fully.
19. Describe the Mature Person-to-Person Philosophy in regard to individuals and nations.
20. Discuss the roles of the United States, the Communists, and the United Nations as outlined in this chapter.

Chapter V

21. Discuss the behavior of some of our present leaders in government.
22. Describe what type of people vote for immature leaders.
23. Name some factors which influence people to vote for a particular candidate.
24. What type of individual would make a good leader? Describe in detail.
25. When will we have more mature leaders? Explain.

Chapter VI

26. Write about the constant pressures which exist between people.
27. Discuss aggression, including its control, as described in this chapter.
28. Illustrate and explain Man's Life Cycle.
29. Describe some of the effects of parental influence on children.
30. Discuss the present institutions for the attainment of world peace.

Chapter VII

31. Discuss in detail dealing with a bully.
32. Discuss the importance of young people concentrating on their personal experiences and not on world problems.
33. Discuss dealing with parents.
34. Discuss dealing with teachers and peers.
35. Describe the mature type of behavior in oneself.

Chapter VIII

36. Why are goals in life necessary?
37. Discuss motivation in regard to goals.
38. How does a person's sense of values influence his life's goals?
39. Why do some people seem to have more opportunities than others?
40. Why is it important for a person to be successful with his lifework?

Chapter IX

41. Why is it so important to make a good choice of a marital partner?
42. Why do men and women become attracted to each other?
43. Discuss how husbands and wives might react to each other.
44. Explain the Railroad Track or Parallel Track Concept of Marriage, and the Unparallel Track Concept of the Origin of Schizophrenia.
45. Why are extra-marital relations and divorce considered to be immature behavior?

Chapter X

46. Explain the development of insecurity, anxiety, and emotionally-related problems in a person as being due to his early relationship with his parents, especially the mother.
47. Discuss the disciplining of children fully.
48. Discuss the raising of different numbers of children and adopted children in a family.
49. Write about the expected behavior and the daily routine of children.
50. Discuss the development of aggression in a person in relation to his parents' inability to "give", sibling rivalry, inadequate disciplining, and overprotection by parents and the government.

GLOSSARY

aggression—attacking action directed at oneself or another, written, spoken or physical.

belittle—to consider someone as less important than he apparently is; to minimize; to depreciate.

complement—something added to a deficiency to make a complete or perfect whole.

dependent—needing and relying on someone or something else for aid and support; being subordinate.

empathy—placing oneself in the position of another person, being aware of his thoughts and behavior, and trying to feel as he does.

exploitation—selfishly promoting self-gain from taking advantage of others.

insight—understanding of the true origin, nature, and mechanisms of one's attitudes and behavior.

maturity—the full development of an individual.

motivation—a condition which moves a person to action.

negativism—resistance to suggestions or advice by doing nothing, something different, or the opposite.

neurotic—pertaining to psychoneurosis, a relatively minor emotional illness with symptoms of anxiety, depression, obsessional thoughts, compulsive acts, or various physical complaints without evidence of true organic disease.

overcompensation—an exaggerated striving in which a person consciously or unconsciously tries to correct a real or imagined unacceptable character trait by replacing it with an opposite trait.

pathological—pertaining to an unhealthy condition.

peer—a person of equal rank or standing.

personality—the sum total of an individual's emotional, intellectual and physical characteristics, and his behavioral patterns of adjustment to his environment.

philosophy—a system and method of attitude and guidance in regard to behavior.

potential—latent or hidden ability, not yet actual, but capable of achieving expression.

psychiatry—the medical science which deals with the origin, diagnosis, prevention, and treatment of emotional or mental disorders.

psychological defenses—mental mechanisms operating unconsciously in an attempt to resolve emotional conflict and alleviate anxiety.

psychosis—any severe form of emotional or mental illness, including schizophrenia.

psychotherapy—a type of treatment for emotional illnesses principally based upon verbal communication with the patient.

rationalization—a psychological defense mechanism in which, without awareness, a believable explanation for one's ideas, feelings, or acts is made up by a person for the relief of anxiety, but the true motivation remains in the unconscious.

schizophrenia—a psychosis marked by withdrawal from reality with delusions, hallucinations, and emotional and intellectual regression.

security—freedom from any threat; feeling confident and safe.

sibling—a brother or sister.

unconscious—without awareness; not consciously realized and willingly acted upon.

INDEX

Communism
  apathy of free people to, 65
  not best form of government
    and, 70
  classless society and, 71
  coexistence and, 94
  concessions in World War II
    to, 95
  distorted culture and, 64,
    67, 99
  expansion and, 96
  exploitation and, 20, 68, 71
  false prosperity and, 68
  freedom, basic desire for,
    and, 99
  immaturity and, 68, 98
  insecurity and, 68
  intent of, 104
  less than 10%, 65
  living conditions under, 66,
    67
  loss of feeling and, 64, 70
  loss of individuality and, 70
  personal gain and, 24
  personality gap and, 64
  promises and, 24
  reason for free people's
    apathy to, 66
  slavery and, 65, 99
  social misfits and, 71
  supremacy of the individual
    and, 69
  sympathizers to, 65
  as a threat to peace, 64, 71,
    72
  tolerance of, 66
  undeveloped countries
    and, 71

Compensation, 158
Cultural trend
  attitudes and, 58
  behavior and, 153
  materialistic and hedonistic,
    135, 168
  pathological, 20, 32, 37, 103,
    133, 141
  potential and, 20
  as a threat to peace, 20, 38
  universal, 146

Dependency
  as a form of exploitation,
    43, 149, 151
  hostility and, 22
  inviting attack, 52
  overprotection and, 205
  parents studying modern
    mathematics and, 207
  peace institutions and, 142
  responsibility and, 126, 127
  subjugation and, 25
  weakness and, 25, 52

Disarmament, 95, 100
Discipline, lack of; see also
    Restrictions
  exploitation and, 211
  immature, insecure parents
    and, 34, 35, 140, 186, 187
  immature spouse and, 35
  ogre father and, 35
  rebellion and, 34, 211

Dishonesty and corruption, 72
Divorce, 195, 196
"Doves" and "hawks", 96
Drives and needs
  aggressive, 71, 72

236

fulfillment in marriage of, 195

leaders', 18, 61, 62

of males and females, 18, 184, 187

between parents, and parents and children, 186

pathological, 188

security and, 183

sexual, 182

similar, 59

sublimated, 71

Dying

controlled by others, 17

in war, 56

Educators, 53, 152

Emotional illness, 18

Emotional immaturity

in all the world, 18, 55, 94

not apparent, 32

and changing one's mind, 176

characteristics of, 18, 33, 35-37, 44, 161

collectively, 19

Communism and, 18

credit buying and, 45

culture and, 18

and the "deadbeat", 44

detrimental to civilization, 226

development of, 186

divorce and, 195

exploitation and, 19, 20, 78, 79

failure with goals and, 165

family and, 18

hand-outs and, 24

Head Start and, 29

and helping people, 44

illicit sexual relations and, 192-195

from immature parents, 33, 35, 140, 141

immediate gratification and, 182

individually, 19

introverts and extroverts, and, 45

jealousy and, 61

being "just a number" and, 46

lack of discipline and, 35, 217

material gifts and, 217

mental health clinics and, 28

misbehavior and, 39

overcharging and, 45

overcompensation and, 44, 226

overprotection and, 217

relationships and, 19, 186

slipshod services and, 44

social problems and, 40

social professions and, 46 53

being ruled and, 108, 109

status and, 32

in the United States, 22

war and, 18

Welfare State and, 24

Emotional maturity

absolute, 78

adaptation to married life and, 191

adulthood and, 54, 161
in all areas, 138, 170, 171
atomic war and, 17
behavior and, 77-79
collectively, 98
commensurate with chronological age, 78
containing leaders and, 105
culture and, 20
and dealing with exploitation individually, 78, 79
as a nation, 101
demise of politics, political parties, and politicians and, 120, 121
development of, 141, 163
freedom and, 20
helping the exploited and, 79, 84, 87, 94, 101, 105, 112, 150, 157, 216
ideal government and, 109, 112
independence and, 205
independent voting and, 120
individually, 98
legislators and, 120
of males and females, 183
new concept of, 78, 161, 202
over-all, 20
permanent peace and, 145
from pressuring, 30
progress of civilization and, 225, 226
progressive and dynamic, 77
raising of children and, 20
relative, 77-79

Exploitation; *see also* Aggression *and* Struggles

adjustment to life and, 17
by belittlement, 42, 43, 151, 185-187
bureaucracy and, 152
business, 43, 152
by children, 215

under Communism, 49
comparing oneself with others and, 167

courtship and, 196
cultures and, 20
dependency and, 43, 149, 151

development of, 204, 205
gifts to children and, 155
between husband and wife, 32

inequitable tax laws and, 126, 152

lack of, 126
lack of discipline and, 155, 186

means of, 79
of the middle class of people, 126

obvious and subtle, 151
overprotection and, 155, 186

personal security and, 20
politicians and, 24, 152
prevalent, 59
prevention of, 149, 150, 158
sex and, 194
status and, 150
weakness and, 127
and the wealthy, 49

and the wealthy and lawyers, 111

Government aid, 25, 29, 30

Hand-outs
allowances and, 209
excessively strong or large government and, 25
due to immature parents and children, 33
loss of freedom and, 22, 134, 152
mental health clinics and, 27
personal gain and, 26, 152
in the United States, 22-25
unshouldering responsibility and, 156

Head Start, 29
"Hecticity", 135
Hedonism, 135
Helping people, 50, 59, 199
Honor, 153

Illicit sexual relations, 192-195
"Immature-Mother Syndrome", 40
Immature nationalism, 50, 51
Immature People Concept of the Origin of War, 61
Immaturity; *see* Emotional immaturity
Immediate gratification; *see also* Sexual gratification
credit buying and, 34
immaturity and, 35
lack of discipline and, 213
not in marriage, 197
Impotence and frigidity, 192

Insecurity; *see also* Emotional immaturity
concept of transmission by parents of, 200, 201
of everyone, 199
joining groups and, 44
loss of freedom and, 23
nightmares and, 207, 208
in the United States, 22

Jews, annihilation of, 51

"Keeping up with the Joneses"
development of, 204
false security and, 170
sibling rivalry and, 224
values and, 169

Labor and Management
economic depression and inflation, and, 50
Socialism and, 50
struggles and, 126
Leaders; *see also* Politicians
achievement of potential and, 119
common good and, 119
dependency of people and, 24
exploitation and, 48, 49, 61, 111
with a famous name, 113
favoritism and, 111
followers of, 62, 113
as "foreign experts", 118
"gimmicks" and, 118
hand-outs and, 24, 111
home environment and, 113, 118
ideal, 115, 116, 119
ignorant, 24

241

creating the Relatively Mature Person, 92
defense of one's reputation or property and, 88
definition of, 84
democracy and, 133, 146
disciplining and, 155
everyone a Pressure Psychotherapist and, 90
everyone practicing, 89, 90, 198
family and, 189, 217, 218
gifts to children and, 155
guide for living and, 180, 181
with individuals, groups, and nations, 85
job and, 177
leadership and, 120
losing the need to exploit and, 92, 100, 130
love and limits and, 148
marriage and, 197
mature higher authority and, 87
mature individuals and, 198
mature leaders and, 198
modern world and, 163
next generation and, 131
and not only person-to-person, 91
overprotection and, 155
personality and, 85
physical violence and, 87, 88
practiced by the immature and relatively mature, 90
practiced by relatively mature nations, 103

present older generation and, 130
present younger generation and 131,
rationalized aggression and, 104
realization of one's potential and, 142, 168
relative maturity and, 85
rigid psychological defenses and, 147
"saving face" and, 105
self-confidence and, 147
teasing and, 215, 216

Maturity; see Emotional maturity
Medicaid, 30
Medicare, 25, 30
Men of good will, 143
Mental health
  adaptation and, 136
  clinics, 28
  subsidization, 30
  workers, 28
Minimal age, 117

Misbehavior
  and constant belittlement, 218, 219
  the law and, 40-42
  parents and, 139

Mother's role
  with child, 200, 201
  different from father's, 138
  in disciplining, 216-218
  and less time with family, 33
  materialism and, 34

nurseries and, 34, 137
part-time job and, 137
and reasons for full-time
   job, 137, 138
security and, 179
in talking to her child, 223

Motivation
   of children, 224
   of Communists, 68
   of leaders, 105, 114, 165
   in life, 165
   of people promoting war,
      68
   to succeed, 134

Neurotic motivation
   of candidates, 115
   displaced, 186
   emotional conflicts and, 59
   of leaders, 48
   of parents, 223
   progress and, 43
   success and, 43, 153
News distortion, 46

Nurseries
   under Communism, 64
   government-controlled, 29
   immature children and, 190
   inadequate wives and
      mothers, and, 137
   working mothers and, 137

Old age
   goals and, 173
   Mature Person-to-Person
      Philosophy and, 148
   useful life and, 127, 170

Opportunity
   achievement and, 127, 134

to act, 175
modern living and, 18
recognition of, 175
in the United States, 21

Orientation
   maturity and security, and,
      171
   wisdom and, 142

Overcompensation
   courtship and, 196
   immaturity and, 44
   of father, 216, 217
   of females, 185
   of leaders, 26
   of males, 184
   perfectionism and, 217
   of students, 158

Overprotection
   behavior and, 36
   of children, 139
   school phobia and, 207
   way of life and, 55

Panic, 51
Parallel Track Concept of
   Marriage, 187

Parents
   concept of transmission of
      insecurity and, 200, 201
   concept of transmission of
      security and, 200
   as chief disciplinarians,
      216-218
   as poor disciplinarians, 140
   influence on children of,
      199, 223-225
   insecurity of, and children,
      40, 140

Relationship
  attention-seeking, 212
  complementary, 183, 187, 188
  dominant-subordinate, 151, 152, 183, 185
  esteem and dignity, and, 193
  between government and people, 112
  between husband and wife, 185
  mature parental, 35, 154, 185, 186, 189
  pathological complementary, 187-189
  pathological parental, 141, 188, 189, 203, 215
  sexual, emotional, and social, 192

Respect
  behavior of adults and, 154
  between boys and girls, 157
  between parents, 186, 187
  between parents and children, 186, 187, 202, 203
  restrictions and, 211

Responsibility
  of adolescents, 160
  authority figures and, 139
  credit buying and, 34
  dependency and, 126, 127
  development of, 204, 208
  expectation and, 205, 206
  government clinics and, 28
  individuals and, 30
  insecurity and, 28

of parents, 189
from teasing, 215, 216

Restrictions; see also
    Discipline, lack of
  creativity and, 219, 220
  forceful, 212
  inadequate, 55, 210
  punishment and, 211, 212
  security and, 148, 204, 205
  "spoiled" children and, 213
  starting before age one, 210
  strength and, 148, 204, 211

Schizophrenia, 188

Security
  by belittlement, 42
  choice of career and, 178
  concept of transmission by parents of, 200
  conjoined with maturity, 134
  from exercising potential, 23
  false, 26, 42, 105, 113, 127 167, 170, 184
  from false reassurance, 42
  from fostering dependency, 42
  from free enterprise, 23, 128
  progress of civilization and, 134, 135
  search for,
    by Communists, 68
    in a democracy, 69
    from parents, 203
  status seekers and, 42
  from success, 134, 200
  worthwhile endeavors and, 172